Blood *on the* Doorstep

A CENTURY FOUNDATION/
COUNCIL ON FOREIGN RELATIONS BOOK

Blood *on the* Doorstep
The Politics of Preventive Action

Barnett R. Rubin

THE CENTURY FOUNDATION PRESS
New York

Blood on the Doorstep may be ordered from the Brookings Institution Press, 1775 Massachusetts Avenue, N.W., Washington, D.C. 20036. Telephone 1-800-275-1447 or 202-797-6258; fax 202-797-6004; web www.brookings.edu.

Library of Congress Cataloging-in-Publication data

Rubin, Barnett R.
  Blood on the doorstep : the politics of preventive action /
Barnett R. Rubin.
  p.   cm.
"A Century Foundation/Council on Foreign Relations book."
Includes bibliographical references and index.
  ISBN 0-87078-473-0 (cloth : alk. paper)
  ISBN 0-87078-474-9 (pbk. : alk. paper)
  1. Conflict management—Case studies. 2. Political
violence—Prevention—Case studies. 3. Ethnic groups—Political
activity. 4. World politics—1989B 5. Pacific settlement of
international disputes—Case studies. I. Title.
JC328.6 .R83 2002
327.1'7—dc21   2002012074

9 8 7 6 5 4 3 2 1
The paper used in this publication meets minimum requirements of the
American National Standard for Information Sciences—Permanence of Paper
for Printed Library Materials: ANSI Z39.48-1992.

Typeset in Minion

Composition by
Oakland Street Publishing, Arlington, Virginia

Printed by
R. R. Donnelley and Sons, Harrisonburg, Virginia

Contents

PART TWO

PREVENTING VIOLENT CONFLICTS:
ANALYTICAL FRAMEWORK AND STRATEGIES

Foreword

E ver since the attacks on September 11, 2001, Americans have felt belea-
guered in a way that they did not even during the most dangerous
moments of the cold war. The breakup of the Soviet Union, the booming
economy of the 1990s, the apparent global triumph of Western ideas, and
the recognition of American military superiority made national insecurity
and uncertainty seem almost impossible. Yet today Americans are asking
such basic questions as, Why do they hate us? Who are they? And what can
we do to feel safe again? Indeed, the focus of public attention has changed
in a way that would have seemed preposterous just a year ago.

To be sure, for the past two decades globalization has been central to
every informed conversation about current affairs. But the globalization
being discussed had very little to do with terrorism or the projection of U.S.
military and diplomatic power abroad. Globalization was seen by most as a
development almost independent of governments, a relatively benign system of commerce that added to economic growth and wealth (whether for
all or only the wealthiest was, of course, at issue).

Today, we all comprehend that global interests are inevitably accompanied by global risks. Yet our understanding and our ability to act effectively
is limited by the fact that we have not invested in international affairs as we
should. To take one obvious example, for several years opposition in
Congress resulted in the suspension of the training of new classes of foreign

service officers. Defining our role in the world narrowly assumes that we have the luxury of picking and choosing when to be involved—and where. But, as we now know, we cannot choose our enemies. The establishment of the Center for Preventive Action in 1994 was a recognition of these realities.

The center was an innovative and significant experiment in citizen activism and diplomacy. When Leslie H. Gelb, president of the Council on Foreign Relations, first approached us (we were then known as the Twentieth Century Fund) about participating in the project, we were impressed by its mission, the stature of the participants, and the commitment to the project by David Hamburg, then president of the Carnegie Corporation. The fact that John Vessey, former chairman of the Joint Chiefs of Staff, had agreed to serve as chair of the center was further evidence of the quality of the endeavor. The effort was greatly strengthened by the choice for founding director of Barnett Rubin, who has long been an adviser to both the U.S. government and the United Nations and now is director of studies and senior fellow at the Center on International Cooperation at New York University.

During his tenure at the Center for Preventive Action, Rubin led in-depth work on the Balkans, Central Asia, Central Africa, and West Africa and became a leading expert on Afghanistan. In this book, he brings his research and experience together to provide an intellectual framework that helps us to understand the significance of apparently remote conflicts and the prospects for action to help reduce the threat of violent outbreaks. He has firsthand knowledge of how rapidly the concept of preventive action is evolving; he emphasizes, for example, the importance of the emergence of the Internet over that period as a means of rapid communication among nongovernmental participants. The growing body of studies of preventive action is itself a good sign that this approach to foreign affairs is gaining strength. It is hard to overestimate how fundamentally different this emphasis is from the great-power political analysis that characterizes virtually all previous work. But scholarship on preventive action remains a very young field, and in this sense Rubin is a pioneer. In the chapters that follow, he identifies the opportunities for preventive action but is fully realistic about the obstacles.

One aspect of the Century Foundation's collaboration with the Council on Foreign Relations and the Carnegie Corporation was that we published the results of the work of the Center for Preventive Action. This book follows others in the Preventive Action Reports series: *Cases and Strategies for Preventive Action, Toward Comprehensive Peace in Southeast Europe,* and *Calming the Ferghana Valley.* More generally, we have sponsored numerous projects examining the problems that have emerged in Europe and Asia since the breakup of the Soviet Union, with a particular emphasis on regions that were ripe for ethnic and religious conflict. In the early 1990s, we supported Steven Burg's *War or Peace? Nationalism, Democracy, and American Foreign Policy in Post-Communist Europe* and Jonathan Dean's *Ending Europe's Wars: The Continuing Search for Peace and Security.* We also began focusing on the issues of human rights and international law arising from ethnic unrest in such studies as David Callahan's *Unwinnable Wars: American Power and Ethnic Conflict,* and we established a task force to examine the construction of a new international legal order whose conclusions are presented in *Making Justice Work: The Report of The Century Foundation Task Force on Apprehending Indicted War Criminals.* Most recently, we issued Richard Kauzlarich's white paper "Time for Change? U.S. Policy in the Transcaucasus," and we have ongoing projects that are looking at these troubled regions of the world, most notably a work on Central Asia by Karl Meyer.

This book is especially timely. There has always been a strong case, morally and historically, for concerted efforts to prevent the outbreak of deadly conflicts. Recent events have underscored the practical and political reasons for giving such activity a high priority. We are indebted to Barnett Rubin for his many contributions to this field and for the splendid job he has done in preparing this book.

RICHARD C. LEONE
President
The Century Foundation
June 2002

Acknowledgments

This book would not exist without the vision, commitment, and determination of Leslie H. Gelb, president of the Council on Foreign Relations. Since our first conversation, in July 1993, about his plans for what he then called a Center for Preventive Diplomacy, Les has shown unwavering commitment to the effort to push the question of how to stop mass killing into the forefront of U.S. foreign policy. By hiring me to establish and direct what became the council's Center for Preventive Action (CPA), Les gave me a great opportunity and responsibility. This book is my attempt to discharge that responsibility and share what I have learned from that opportunity.

I could not have carried out these responsibilities without the support of other, equally committed and visionary colleagues. Little in my previous career (or so I thought) had prepared me for a partnership with a former chairman of the Joint Chiefs of Staff, but General John W. Vessey, retired, of the U.S. Army, who became chair of the CPA's advisory board, taught me a great deal about leadership and adherence to principles. He read and commented on this manuscript and shared leadership of the study group that discussed draft chapters, despite the difficulty of squeezing in trips to New York from his home in Minnesota. Nothing I write here can adequately convey my debt to him.

Such a project requires financing, and I am grateful to both the Carnegie Corporation of New York and The Century Foundation (formerly the Twentieth Century Fund) for the support they offered to the CPA; but the participation of their leaders went far beyond funding. One of the great privileges of this experience has been getting to know David Hamburg, who was president of the Carnegie Corporation as well as cochair of the Carnegie Commission on Preventing Deadly Conflict during my term as the CPA director. David's unswerving support, encouragement, and friendship have inspired me increasingly over these years. His acute comments on this manuscript, as he worked on his own, parallel effort, helped me persevere and pushed me to raise my sights. Richard Leone, as president of the Twentieth Century Fund, showed the vision and daring of the small foundation by seeding this effort with a start-up partnership in 1994. He then took on cosponsorship of the CPA's annual conferences and publications program, which culminated in this book.

Equally important to my ability to finish the book was the generous support of Shepard Forman, the director of New York University's Center on International Cooperation, where I now work. The time Shep allowed me away from my duties there to complete this book made him a full partner in the effort.

My daily companions in this effort during my six-year tenure at the Council on Foreign Relations were the CPA's junior staff. As I said at one of the farewell parties we held as they outgrew these positions, no matter how long I live, or how many people I have working for me, I don't think I will ever have a better staff. Darren Kew started up the center with me and prepared the grounds for our Nigeria and Burundi projects, as well as the first annual conferences. Anya Schmemann ran the projects on the Balkans and Central Asia with deft efficiency and considerable diplomacy and oversaw administration as assistant director. Fabienne Hara raised our work on Burundi and the Great Lakes to the highest level. Her comments on the Great Lakes chapter of this book were invaluable. Susanna Campbell oversaw annual conference preparation and production of our in-house publications, took over as Great Lakes coordinator at times, and gave key advice on the writing of this book, especially on how to get started. Nana-Oye Addo-Yobo saw our Nigeria project through, including our mission to the country and collaboration with the Carter Center—demanding tasks that she carried out with skill and equanimity. Kurt Low ran the Great Lakes project during his short stay. Veronique Aubert took over that project and gave it her own special touch of depth and concern, in addition to helping on this book. Negar Katirai and Parag Khanna helped draw my tenure to a close and provided yet more research support. Their subsequent achievements in academia, advocacy, human rights organizations, foundations, conflict prevention networks, and the United Nations are, to me, one of the CPA's proudest legacies.

Many of the CPA's board members participated far more actively than is usual for what is often a purely honorary appointment. Deputy chair Sam Lewis chaired sessions at our annual conferences, and deputy chair Frances FitzGerald reviewed this book in manuscript and offered suggestions and encouragement. Lionel Rosenblatt of Refugees International cofounded the Great Lakes Policy Forum with us, along with John Marks and Susan Collin Marks of Search for Common Ground. Seymour Topping generously gave of his time to chair our working group on the South Balkans and participated actively in follow-up activities. Roy Williams contributed his knowledge of humanitarian operations in the Balkans. As chair of our working group on Nigeria, Pearl Robinson provided our work with both intellectual and political leadership. William Howard made a major contribution to our work on religion and conflict there. Gay McDougall, Vivian Lowery Derryck, and Donald McHenry also contributed to that project. Our working group on the Ferghana Valley was honored with the chairmanship of Senator Sam Nunn, who was not a board member, and benefited from the help of R. Scott Horton on the mission and follow-up. As executive director of the Carnegie Commission, Jane Holl Lute cosponsored our annual conferences and provided ideas that pervaded the CPA's work and found their way into this book. Antonia Handler Chayes played a vital role as cochair, with General Vessey, of the study group on the book manuscript. Others whose participation in that study group helped me greatly include Michael Lund, who also contributed his work on Burundi, Wendy Luers, Pearl Robinson, and Donald W. Shriver Jr., all board members. Ahmedou Ould Abdallah, whose support of the Burundi Policy Forum had been key earlier, and Andrea Bartoli, of Columbia University and the Community of Sant' Egidio, provided important insights. David Rieff's comments on a complete draft helped strengthen it further.

Board members provided most of the leadership for our projects, but consultants did much of the work, a great deal of which has found its way, with the added, if sometimes questionable, benefit of hindsight, into this book. They include Steven L. Burg and David Phillips on the South Balkans, Michael Lund on Burundi, Peter Lewis on Nigeria, and Nancy Lubin, assisted by Arsalan Zholdasov and Keith Martin, on the Ferghana Valley.

Both the study and practice of conflict prevention are collaborative activities, and I learned much from many partnerships other than those already mentioned: with colleagues at the Council on Foreign Relations, including Salih Booker, Michael Clough, Ruth Wedgwood, Robert DeVecchi, Arthur Helton, and others, especially the military fellows over the years; Ambassador Lakhdar Brahimi, who also commented on portions of the manuscript; Anthony Richter of the Open Society Institute, an important partner on Central Asia; Kumar Rupesinghe and his successor, Kevin Clements, at International Alert, as well as staff such as Eugenia Piza-Lopez and Tony Jackson; David Nyheim of the Forum on Early Warning and Early Response, as well as FEWER board members Howard Adelman, Sharon Rusu, Josephine Odera, Bethuel Kiplagat, and Valery Tishkov; President Jimmy Carter, Harry Barnes, and Joyce Neu of the Carter Center; Hassan Ba of Synergies Africa; and all those countless people who spoke at our conferences, participated in our meetings, and responded to our writings.

A few people made special contributions to the completion of this book. Larry Korb, director of studies at the Council on Foreign Relations, followed the manuscript's progress with great interest and attention. My successors at the CPA, Fred Tipson and William Nash, pushed me to clarify what lessons they could learn from my experience. Charles S. Graybow, Andrea Armstrong, and Marisa Jamerson of New York University's Center on International Cooperation provided indispensable help with final revisions, and I thank Shep Forman again for making their time available.

I cannot name everyone who provided me with an idea or an inspiration. I apologize to all those left out. I regret the errors this book may contain, but daring to make them was an indispensable precondition for approaching such a subject. I alone am responsible for them, and no one will be more interested than I in seeing them corrected or debated.

You know, of course, what is coming last. Though it may be a convention, it is still true. Knowing that there was someone to share my life with made it possible to devote myself to this work. Thank you, Susan, for being there.

1

What Is at Stake?

I said, with tricks and spells I will hide my inmost secret.
It will not stay hidden, for blood overflows my doorstep.
—ABU ABDULLAH MUSHARRAF IBN MUSLIHUDDIN SHIRAZI,
known as SA`ADI, *Ghazaliyat*

On July 1, 1994, when the Council on Foreign Relations established a Center for Preventive Diplomacy, the Rwandan genocide was drawing to a close, and refugees (and fugitives from justice) were inundating the region around Goma in neighboring Zaire (as the Democratic Republic of the Congo was then called). Over the next several years, the Center for Preventive Action (CPA), as it came to be called, issued numerous reports and documents arguing that such seemingly obscure and distant conflicts, dismissed by many "realist" thinkers as remote from the United States, had the potential to damage our country's interests in unforeseeable ways. The world has become so linked, we argued, that no threat to human security is unconnected to our own.

The events of September 11, 2001, provided more shocking evidence for this proposition than we ever imagined was possible. A global underground network, al-Qaida, had exploited the destruction of Afghanistan to turn that country into a base for unprecedented attacks against the United States itself.

The loss by the people of Afghanistan of any ability to control their own destiny, the descent of their country into the condition of a "failed state" in which no authority had any stake in the international system, enabled a small extremist group to stage the most devastating attack ever on U.S. soil. Further revelations indicated that al-Qaida was seeking to establish itself in another failed state, Somalia; that it had partly financed itself through illicit traffic in diamonds promoted by wars in western and central Africa; and that it was attempting to spread its influence in areas unsettled by civil wars in the Philippines, Indonesia, the Balkans, and the Caucasus. All these holes in the fabric of international society turned out to be not just unfortunate tragedies to be met with charity but threats to the integrity of global society as a whole.

The CPA never aspired to address issues at the center of U.S. foreign policy concerns. Our goal was more modest, as our founding document noted: "to study and test conflict prevention—to learn whether and how preventive action can work by doing it." We went on to argue that "many of today's most serious international problems—ethnic conflicts, failing states, and humanitarian disasters—could potentially be averted or ameliorated with effective early attention. Yet few have attempted to put this idea into practice, and even fewer have evaluated such attempts."

We promised to "use the unique resources of the membership of the Council on Foreign Relations to fill these voids of action and understanding." To do so, the CPA carried out a number of case studies, assembling diverse working groups to explore ways to prevent violent conflict and to promote implementation of at least some of our recommendations, partly through partnerships we developed with other organizations. The CPA held meetings and conferences to discuss both its case studies and general issues in the field and tried to develop institutions to promote coordination and information sharing. I also integrated the work I continued to do on Afghanistan, on my own and for several United Nations agencies, into the framework of the CPA—hardly anticipating that this case might ultimately provide the strongest argument for what we were doing. This book, along with the CPA's previous publications and other activities, is an attempt to keep the promise to fill the "voids of action and understanding."

The engagement in this task of the Council on Foreign Relations, the most venerable and establishment oriented of U.S. foreign policy organizations, which had been so identified with the core issues of the cold war, signaled a shift in the terrain of international affairs—if one smaller than that which occurred after September 11. For most of those professionally concerned with foreign policy in the United States, these "teacup wars" seemed marginal diversions from the big business at hand—managing the breakup of the Soviet Union and the decline of Russia, integrating or deterring China as it becomes an economic and military power, creating a new North Atlantic relationship between the United States and a uniting Europe, reaffirming and strengthening the security relationship with Japan, creating a financial and trading architecture to safeguard prosperity, and defending the nation's land and people from the terrorism or ballistic missiles of outlaw regimes and movements.[1]

Yet even before September 11, more often than many would like, the foreign policy and security establishment found itself dragged reluctantly into the muck of dirty wars. The military continued to train and equip its troops to fight and win the nation's wars against powerful, threatening states, even as actual military deployments increasingly involved special forces deployments in places like Afghanistan, coercive diplomacy in civil wars, peacekeeping among hostile ethnic groups, and protection of humanitarian operations in the institutional vacuum of failed states.

By one careful estimate, excluding the cost to the victims themselves, these deadly conflicts cost major powers $199 billion in the 1990s—even before the additional confrontations in Kosovo and East Timor, not to mention the war in Afghanistan and whatever further stages the "war on terrorism" may include. Even removing the estimate for the Persian Gulf war ($114 billion), a classic interstate conflict, leaves a total of $85 billion, plus nearly $5 billion for the Kosovo war, more for East Timor, and billions for postconflict reconstruction in both cases. Careful estimates of the cost of preventive efforts in those same conflicts show that their cost to outsiders invariably exceeded the cost of even the most robust preventive efforts.[2] The case of Afghanistan can only strengthen these arguments.

The spectacles of atrocity that appeared intermittently on the television screen puzzled the general public. Apparently innocent victims evoked sympathy, and the checks that poured in to relief organizations bore out the willingness of some to make private contributions, even if the government's public role remained confused. Who these suffering or violent people were, however, and why some of them engaged in orgies of killing remained opaque. In some common images, with the end of U.S. and Soviet dominance, "global chaos" was spreading, "ancient hatreds" were becoming unfrozen, and irrational people in the most foreign of foreign places—the Balkans, Africa's heart of darkness, Central Asia—were reviving their traditions of slaughtering their neighbors. When U.S. policy turned toward intervention in the Balkans, the former view, which had provided a rationale for inaction, gave ground to an opposing, and equally simplistic, narrative: that violence derives from the manipulation of evil leaders—a view that is consistent with the tendency to personalize and demonize enemies in a media-driven foreign policy.[3] The focus on Osama bin Laden as the source of terrorism manifests the same tendency. The source of this evil and hatred, however, remains equally unexplained.

As we were setting up the CPA at the Council on Foreign Relations, nightly news broadcasts showed masses of Rwandans streaming across border crossing points into the barren lava soils of eastern Zaire, dying by the thousands of cholera. These images prodded the Clinton administration into sending the military on its first African mission since Somalia. Alarmed by the domestic political backlash against the killing of eighteen Army Rangers in the streets of Mogadishu—an event for which the White House had made the United Nations a scapegoat—the administration had blocked international action to stop the Rwandan genocide. After the military victory of the Rwandan Patriotic Front effectively halted the genocide, however, the administration, confronted with TV images of dying children, flung troops into the breach to help the United Nations high commissioner for refugees and scores of private organizations stem a cholera epidemic and set up tents, water supplies, and health care facilities to sustain the "refugees."

These dying Africans on the screen seemed to qualify as refugees by their very appearance. Far from being the genocide's victims or survivors, however, these were the perpetrators and their hostage constituency. The establishment of the humanitarian infrastructure that saved their lives also empowered fugitives guilty of genocide, who used the resources of the humanitarian operation to rearm and launch a new round of war. A purely humanitarian response, one that was not integrated into a strategy to prevent further wars, ultimately fueled more killing. The unanalyzed images of suffering guided action as poorly as the unanalyzed images of violence that had inspired the decision to oppose earlier intervention. And we—the distant spectators and decisionmakers—were actors and participants in this conflict, whether we willed it or not. The protagonists manipulated the reactions of the wider world. At the center of Joseph Conrad's *Heart of Darkness*, after all, was not an African "savage" but a corrupted, horrified, and uncomprehending agent of European civilization.

Understanding and approaching the prospect of such conflicts matters, not only because of sentiment, morality, or human solidarity but because, in a globalized world, *foreign policy* is an obsolete concept. The term conjures up the image of a domestic society—literally, one within the walls of a house—sending forth envoys to deal with other such societies, with their foreign ways and foreign interests. Even the somewhat broader term, *international affairs*, evokes a world of cooperation and commerce among a professional élite representing nations. When communication and money cross all borders at the speed of light, however, all the things that communication and money can provoke or purchase will not be far behind— weapons, consumer goods, symbols of struggle, images of agony, information and disinformation, organized crime, and organized beneficence.

This is a world not only of foreign policy or international affairs but also of globalized or transnational relations. Scholars call cross-border links in which at least one actor is not a state "transnational," as opposed to international, relations. Globalization, especially of communication and transportation, has led to an explosion of transnational relations. This is perhaps best known in the economic field, in which the term *transnational corporation* captures the nature of that institution better than the older term, *multinational*, and investment surges around the world in what Thomas Friedman calls the "electronic herd."[4] Transnational relations now also involve all sorts of people and interests, however, from those promoting principled issues like human rights, religion, the environment, or the prevention of violent conflict, to organized crime, arms dealers, smugglers, and terrorists. These networks modify the environment in which the still-sovereign state acts and change the process through which it can define and act on interests.[5] States remain the most powerful institutions in this transnational field of relationships, but the problems they confront and the strategies available for confronting them have changed.

A balance of power, military hegemony, or interstate agreements are far from sufficient to produce stability in such an environment. The interstate concept of stability assumes what is today most in question in much of the world: the integrity of states, the components of the international system and the parties to international agreements or strategies. Insecurity spreads more quickly and is harder to manage when these components disintegrate than when conflicts arise among well-organized states. One of the firmest results of research in the field of international conflict is that armed conflicts among states are far more likely to be settled peacefully than those involving nonstate actors.[6] Seemingly domestic conflicts in today's world spread quickly: Civil wars become transnational wars. Fighters network across borders, creating regional alliances, war economies, and even global terrorist networks that outpace the networks of nongovernmental organizations or other peacemakers. As violence propagates so does disease: war and social disintegration have done much to spread HIV/AIDS in Africa and may do as much in Asia.

In those regions of the globe where peace prevails, its pillars are strong states engaged in accountable governance that regulates transnational actors as well as purely domestic ones. The absence of an accountable state in Afghanistan enabled al-Qaida to root itself there. The Carnegie Commission on Preventing Deadly Conflict has rightly argued that the ultimate goal of prevention must be the creation of "capable states."[7] A strong or capable state is not the same as a despotic state. Rulers often resort to terror precisely when they have few means by which to govern their population and so instead seek to terrorize or prey upon it.[8] International conflict prevention substitutes transnational governance processes for weak or defective national ones while trying to strengthen states and societies for more effective national governance within the globalized context. At the same time, globalization has to some extent deprived states, even strong ones, of capacities for domestic governance they once enjoyed, so that global governance through transnational networks becomes a permanent complement to national structures.[9]

No state, of course, has an undifferentiated interest in monitoring humanitarian concerns and security threats around the globe. Even if the United States is an "indispensable nation," as the former secretary of state Madeleine Albright has observed,[10] it has made itself less indispensable in some regions of the world than in others. At least before the events of September 11, which demonstrated the obsolescence of such a concept, the United States showed greater concern for crises in Europe, where it has fought two world wars, than in Asia or Africa. Even in Europe, when such crises did attract its attention, the United States reacted with concern for state interests such as upholding the prestige of the North Atlantic Treaty Organization (NATO) and maintaining U.S. preeminence rather than with a so-called humanitarian agenda, addressing the collapse of states. Although its unique global scope causes many around the world to regard it almost as a second—and more powerful—United Nations, the United States remains a state with particular and parochial interests that coexist in a permanently unresolved tension with its global vocation.

Yet seeking to prevent such violent conflicts becomes more necessary as the United States becomes more intimately tied to global society. In their growing dealings with all manner of actors around the world, Americans and their government rely on a thick network of norms, agreements, laws, and, yes, values. The debate over the universality of values such as human rights results precisely from the increased intensity and frequency of transnational interactions that require common understandings. In the fight against terrorism, for financial transparency, for confidence-building measures and arms control, the United States continually tries to strengthen norms and values that are an indispensable part of the software that keeps the world running.

It is therefore misleading to distinguish interests and values as if they were mutually exclusive categories or inevitably opposed. No one would do so in domestic politics, in which groups legitimate claims in the language of justice or fairness. Internationally as well, the United States has an interest in promoting certain values. The mass killing, injury, pillaging, and flight of other human beings undermines those values both indirectly, by multiplying cynicism, and directly, by destroying the institutions that can realize those values in the societies so affected. How close we can come to realizing the goal of preventing violent conflict and how many resources we should spend or sacrifices we should make in pursuit of that goal remain open questions. But they are questions that the circumstances of the past decade have placed on the agendas of the United States and the world.

That does not mean that exerting American power can prevent all eruptions of violence around the world. American power is limited. Its use is accountable to the people of the United States and their representatives, not to a purely global agenda, and, in any case, it is not always the most appropriate or effective remedy. Often enough the exercise of U.S. power aggravates or causes conflict, rather than the reverse. Nor is there an effective remedy for every problem that history poses. But the United States and its people participate in a worldwide community that regulates itself across borders in more ways than most people realize: through the international postal union and through product standards that make global communications possible, as well as through multinational agreements on development, human rights, or trade. Exercising commensurate global responsibilities in cooperation with others has become essential to our own security and well-being.

Is such action possible? Conflict and even violence will not disappear from human affairs. Paradoxically, perhaps, episodes of violence sometimes establish the foundations for a lasting peace. Promoting preventive action and conflict resolution does not require a belief that organizational reforms will end the scourges of history or abolish war. Few people seem to doubt, however, that political action can make the world a more dangerous or threatening place. It can also make it a safer place.

Of course, if conflict truly springs from irrational wells in the human personality or from deeply rooted cultures of hate, it will be extremely difficult to prevent. On the other hand, if violence results from the manipulations of a few evil men—Saddam Hussein, Slobodan Milosevic, Osama bin Laden—it may be that all that is necessary is the courage and resources to stand up and defeat them. The sources of conflict, however, are neither as remote and unchangeable as the former argument proposes nor as simple to confront as the latter.

In my experience, what is most difficult to convey about foreign conflicts is not the foreign cultures, beliefs, or hatreds that make others different from us; it is rather the radically different circumstances that make people just like us behave differently. It is those situations—desperate impoverishment, fear for one's life, collapse of institutions that once made sense of existence and gave a sense of security, the threat that not using violence will leave one prey to the violence of others—that propel people into bloody conflict. And these situations are not as far from us as we sometimes think. Often enough, when tracing back the links that lead to violence, one finds global institutions—arms dealers, banks, markets, corporations, intelligence agencies, governments, international organizations—whose immense power and resources form the context for the decisions of local actors. Opportunism and evil exist, but they find their opening when people become desperate and lack alternatives.

2

Conflicts and Their Causes: Acres of Desolation

What has made it impossible for us to live in time like fish in water, like birds in air, like children? It is the fault of Empire! Empire has created the time of history. Empire has located its existence not in the smooth recurrent spinning time of the cycle of the seasons but in the jagged time of rise and fall, of beginning and end, of catastrophe. Empire dooms itself to live in history and plot against history. One thought alone preoccupies the submerged mind of Empire: how not to end, how not to die, how to prolong its era. By day it pursues its enemies. It is cunning and ruthless, it sends its bloodhounds everywhere. By night it feeds on images of disaster: the sack of cities, the rape of populations, pyramids of bones, acres of desolation.

—J. M. COETZEE, *Waiting for the Barbarians*

What were these conflicts the Center for Preventive Action sought to prevent? In writing the CPA charter, we called attention to "ethnic conflicts, failing states, and humanitarian disasters." We could have added "genocides" and "civil wars." The cases we chose reflected this focus: none primarily involved the threat of war among states or other threats, like terrorism, that directly target U.S. citizens. Instead, we concentrated on a class of violent events that is emerging as one of the most difficult and intractable issues in global affairs. These deadly conflicts kill more people than any other type of political event and thus constitute one of the greatest actual threats to humanity. By one rather conservative estimate, in the ten years following the end of the cold war, more than 4 million people died violent deaths in such conflicts, and the number of lives lost owing to destruction of basic economic and social infrastructure, such as water resources, food supplies, and health care, is incalculable.[1]

9

Yet for the most powerful states, first of all the United States, the relation of such conflicts to the national interest remains undefined or controversial. Before September 11, the United States seemed to think that it could combat international terrorism without seriously addressing the problems, notably in Afghanistan, that enabled it to operate. Because the United States and other powerful governments and their publics felt that humanitarian emergencies required some response, whether for purely altruistic reasons or because they threatened in some way the fabric of international life, the global system assigned these tasks to international institutions charged with preventing, managing, or ending such conflicts as a kind of international public good. As for other types of public goods, the institutions responsible for providing them were underfunded and often overridden by direct interests. In the aftermath of September 11, the United States suddenly turned to the United Nations (UN), asking it to perform all kinds of activities that the Bush administration had previously opposed (notably, "nation building"), only to find it understaffed and underequipped after years during which the United States had withheld its dues and insisted on no growth in the organization's budget.

Contemporary Conflict: Multiple Perspectives

The predominant form of contemporary conflict escapes strict classification. The philosopher Ludwig Wittgenstein has cautioned against applying definitions too rigidly to real phenomena. He suggests that the instances of any concept will not necessarily share any single trait. Rather, they will resemble one another as the members of a family do, some sharing some traits and some sharing others.[2] So it is with the set of conflicts that concern us here. Each of the terms to which I refer above—*ethnic conflict, failed state, humanitarian emergency, genocide, civil war,* and *transnational war*—captures an aspect of contemporary conflict, but no one concept suffices to define the family resemblance.[3]

Each of these terms favors a different diagnosis and response. *Ethnic conflict* emphasizes the identity of the contenders: they are cultural groups, not ideological movements or social classes. The focus on identity favors prescriptions such as interethnic reconciliation or ethnic partition. A focus on *wars* concentrates on the means used in the conflict—namely, organized violence between two or more parties. War carries with it a whole conceptual apparatus of organized groups contending over political goals, of its opposite, peace, and of the means used to prevent or end it, including diplomacy, negotiations, confidence-building measures—or victory. The concept of a *failed state* singles out structures rather than actors. To end or prevent violence, it implies, actors will have to do more than change behavior: they will have to construct institutions. Terms such as *genocide, war crime,* and *crime against humanity* draw attention to violent actors and the need for justice and accountability. Like *humanitarian emergency,* they also spotlight the consequences for the civilian populations. By evoking the offense of such acts to internationally recognized standards of conduct, these terms also evoke the duty of others to act to end the offense, punish the offender, or aid the victims.

Ethnic Conflict

An ethnic conflict is one in which the contenders are defined by cultural criteria. Ted Gurr, one of the leading scholars of the subject, prefers the term *ethnopolitical* conflict, and, indeed, "ethnic conflict" per se does not exist. The contenders are always political or military organizations that define goals or recruit supporters in ethnic terms, never unmediated ethnic groups themselves.[4]

The phenomena denoted by the term *ethnicity* bear only a weak family resemblance to one another. *Ethnicity* identifies groups according to differences in language, in religion or other aspects of culture, in physical or "racial" characteristics, or in political status, such as the Hutus and the Tutsis in the Great Lakes region of central Africa, though racial mythologies have provided rationales for their differences.

Ethnic conflicts differ in a number of ways. Groups may be "ranked" or "unranked": Ranked groups occupy different statuses in the social hierarchy; racial groups in South Africa or the United States and the Hutus and Tutsis are two examples.[5] Unranked groups, on the other hand, do not differ systematically in social status. Some groups, usually unranked, claim territories as their homeland, whereas others demand nonterritorial rights within a common land.

Ethnic conflicts also differ by the number and relative size of the groups involved. Conflicts among two groups are more likely to become polarized and violent than claims in more diverse, multiethnic societies. When a dominant group constitutes a minority that may feel threatened with extinction if it gives up its privileges, conflicts can be particularly intense. Only extraordinary leadership enabled South Africa to emerge relatively peacefully from a conflict of this sort, and similar conflicts continue to rage in both Rwanda and Burundi.

Ethnic identity is as much a political project as a reality. Whether a conflict is "really" ethnic can itself be a stake of the conflict. Despite the appearance that the conflict between the Hutus and the Tutsis is possibly the most polarized and violent in the world, members of both groups often argue that the conflicts in Rwanda and Burundi are not "really" between Hutus and Tutsis but in fact about poverty, ideology, or power. The meaning of this denial varies with the speaker. For Tutsis in the governing élite of post-1994 Rwanda, it means that their rule is legitimated by the struggle against the "ideology of genocide." For one leader of the Burundian political party FRODEBU (Front pour la Démocratie au Burundi [Front for Democracy in Burundi]), Augustin Nzojibwami, the denial legitimates the party by explaining the predominance of Hutus therein as the result, first, of simple demography (Hutus represent 85 percent of the population) and, second, of the appeal that a movement for democratic change held out to the more deprived sectors of society. Nzojibwami was implicitly countering charges like those made by my Tutsi driver on the way to the interview, who warned me that FRODEBU had a "côté génocidaire."[6] Other Hutus, who insist on the ethnic or racial nature of the conflict, charge Tutsis with seeking to obscure their dominant position.

Even in the Balkans, where ethnicity (or nationality) seems indisputable, its role is a political issue. Kosovar Albanians insisted on the nationalist nature of their struggle, especially when Serbian democrats (or well-meaning westerners) tried to convince them that the fundamental issue was the lack of democracy and violations of human rights in Milosevic-ruled Yugoslavia.

Ethnicity is thus a contested terrain. Outsiders can easily be tempted to think they understand a conflict once they have labeled the principal actors and listed their grievances. Ethnicity may structure conflict, however, without causing it. Institutional breakdown may throw people back on group solidarity, or leaders may use such solidarity to mobilize people. Outsiders can too easily structure programs in ways that strengthen rather than bridge differences, whether by assuming the reality of contested identities or by overlooking group feelings whose importance must be acknowledged.

Civil War

One prominent set of studies defines war as organized political violence leading to at least a thousand battle casualties in a given year, with every side suffering at least 5 percent of total losses.[7] The number of interstate wars—and, in particular, the number of wars among major powers—has clearly declined. Analysts differ as to whether the decrease is a consequence of nuclear deterrence, the spread of democracy, social factors that inhibit developed societies from accepting casualties, the gradual delegitimation of war as an extension of diplomacy, or other causes, but the result is clear.[8] The Persian Gulf war, the Ethiopian-Eritrean war, and the tense situation between India and Pakistan remind us that interstate war has not disappeared, but most wars today are commonly known as "civil" or "intrastate" wars, though these terms overlook the cross-border character of most such conflicts.

The combatants in this type of war include many protagonists other than armies organized by states. Members of the fighting groups may not be differentiated from the rest of the population. The victims of war are similarly undifferentiated, or differentiated in the opposite way. Civil wars do not consist primarily of engagements between opposing military units. Fighters may attack targets that are economically or symbolically important to the enemy. Civilians are principal targets; beginning with World War II, civilian casualties have outstripped military ones in every war, and the imbalance continues to rise.[9] Some earlier colonial wars, of course, also resembled campaigns of extermination more than interstate war.

Many contemporary militias are not organized hierarchically into a coherent structure. Instead, the units are more fluid and fragmented, making it far more difficult to structure negotiations or for those engaged in negotiations to reach meaningful agreement. The goals of the fighters are similarly fluid and fragmented, as local social or economic conflicts or interests obscure to outsiders may loom larger than any political goal.

The term *civil war* conveys a misleading image of a fight within borders. *Transnational war,* a term suggested by the British scholar and activist Mary Kaldor, better captures the relationship of the combatants to the international system.[10] Many parties to so-called civil wars receive significant support from, or are even organized or goaded into fighting by interested states. Other insurgents receive support from diaspora communities. When a delegation of the Center for Preventive Action's working group on the South Balkans met with the Serbian president Slobodan Milosevic in December 1995 to discuss the Kosovo conflict, Milosevic memorably told us that the "Albanian extremists" were supported by "your doormen on Park Avenue." Perhaps it was an exaggeration, but in Pristina, Albanian nationalist activists explained to us how they taxed the income of Kosovars abroad. Diaspora networks also fund guerrillas through various contraband activities, such as the drug trade, smuggling, and car theft.

Especially when conflicts are linked to the collapse, disintegration, dissolution, or failure of states, regional conflicts link up into conflict systems.[11]
In their 2001 annual review of world conflict, the Swedish peace researchers
Peter Wallensteen and Margareta Sollenberg find that ten out of fourteen
major armed conflicts "spilled over" into their neighboring states—thus
belonging to what the authors identify as "regional conflict complexes."[12] For
instance, the Great Lakes region of central Africa includes linked conflicts in
Rwanda, Burundi, and the Democratic Republic of the Congo (the core) that
are in turn linked to conflicts in Uganda, Sudan, Angola, Zimbabwe, and
elsewhere. The Balkans has seen conflicts in Croatia, Bosnia-Herzegovina,
Kosovo, Macedonia, and Albania, with potentially wider links especially
owing to overlapping claims on Macedonia. Southwest Central Asia includes
conflicts in Afghanistan, Uzbekistan, Tajikistan, Kyrgyzstan, Pakistan, and
Kashmir, with links to Iran and the broader India-Pakistan confrontation.

The economic networks that sustain conflict are also likely to involve
transborder alliances.[13] Afghanistan's Taliban depended on trade in both
drugs and smuggled consumer goods that involved cooperation with trading and security organizations in Pakistan.[14] Many of the military activities
in the Great Lakes region are financed through the smuggling of gold, diamonds, coltan, and other precious goods through networks that reach from
the Congo or Angola, where these items are found, to the neighboring and
West African countries through which they are smuggled and, of course, to
the developed countries where they are sold. The trade in small arms and
ammunition, essential to all such conflicts, also involves transborder ties.
Often these ties span huge distances, as when Uzbek or Ukrainian pilots fly
surplus weapons from the former Soviet Union into Africa, or when Serb
mercenaries die defending Kisangani in eastern Congo from rebels supported by Uganda and Rwanda. Hence these conflicts form an integral part
of today's globalized economy.

Failed States

Differences among the actors in a conflict—whether "ethnic" or not—may
explain how the conflict is structured, but they do not explain why conflict
breaks out or why it escalates to war. In peaceful societies, institutions manage conflict, and violence may erupt when these institutions, especially states,
collapse. Such breakdown of basic governing capacity defines the failed state.
Somalia, Afghanistan, Albania, Liberia, Sierra Leone, the Democratic Republic of the Congo, and Haiti have also at one time or another been candidates
for that label.

Before the failed state became another emblem of the supposed chaos of the post–cold-war world, scholars of postcolonial Africa analyzed states that enjoyed international recognition (juridical statehood) but lacked the capacity to govern (empirical statehood).[15] Countries ruled by colonial administrations designed for domination or exploitation could not become coherent states or nations simply by virtue of legal independence. The international rights to which juridical sovereignty entitles them are one of the major resources of the rulers of such states. Because they have limited ability to extract resources from the societies they nominally rule, such rulers rely on controlling exports of extracted goods (oil, gold, diamonds) or foreign aid. They have few incentives to govern, rather than simply maintain power for the sake of private gain. Faced with losses of revenue, they may cease paying government employees, including the army and police, and fail to maintain essential government services. Combinations in various degrees of kleptocracy and anarchy can result in the collapse of basic government functions.

When authority collapses in this way, some form of conflict inevitably breaks out, though the conflict need not be ethnic. In Albania, Somalia, and Tajikistan, the fighting was largely political or clan-based conflict within single ethnic groups, though the phenomenon labeled as "clan" differs.[16] In each case, the state collapsed because financial crisis or loss of external support resulted in conflict, not the reverse. The collapse of state power can create a security dilemma for the unprotected population, which falls back on associations based on ethnicity or clan as a means of self-defense. As Michael Ignatieff has put it, "Ethnic hatred is the result of the terror that arises when legitimate authority disintegrates."[17]

One must be careful not to apply the concept of failed state rigidly. States vary along a continuum of capacities. Some are more failed than others, and states that fail may do so in different ways. Analysts often claim that the Rwandan government's ability to organize the killing of hundreds of thousands of people in three months in 1994 shows it was not a failed state; but that state's ability to mobilize to kill was not matched by an ability to provide security or livelihood. Indeed, in the absence of the latter it created a support base through genocide and predation. Furthermore, the term *failed state* may be misleading, if it is understood to indicate a purely internal failure. States are units of an international state system, not independent entities juxtaposed to one another, and most failed states are legatees of colonial conquest that collapsed when a change initiated from outside the state altered the ability of its rulers to mobilize resources. The mix among the exogenous collapse of institutions, preexisting conflicts, and the manipulation of the latter by predatory leaders varies, but all contribute to the mix in most failed or failing states.

Genocide, Politicide, and Massive Human Rights Violations

Not all mass violence takes place in war, though war usually provides the context in which such violence occurs. By the time of the 1994 genocide, the Rwandan government had been fighting the Rwandan Patriotic Front for four years. The overwhelming majority of those slaughtered in the genocide, however, were no more victims of combat than were those gassed in the Nazi concentration camps.

The term *genocide* itself became part of the battle. At a time that the United States was opposing UN action, officials refused to answer clearly whether genocide was taking place: they sought refuge in the euphemism "Acts of genocide may have occurred." For genocide is not simply a phenomenon, like ethnic conflict, state failure, or war. It is also a crime, defined by an international treaty that obligates its signatories to prevent and punish it. Because the Clinton administration (like many others around the world) did not want to assume this obligation, it sought refuge in obfuscation and, in a mark of its particular style, subsequent expressions of regret.

The 1948 Genocide Convention defines the crime as any of several acts, including killing, performed with the intent to destroy a racial, religious, or ethnic group in whole or in part. The genocide that led to the coining of the term and the drafting of the convention, that of the Nazis against the Jews, was an attempt to destroy all Jews by killing them, an attempt not duplicated until the Rwandan events of 1994. The language of the covenant, however, is more elastic, and its boundaries are contested. Not all mass killing aims to eliminate racial, religious, or ethnic groups. The purges by Stalin or the Khmer Rouge killed millions of people for political rather than ethnic reasons. Some scholars have therefore coined the term *politicide* to denote politically motivated mass killing.[18]

The precise nature of the intent required is also contested. How much of a group must the perpetrators intend to kill?[19] More common than an attempt to eliminate an entire group is the systematic killing of men of military age, combined with other killings of civilians, atrocities such as rape, and mass population expulsions. This pattern has come to be known as "ethnic cleansing."

Because the Genocide Convention obligates the parties to prevent, halt, and punish the crime of genocide, arguments about its definition are not purely conceptual. No other human rights treaty imposes a comparable obligation. Those who seek military intervention in conflicts may argue that one side is committing genocide, hoping thereby to establish a legal obligation to intervene that should transcend mere policy debates. Some made this argument during the campaigns of ethnic cleansing in Bosnia and Kosovo.[20]

Like other prisms for observing conflict, this one magnifies certain aspects, with implications for action. *Genocide, war crimes,* and *crimes against humanity* (which, together with "aggression," constitute the mandate of the International Criminal Court) depict aspects of conflict as crime and lead to "the struggle for justice," in Aryeh Neier's term.[21] That struggle focuses on the actions of individuals, actions for which they are responsible regardless of the conditions that promote such abuses.

Humanitarian Emergencies

Intergroup conflict, institutional collapse, wars, and human rights violations cause immense pain to the millions of people who are killed, wounded, tortured, arrested, or forced to flee their homes and countries, who see their houses, property, and sources of livelihood destroyed or stolen, who fall ill with preventable diseases, lose their limbs to land mines, and suffer from thirst, hunger, and malnutrition. Women, children, and the elderly suffer disproportionately. Over the past century, and especially since World War II, a network of organizations has emerged to care for these victims. This system has defined those situations that require extensive assistance as "humanitarian emergencies."[22]

This concept thus focuses on the effects of conflict on the victims and the efforts of the rest of the international community to relieve their suffering. *Humanitarian emergency,* like *genocide* or *human rights violation,* is a normative concept that inherently calls for action and has been incorporated into the operational code of a set of organizations.

The Finnish scholar Raimo Väyrynen has defined death, displacement, disease, and hunger as the four horsemen of the humanitarian apocalypse. Measuring these indicators among populations, he finds three main clusters of humanitarian disasters, only two of which are attributable to conflict:

—violent humanitarian crises mainly resulting from war, with high casualties and displacement but little disease or hunger, usually the result of civil wars in middle-income countries, such as the former Yugoslavia;

—poverty crises mainly owing to hunger and disease, as found in a number of very poor countries without pervasive conflict (Niger, India); and

—totalistic humanitarian crises, involving all "four horsemen," generally owing to enduring civil war in very poor countries, such as Afghanistan, Tajikistan, and many African cases.[23]

That levels of distress comparable to that produced by violent conflict can result from intense poverty or social discrimination reminds us of the relation between conflict and seemingly more mundane problems. People already in dire circumstances more willingly accept the risks of violence. Conflict arises not just from intergroup hatred, technologies of violence, institutional failure, or the criminal acts of leaders but also from desperate competition for scarce resources. Furthermore, though conflict resolution and alleviation of poverty may appear to be different problems, both are related to a common task, that of building institutions for sustainable development.

The humanitarian perspective has a certain purity: even if we cannot stop violence or determine who or what is to blame, at least we can relieve the suffering it causes. Far from being wildly idealistic, the humanitarian approach, especially as practiced by the International Committee of the Red Cross, can incorporate a clear-eyed realism or even pessimism about what is possible and what is not.[24] Yet alleviating suffering in the context of conflict is a political act, however it is intended, because in most contemporary conflict inflicting suffering on civilians is an intentional goal rather than an unintended consequence of violence. The critique of the political manipulation of humanitarian action has generated an extensive debate—notably within humanitarian organizations themselves.[25]

Causes of Conflict

The recognition of the inadequacy of a purely humanitarian response to conflict has been one of the major impulses behind the development of the fields of conflict prevention and resolution. Rather than merely alleviating the symptoms of conflict, in ways that may even aggravate the underlying problem, international actors should confront the causes. What are they?

When people debate what causes a violent conflict, they are often engaged in a disguised discussion about what to do. The thesis that most contemporary wars are ethnic conflicts derived from deep-rooted hatred supports policies of isolating conflicts until they burn themselves out or separating groups through partition. Supporters of a contrasting view, that political leaders manipulate people into conflict as part of a strategy to seek power, argue for firm action against the leaders responsible.

Both of these explanations underestimate the effects of changes in political and economic structures that determine actors' incentives and opportunities. The weakening of institutions or the loss of livelihood or security pushes groups into conflictual relations and creates opportunities to profit from the use of violence. Conflicts occur more frequently in impoverished, poorly educated, polarized societies with weak states and resources that can be looted because these structures favor violence, not because such societies' cultures are more permeated with hate or their leaders more evil. Some such societies experience genocide and others more mild forms of instability or violence partly because of choices among alternatives that still exist under these hard conditions. Measures aimed at both structures and actors are necessary—indeed, they are interdependent—but the former, though they take more time, will provide more permanent solutions. Strategies aimed at individuals will be no more than stopgap measures, as the same structures eventually reproduce the same conflicts.

The quest for the causes or sources of conflict poses several different questions at different levels of analysis.

—Why are there more, fewer, or different types of conflicts in the world at one time than at another?

—Why are conflicts more likely to involve certain units, whether regions, countries, or minority groups, than others?

—Why does conflict break out in a certain place at a certain time?

These questions, all relevant to the prevention of conflicts, have different, if related, answers. The levels of analysis appropriate for answering these questions correspond to those developed by Kenneth N. Waltz in *Man, the State, and War*.[26] Waltz distinguishes three levels of causation—the structure of the international system, the internal structures of states, and the nature of the human individual. Is war the result of humanity's propensity to violence, the political nature of certain regimes, or the anarchy—lack of governing authority—of the international system? With appropriate changes, these same distinctions are useful to understanding the sources of today's transnational conflicts.

Global Systemic Sources of Conflict

Trends in the overall prevalence and nature of mass violence result from sources of conflict and peace at the global level. The common term *post–cold-war conflict* implicitly assumes that the change of the global strategic structure has affected conflict in ways that explain the decline in war, the relative increase in civil wars, and the perception of a rise in "chaos."

Although some global factors result from major historical shifts that are hardly amenable to policy choices, others can be affected by institutional change. The changes in 1989–92 included three linked but different phenomena:

—the thawing of relations between the United States and the USSR and the freeing of the USSR's external empire in Eastern and Central Europe;

—the breakup of the USSR and subsequently of Yugoslavia into component republics;[27]

—the abandonment of communism or state socialism as a political and economic system by the USSR and all of the socialist states of Europe, combined with the adoption of extensive market reforms in China.

The end of U.S.-Soviet confrontation changed the strategic structure of the global state system from antagonistic bipolarity to more cooperative bipolarity in 1989–91. After 1991, the breakup of the USSR into weaker states and the economic and military decline of all the successor states, especially Russia, effectively ended bipolarity, creating a world with one superpower, albeit an ambivalent one challenged by emergent multipolarity.

The end of global strategic competition transformed the processes by which conflicts were prevented or aggravated. A global zero-sum competition no longer invested every bit of territory with strategic meaning. Global competition had escalated local disputes during the cold war, as the superpowers flooded arms into wars that they perceived as strategic conflicts they wanted to win rather than chaotic violence they might want to prevent. UN Secretary General Dag Hammarskjöld then defined the main task of preventive diplomacy as keeping local disputes insulated from cold-war competition.[28] The end of this competition reduced the prevalence and intensity of war and armed conflict in states and regions in which conflicts had been aggravated by such intervention (Central America, Southeast Asia).

In some areas, however, regional powers now felt freer to act on local interest without reaction from major powers, as Pakistan and Iran did in Afghanistan. Some states that had depended on politically motivated flows of foreign aid (Somalia, the Democratic Republic of the Congo) became weaker as those flows decreased and consequently more vulnerable to insurgency and state collapse. Some guerrilla groups and governments that had relied on superpower patronage and cold-war ideology now turned to the increasingly globalized international market for conflict resources and to ethnic appeals for legitimacy.[29] The transformation of these conflicts from parts of a global struggle to local or regional wars covertly linked to the global economy made them harder for international publics or policymakers to pigeonhole. The cold war had provided a ready-made framework through which to misunderstand politics around the world, and its absence without a comparable replacement led to a perception of "chaos."

The breakup of the Soviet Union and Yugoslavia sparked new conflicts. The division of these multinational states into component republics was accompanied by revolts and violence, nearly all of which started in the years 1988 to 1992. Since that time, however, though some of these conflicts have occasionally become more aggravated, efforts at peacemaking, state building, and conflict management have reduced the level of violence in most of these regions, and few new conflicts have started.[30] It remains to be seen whether the now more fragmented state systems of the Balkans, the Caucasus, and Central Asia will be able to achieve long-term stability.

Finally, the collapse of communism as a social and economic system in Europe (and its de facto abandonment in China) gave free-market capitalism an uncompetitive monopoly in the marketplace of economic ideas. Not only did Leninist state socialism disappear, but models of regulated or state-centered capitalism with a large public sector were also discredited.[31] The globalization of capital gave rise to an inchoate new superpower—what Thomas Friedman calls "Supermarkets."[32] Both financial markets and corporations moved resources around the world electronically in response to shifts in government policy, rumors, or fluctuations in expectations. These trends all created pressures to relax or abolish state controls on the economy. Such changes sometimes released economic energies and weakened predatory regimes, but they also dismantled programs that dispensed political patronage and provided employment. The adoption of a market-based model as a goal did not improve understanding of how to make the transition, and countries that bogged down in stalled transitions or were shocked by crashes fell prey to elements of the failed state syndrome. Criminal syndicates controlled much of the economy, and politics or militaries that had once served rulers as agents of repression fractured into self-serving, profit-seeking ventures. As a result, institutions, including newly introduced democracy, lost legitimacy and the ability to regulate or resolve domestic conflicts.

These economic transformations linked the end of the cold war to what some now call the "age of globalization." That same transition affected the resources for conflict in a number of ways, through its effects on markets for arms, drugs, and financial assets. Warlords often fund violence through trade in primary commodities whose origins are difficult to identify. Some of these are illegal (coca and opium), while others are licit (coltan and diamonds). Whereas these commodities are produced in poor, conflict-ridden countries and sold for huge profits in rich, peaceful ones, the arms market has the opposite structure, making the two natural complements. Indeed, these two types of commodities could constitute a classical model of gains from comparative advantage in international trade, just like David Ricardo's model of British cloth being exchanged for French or Portuguese wine.[33]

The end of the cold war led to a glut on arms markets, especially of small arms and light weapons. Among the factors that have contributed to their uncontrolled proliferation and consequent drop in price are:

—the reduction in size of major militaries, such as those of the United States and the successor states of the USSR, especially Russia, creating large surplus stocks;

—the termination or winding down of a number of conflicts, such as those in Mozambique, Central America, and Indochina, leading to sales of weapons by former combatants;

—the continued dependence for employment on arms production and sales of a high proportion of the population in countries such as Russia, Belarus, Ukraine, and Bulgaria, with the result that these governments and companies have actively sought out new markets, especially in Africa; and

—the expansion of the North Atlantic Treaty Organization (NATO), which requires new members to upgrade to modern equipment compatible with NATO standards and junk much Warsaw Pact–era material, which ends up on secondary markets.

The easy availability of powerful automatic weapons accelerates the escalation of disputes. The mere knowledge that one's opponent in a local dispute may have access to automatic weapons creates a security dilemma that gives rise to arms races in local conflicts, just as the same mechanism did in the global strategic arms arena during the cold war. Furthermore, when combatants obtain arms through diffuse commercial networks rather than through centralized aid pipelines, their organizations are more likely to become fragmented, rather than polarized, as occurred during the cold war.

The sale of commodities to developed countries often pays for those arms. Page 3 of the first section of the Sunday *New York Times* of August 22, 1999, featured an article on the wrenching problem of Sierra Leone: how to make peace with the Revolutionary United Front, a rebel group that had committed such atrocities as chopping off people's hands and arms with machetes simply to punish them for voting or to attract attention. The government had previously paid a private South African firm, Executive Outcomes, to provide security for national elections by assigning rights to some of the country's diamond resources. On this page of the newspaper of record, next to a photo of a man holding two children in the bandaged stumps of his arms, the text noted that the peace agreement left the rebels in charge of the country's lucrative diamond mines. To the right of the article an advertisement for Tiffany's displayed a delicate bracelet of innumerable small diamonds that can hang brightly on the wrist—at least, of those who still have wrists. The war in Congo is financed not only by traditional treasures like gold and diamonds but also by the sale of coltan, an ore containing the rare metal tantalum, which is used in the manufacture of high-technology products from computer chips to mobile phones.[34]

The trade in illegal drugs that funds so many wars also exploits globalization. The high-volume transfers of funds that make the trade possible rely on offshore banking and money laundering. The mafias that transport, refine, and market the product from the Afghan or Colombian peasant to the streets of New York or Amsterdam rely on a full array of contemporary transport and communication. Because their business is illegal, drug traders must organize or at least rent their own security, rather than paying taxes and benefiting from public order, so they are naturally linked to arms traders and armed groups, which in turn benefit from the funds derived from the trade.

Corrupt rulers who gut institutions and stay in power by playing groups against one another also rely on offshore banking and secrecy laws to move their wealth around the world and evade detection. Some such money comes from international financial institutions or other sources of aid, and rulers may be able to use the threat of default to keep aid coming as their predecessors used the threat of switching sides during the cold war.

Although globalization has broadened horizons and offered new opportunities for many, the shifts in opportunities it provokes can also promote conflict. According to the United Nations Development Program (UNDP), between 1980 and 1999 malnutrition was reduced worldwide, and between 1970 and 1999 the percentage of people in rural areas of the developing world with access to safe water increased. The developing world also saw increases in life expectancy and adult literacy and decreases in the infant mortality rate. The benefits, however, were unevenly distributed and did not reach everyone. "Global inequalities in income," according to the UNDP, "increased in the twentieth century by orders of magnitude out of proportion to anything experienced before."[35] Although indicators of well-being are rising for many,

between 1987 and 1993 the number of people with incomes of less than $1 a day increased by almost 100 million to 1.3 billion—and the number appears to be still growing in every region except South-East Asia and the Pacific. . . . In the past 15–20 years more than 100 developing and transition countries have suffered disastrous failures in growth and deeper and more prolonged cuts in living standards than anything experienced in the industrial countries during the Great Depression of the 1930s. As a result of these setbacks, the incomes of more than a billion people have fallen below levels first reached 10, 20 and sometimes 30 years ago. . . . The share of the poorest 20% of the world's people in global income now stands at a miserable 1.1%, down from 1.4% in 1991 and 2.3% in 1960.[36]

At the same time that these disparities are growing, the increase of global communications, and especially television, has made people more aware of them.

The Great Depression provided the backdrop for the rise of fascism and World War II. It is hardly surprising that even harsher economic declines have provoked many violent conflicts. In much of the world, the young men who furnish the recruitment pool for militias of all sorts are losing opportunities for education and employment and, along with those, for stable marriage and family life. Several empirical studies have found that the proportion of young men in the population or the presence of a "youth bulge" is a statistically significant predictor of civil war or state failure.[37] For such youths, violence becomes an alternative career.

These trends affect the likelihood and character of conflict worldwide, but they do so through differential impact on societies. Although global reforms to reduce these background effects are desirable, so too are more targeted measures to reduce factors that make some societies or groups more vulnerable than others.

State-Level Sources of Conflict: Structures, Cultures, Institutions

Just as the international system as a whole includes structures, institutions, and patterns of interaction that are relatively independent of the parts of the system they affect, the units of the system (nation-states or, more loosely, "societies") also have characteristics relatively independent at any given moment of the individuals that constitute them. Study of the structural characteristics of societies is most likely to answer questions such as, Why are conflicts more likely to occur in certain places rather than others? A number of academic and official efforts to develop global, cross-national early warning systems have attempted to address the first problem by identifying indicators that either statistically predict the various phenomena to be prevented or provide ways to assess comparative risk.[38] These state-level factors are equivalent to what others have called structural, cultural, or institutional sources of conflict.[39]

Social structures and institutions affect both the demand for and the supply of conflict. The former—namely, the motives for which people fight—generally receives the most attention. In the general image of conflict, people take up arms to redress grievances. Every society has such grievances, however, yet in only some do people seek redress through violence. Political violence requires more than will. It needs money, equipment, and people (usually young men), as well as the opportunity to organize without immediately being arrested or killed. These require various forms of both financial and social capital.[40]

Recent studies have proposed two major hypotheses on what economic structures promote conflict: inequality among identity groups, and the presence of economic returns to violence. A study by the United Nations University has found that élites use political and socioeconomic inequality among identity groups—what sociologists refer to as "horizontal" inequality—to mobilize people to compete for power and resources.[41] Though poor people may seek more resources, poverty alone does not prod them into collective action, identify an enemy, or provide the resources they need to mobilize. Impoverishment without social capital for revolt is more likely to lead to violent crime, as has occurred in many third-world megalopolises. When economic fault lines coincide with cultural groups or political territories, economic disparities are far more likely to be translated into conflict.

Ethnic groups are not just groups with more or less common interests or values, and hence grievances; they also possess social capital in the form of institutions, symbols, and discourses of justice. In ethnofederal states like the USSR or Yugoslavia, they even possessed ethnonationally defined institutions with territories and economic resources. The combination of economic decline with distributional struggles among identity groups (in other words, of high demand for and high supply of revolt) underlies many intense conflicts, from the former Yugoslavia to the Great Lakes region of central Africa.

A set of studies by a World Bank team led by Paul Collier has tested alternative models of the risk of civil war—pithily, if inaccurately, described as models based on either grievance or greed.[42] Grievance models emphasize the political or social goals of violence, such as the redress of inequality. Greed models pay greater attention to the availability of resources to finance violence. Violent leaders profit as entrepreneurs of organized violence, as did Jonas Savimbi of Angola and Foday Sankoh of Sierra Leone, who turned the leadership of insurgencies into positions of wealth as diamond merchants. A high proportion of primary commodity exports (a proxy for "lootable" goods) in domestic product and a low national average level of education (a proxy for the cost of recruiting fighters) are significant predictors of the risk of such conflict. Education of women, which has been shown in many studies to provide important social capital for social welfare and stability, is likely to be important to a society's capacity to sustain peace.

Thus countries with weak governments and lots of diamonds, coltan, coca, or opium are particularly prone to civil wars, though the lawless environment and thirst for cash created by wars also stimulates drug production, as in Afghanistan or Colombia. Such wars are hard to prevent, at least through the conventional means of diplomacy such as negotiations, good offices, or mediation. These means address political demands or grievances; but addressing grievances does little to reduce the attraction of quick wealth, and holding dialogues with or among leaders about political demands may accomplish little when leaders are entrepreneurs of violence delivering economic opportunity to their Kalashnikov-wielding followers. The "hurting stalemate" that analysts posit as a condition for negotiated settlements may never hurt enough when the stalemate itself creates the conditions for profiteering.[43]

Static poverty creates fewer grievances than sudden impoverishment. Sudden shocks that deprive people of economic security create intense anxiety and a search for both solutions and scapegoats. In Yugoslavia, the collapse of economic management under the impact of the debt crisis and the strict conditions imposed by international financial institutions set the federal government against the republics and the republics against one another. In central Africa, the collapse of the international coffee agreement in the mid-1980s created an economic crisis throughout the region that helped spark the upheavals in both Rwanda and Burundi.

Cultural analysis of conflict has to a certain extent been discredited by simplistic, essentialist readings, notably that of Samuel Huntington in his *Clash of Civilizations*.[44] Cultures are fields of conflict and contradiction, not of immutable unanimity. They are always changing through the reflection and action of participants as well as interaction with other "cultures." Bounded, permanent, and uniform national or civilizational cultures are political projects, not social realities.

Cultural sources of conflict are real, however, even if they are constructed or manipulated. These include values, constructions of history, and symbols.

These may legitimate, structure, or intensify conflict. We have already noted how identities provide institutional resources or social capital for collective action. When cultures define markers (for example, territory or group membership) that determine the distribution of resources, they can also promote mobilization for conflict over those resources.

Leaders manipulate symbols and identities in times of crisis, but culture is not an infinitely malleable political tool. Demagogic leaders cannot manipulate cultural values or fears that do not exist. Nor do these leaders live in some realm of pure instrumentalism mysteriously insulated from the beliefs of their co-nationals. Every culture includes a variety of potential symbolic and political resources for both conflict and peace that élites transform into political resources.

Somewhat more amenable to transformation than economic and social structure are political institutions. Societies that manage political conflict without violence do so through effective institutions. If the institutions and the processes of interaction within them seem legitimate and fair, those who lose on an issue are less likely to resort to violence. Effective institutions also prevent looting and provide security. The collapse of such institutions is often the cause of conflict, rather than the reverse. Through systems of representation and administration, institutions structure the way that identities are translated into political mobilization. They are vehicles for power sharing or exclusion.

Among institutions it is important to distinguish state structures from political regimes. The latter, including democratic institutions or their absence, and most especially elections, have become an important focus of policy. One of the definitions of the foreign policy goals of the Clinton administration given by Anthony Lake, national security adviser at the time, was "democratic expansion."[45]

Transnational action to prevent violent conflict is at best an inferior substitute for legitimate, accountable governance through democratic institutions. But governance—accountable or otherwise—presumes an effective state in the modern world. Although other forms of governance are possible (such as acephalous tribal structures), these have been largely displaced and disrupted by colonialism and state formation. Those who live in relatively stable societies tend to take the state for granted, like air or water. The existence of an institution that ensures the security of life and property, guarantees contracts, and provides innumerable services forms the background hum of all our activities. We want to be sure to control its potentially dangerous monopoly of violence through laws, free elections, and other safeguards; but much of humanity lacks such basic institutional security. Attempts by groups to provide such security for themselves despite or against the state form a principal source of violent conflict.

The persistence of poor governance through changes of leadership and even across different types of regimes in many countries argues for the fundamental effect of state structures. The postcolonial establishment of universal juridical statehood over the whole globe, regardless of the actual capacity of the state apparatus to exercise domestic or international sovereignty, created many opportunities for civil conflict. Collier and Anke Hoeffler's finding that the percentage of primary commodity exports in an economy was a consistent predictor of the likelihood of civil war may indicate not only the importance of looting for supporting an insurgency but also that states with such dependence are more vulnerable to violent opposition.[46] An economy largely limited to a few commodities enables even a weak state to accumulate control over the society's scarce economic resources. The state's international status as the representative of a given territory and population accords it a monopoly of control of legitimate international exchanges. Hence access to state power and state position is virtually the only route to the accumulation of wealth. As a former UN official in Burundi once told me, "If they don't have the Mercedes of a minister, they have to take the bus like everyone else, and you know what the buses are like in such places." Relatively few positions provide such access, and the competition to control them is acute.

Weak states not only incite or fail to prevent domestic revolts or conflict but are also open to influence and contagion from states in the neighborhood. When states or groups in neighboring countries have ties to parties in a conflict, the conflict is more likely to escalate and resist prevention or resolution. External aid can block development of a stalemate that might force negotiations. It also promotes the development of transnational war economies. Because weak border control and weak national identities are consequences of weak states, they inherently tend to spread, creating regional conflict formations.

The capacity of states limits the possible types of regimes. Within these limits, of course, the type of regime (democratic or authoritarian) affects the likelihood that conflict will escalate to violence. Authoritarianism and repression may indeed suppress violent protest and thus "prevent conflict," but prevention does not constitute a seemingly apolitical quest for "stability," implicitly identified with the status quo. Prevention requires political choices informed by goals and values. Violations of human rights, even ones that fall short of crimes against humanity or genocide, are signs of dangerous tensions that are not being addressed. At the same time, merely addressing the human rights violations as such by removing or punishing actors who commit them may not solve the problem. Many societies lack the capacities—economic, social, and political—to govern themselves without violating human rights. Fair trials with adequate defense, scientific police investigations, and administrative procedures that accurately monitor economic behavior all cost more money and require more skills than summary trials or punishments, torturing suspects until they confess, or taking bribes from the wealthy.

Finally, all "democracies" are not alike. Institutional design matters. Systems that provide little compensation for losers or that concentrate power too much in one authority have an inherent penchant for conflict. One reason that it has been so difficult to establish stable democracy in Nigeria has been that the flow of oil wealth has concentrated control of virtually all the country's resources in the president. No major group felt it could afford to lose an election to such a powerful post. That is why both fiscal and political federalism are vital for Nigeria's future. Systems that provide for power sharing and compensation to losers are likely to be more stable than winner-take-all systems. Modes of power sharing can vary. They involve the design of the executive (presidential, parliamentary, and mixed systems), local government, and administration.[47]

Individual-Level Sources of Conflict: Escalation Dynamics

Systemic or society-wide changes can place actors in situations in which conflict is almost inevitable. Unless these conditions are transformed, violence is likely to recur. Yet how violence does break out and spread depends on actors who mobilize the resources in their environment. Conflicts can also be set off by sudden, usually unexpected events like financial crises or acts of violence that ignite latent grievances or create fear. In the professional jargon of warning and prevention, acts that escalate conflict are known as "accelerators," and sudden events that provoke violence as "triggers."[48]

Escalation can be either vertical—in the intensity of the means used—or horizontal—in the issues, groups, or territories involved.[49] Horizontal escalation includes the processes by which separate conflicts become linked into regional conflict formations.

Some scholars have developed typologies of "accelerators" that classify escalation processes in different forms of mass violence. Barbara Harff, for instance, has developed sets of accelerators for both ethnopolitical conflict and genocides or politicides.[50] The former focus on communal clashes and include

—attacks or clashes with communal rivals;

—new regime policies that threaten a group's status;

—contention between moderate and militant factions within a group;

—formation of paramilitary units or acquisition of arms;

—political action by kindred groups in neighboring countries.

Accelerators for genocide and politicide focus on regime insecurity and include

—formation of coalitions among regime opponents;

—clashes between regime supporters and communal groups;

—increase in external support for communal groups;

—empty threats of external involvement against the government.

Small increases in the level of violence used by either government or non-governmental groups—vertical escalation—are key signs of trouble to come.[51]

Leaders and media often play central roles in the escalation of violence. They may incite fear and hatred to strengthen group solidarity as a basis for their own power.[52] Recognizing the role of individual actors, especially leaders, is central to introducing the moral dimension—in particular, that of personal responsibility—into conflict prevention and conflict management more generally. Analysis of global, structural, cultural, or institutional factors can lead to a kind of "no-fault" approach to conflict, one in which human beings are mere dust motes swirled in the winds of history. Indeed, there is some truth to such an image, which also contains an important moral dimension. Those engaged in conflict prevention or its allied disciplines in the United States and Europe, or in international nongovernmental and intergovernmental organizations, tend to be the beneficiaries of much good fortune, in terms of where they were born, how they were educated, and the opportunities life offers them. Most of those engaged in conflict, including many who commit crimes, are confronted with stresses and narrowed opportunities that some who condemn them will never have to confront. Recognition of these harsh circumstances should induce humility, a recognition of the element of tragedy in violent conflict, and a willingness to work for reconciliation.

To ignore the fact that even in the worst circumstances people retain their status as moral actors, however, is to deprive them of basic human dignity. Even in unimaginably dire circumstances some leaders and anonymous men and women struggle against the odds for nonviolent strategies, or simply to protect their neighbors, while others exploit a conflictual environment, whether sincerely, to pursue political goals, or cynically, for personal power or enrichment. No matter how bad a situation is, political leaders enjoy latitude in calming or exacerbating the potential for violence. The escalation of conflict to massive human rights violations or deportations always involves deliberate planning.[53] Recognition of that fact provides the basis for both deterrence and punishment of leaders as components of conflict prevention.

Escalation also involves psychosocial dynamics, such as the reinforcement of images of the other as enemy and the attribution of malign motives to others and of purely defensive or reactive ones to one's own group. Mass media can be particularly effective in exploiting or reinforcing such phenomena. Changes in the content of mass media toward dehumanizing or demonizing ethnic or political opponents are often signs of impending violence.

Finally, all the causes of escalation are not "out there" in the situation at risk. Some of them result from external intervention. Evidently, external intervention to aid one of the conflict parties can lead to vertical escalation by upgrading the level of weaponry available and to horizontal escalation by involving foreign actors and territories. The pursuit of economic interests or narrowly defined security goals often leads the United States and others to aggravate local conflicts. Even external intervention aimed at prevention can escalate conflict. John Davies and Barbara Harff have found that empty threats of intervention have contributed significantly to the risk of mass killing in a number of cases.[54] During his tenure in Burundi, UN Special Representative of the Secretary General Ahmedou Ould Abdallah argued that "early warnings" of the danger of a "Rwandan-style genocide" in Burundi increased fears and may have provoked violence. After his departure from Burundi in 1996, UN consideration of a preventive armed force and discussion by East African states of a regional security force for Burundi (neither of which ever materialized) seem to have incited the parties to escalate military activity that ultimately, through a cycle of killing and revenge, led to a coup d'état.[55] The NATO military intervention in Kosovo provoked (or gave cover for) a dramatic escalation of ethnic cleansing by the Serbian regime and paramilitaries, while the intervention was structured in such a way as to be unable to stop the crimes being committed. One critic claims that the CPA's Central Asia report may have contributed to conflict by exaggerating ethnic tensions in the Kyrgyz Republic and ignoring local capacities for peacemaking.[56]

In any particular situation, all levels of causality interact. The more intense or widespread the conflict at a given moment, the more intervention must concentrate on reversing or containing the escalation dynamics. Merely inhibiting escalation will be temporary and ultimately ineffective, however, if the longer-term factors that promote conflict remain unchanged. At the same time, addressing the more fundamental causes of conflict in a particular place is difficult or impossible while violence is escalating; and intervention before signs of escalation appear is often politically impossible. Reforming global institutions that facilitate or provoke conflict or creating global institutions that deter or prevent it may be more effective, but these are slow processes, the effects of which are hard to measure. These are the central strategic conundrums of preventive action.

PART One

Case Studies

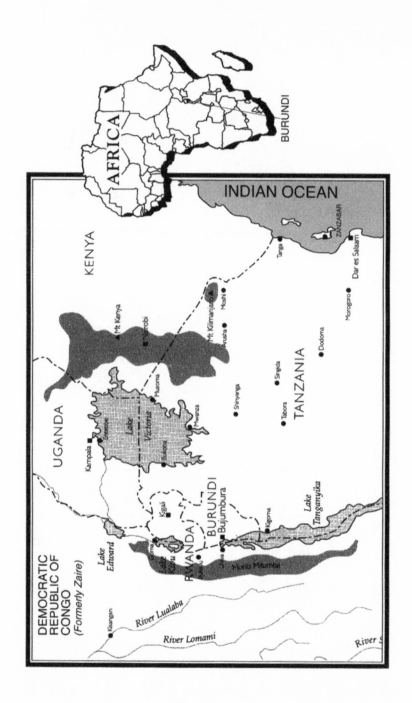

AFRICA

BURUNDI

INDIAN OCEAN

ZANZABAR

KENYA

Tanga

Dar es Salaam

Mt Kenya

Nairobi

Mt Kilimanjaro

Moshi

Arusha

Morogoro

Dodoma

Masoma

Singida

TANZANIA

Lake Victoria

Shinyanga

Tabora

Speke

Mwanza

Kampala

Bukoba

UGANDA

Kigali

BURUNDI

Bujumbura

Kigoma

Lake Tanganyika

RWANDA

Lake Edward

Goma

Lake Kivu

Uvira

Monts Mitumba

DEMOCRATIC REPUBLIC OF CONGO
(Formerly Zaire)

Kisangani

River Lualaba

River Lomami

River S

3

Burundi and the Great Lakes Region of Central Africa: Strengthless Cures, in Vain

> We shall
> let loose indiscriminate death.
> Man shall learn from man's lot, forejudge
> the evils of his neighbor's case,
> see respite and windfall in storm:
> pathetic prophet who consoles
> with strengthless cures, in vain.
>
> .... Now
> The House of Justice has collapsed.
> — *"Chorus of the Furies,"* AESCHYLUS, *The Eumenides*

The Center for Preventive Action began work on the Great Lakes region in support of the international effort to prevent escalation of violence in Burundi in the aftermath of the 1994 Rwandan genocide. Although mass violence between Hutus and Tutsis had already swept Burundi in the fall of 1993, international attention focused on the Great Lakes only after the systematic murder of more than a half million people brought a brief moment of media attention to a region that not even the cold war had made relevant to global politics.[1]

Whatever indicators of conflict potential one uses, the small, densely populated, impoverished, landlocked countries of Rwanda and Burundi, as well as the neighboring areas of Congo, score at the top.[2] Among the poorest nations in the world, these countries depend on coffee exports for the bulk of their foreign exchange. The 2000 Human Development Report of the

This chapter has greatly benefited from comments on an earlier draft by Lakhdar Brahimi, Fabienne Hara, Tony Jackson, Gérard Prunier, and David Rieff.

United Nations Development Program ranked Rwanda 164th and Burundi 170th of the 174 countries reporting indexes of human welfare.[3] In both countries Hutus and Tutsis clash in "ranked" conflict, in which the vertical divide among identity groups largely coincides with and reinforces horizontal inequality of wealth and power. Since the 1990s, nowhere else in the world have people been more likely to be murdered for ethnic or political reasons. Originally separate civil conflicts have fused into a regional conflict formation. Central Africa continues to pose the most difficult test of the international community's ability or willingness to prevent or limit mass violence.

Background

Unlike most contemporary African states, Burundi and Rwanda are based on precolonial political units of the same names and are not artificial or foreign creations. Both have national languages common to all their people (Kirundi and Kinyarwanda) and considerable cultural unity. Nonetheless, colonial powers made both ruling institutions and social structures more rigid, intensifying and concentrating sources of conflict while reducing the multiplicity of institutions to manage them.

Before the arrival of European colonialism these well-watered, hilly countries supported a dense population of farmers and herdsmen who formed chiefdoms and monarchies. The clans of both countries were loosely classified into groups known as Hutu and Tutsi, often identified with those living respectively from agriculture or pastoralism, though the Ugandan scholar Mahmood Mamdani argues that these names fit more closely with political status.[4] The monarchs and most of the ruling stratum were drawn from Tutsi clans, though in Burundi the royal clan (Ganwa) became more differentiated from the Tutsi and hence was (and is) considered more neutral. Nonetheless, although the Tutsi or Ganwa king was paramount, both Hutu and Tutsis had chiefdoms. Hutus, Tutsis, and Twa (a small group of forest-dwelling pygmies) shared, as they still do, a common language, culture, and political unit.

Hutus and Tutsis enjoyed unequal status, but political conflict never opposed these two groups as such until the late colonial period. Crisscrossing the Hutu-Tutsi cleavage were many others—clan, chiefdom, clientele, region—and none of these cleavages necessarily predominated over the others. Kingdoms and chiefdoms expanded and contracted over time, exercising more or less power or sovereignty depending on the fortunes of history and the skills of leaders. Individuals or clans might change affiliation as their status or alliances changed.

The German and then Belgian colonists who took control of these kingdoms faced the classic colonial problem of finding both reliable agents through whom to rule and a usable (mis)understanding of the subject society. The classifications made by colonial powers everywhere affected the pattern of later intergroup rivalries. These practices were based on theories that were current in the metropolitan society of the time: the feudal romanticism of Sir Walter Scott helped define the British notion of "warrior races" that indirectly lay behind the cleavages fueling the civil wars in Pakistan and Nigeria in the 1960s and 1970s.

By the late nineteenth century, when they arrived in the Great Lakes region, Europeans had developed pseudoscientific racial theories, as the writings of Arthur de Gobineau prefigured the ideology of Nazism. The colonialists identified the ruling Tutsis as racially superior "Hamites" and the Hutus as "Bantus," erasing the flexible political character of these identities. Tutsis, who constituted a minority usually estimated at about 14 percent of the population, gained a virtual monopoly on modern education and skills. They dominated the ranks of the colonial administrative apparatus in both countries, which also retained their Tutsi monarchies under foreign sovereignty. Peasants (mostly Hutu) were pressed into labor cultivating cash crops, notably coffee, largely under Tutsi "native authorities."[5] The colonial rulers also hardened the state structure, identifying the local monarchies with the European doctrine of unitary sovereignty, whereas in precolonial Africa (and many other parts of the world, including premodern Europe), ruling authority was layered and shared among different institutions. This terrible simplification of the social structure led to today's political disaster as surely as replacing complex natural forests with uniform eucalyptus plantations leads to ecological disaster.[6]

It should go without saying that the notion that Hutus and Tutsis belong to "races" with distinct mental or social characteristics has no scientific basis. Scholars still dispute why Tutsis are, on average, taller, though there is much variation within each group. Nonetheless, the European racialist ideas took on a life of their own in central Africa. Some Tutsis adopted racial arguments in favor of their own superiority; some Hutus used the myth of racial difference to stigmatize Tutsis as foreign invaders. Other Tutsis, claiming that the colonialists had invented Hutu-Tutsi conflict, stigmatized Hutus who protested against discrimination and exclusion as antinational. Acute competition among the élite of both groups for the relatively few positions of power and wealth stimulated the elaboration of such ideologies. With time, the identities themselves were largely constructed and defined through the history of conflict and violence, becoming a product of the conflicts as much as a cause.

The construction of unitary sovereign states based on a single-crop export economy (coffee), in the absence of development adequate to create a broader middle class with a stake in national institutions, empowered militaristic élites in both countries. In other respects, however, the politics of independent Rwanda and Burundi diverged. In Rwanda populist dictatorships ruled in the name of the Hutu majority, and in Burundi a dominant Tutsi élite clung to power and privilege, which it increasingly identified as key to survival. These élites, drawn in both countries from particular clans and regions (Hutus from Gisenyi in northwestern Rwanda, Tutsis from Bururi in southern Burundi), deployed a nationalist or ethnic discourse to legitimate their rule. During the "Hutu revolution" of 1959–61, which overthrew the Tutsi king *(mwami)*, perhaps 2,000–3,000 Tutsis were killed, and about 150,000 fled the country, largely to neighboring Uganda and Burundi. Many more (at least 10,000) were killed from December 1963 to January 1964, triggering a larger exodus. In Burundi the monarchy was overthrown in 1966, but by a Tutsi military regime that was determined to prevent Rwandan-style political developments in Burundi.

Massive violence reinforced and perpetuated the conflicts. Whereas independent Rwanda started its history with anti-Tutsi violence, Burundi's history since 1965 has been punctuated by Hutu revolts and reprisal massacres by the Tutsi-dominated military. In 1972, in killings that some consider genocide, the Burundian military regime responded to a revolt by massacring perhaps 100,000–200,000 educated Hutus, driving hundreds of thousands of Hutu refugees into Tanzania, with little international reaction.[7] Massacres of Tutsis also punctuated the political development of Rwanda. The desire of élites to retain privileges and the protest of others against exclusion fused with a mutual fear of extermination, accentuated by the threatening and stigmatizing rhetoric deployed by political leaders in search of constituencies.

Wars, Reforms, and Preventive Efforts

The current round of violence and political transformation started in 1990, when the Rwandan Patriotic Front (RPF), an organization composed of and led mainly by Tutsi refugees, invaded Rwanda from Uganda. The RPF's leaders (notably, Paul Kagame, today's president of Rwanda) had served in the guerrilla force and then army of President Yoweri Museveni. The invasion took place a mere three months after the Ugandan government enacted a law depriving Rwandan "refugees" (many of them born in the country) of the right to own land. The invasion signaled the start of a crisis of citizenship throughout the region that also sparked the war in eastern Zaire six years later.[8] Uganda's military—including Kagame, then chief of intelligence—was at that time receiving U.S. training, and Museveni was developing close links to Washington. France, closely linked to the Rwandan regime, sent military advisers to bolster defenses in Kigali, the capital city.

The RPF invasion displaced hundreds of thousands of largely Hutu peasants and set off government-inspired massacres of Tutsis. Development aid, which came with few conditions concerning human rights or political accountability, strengthened the regime at a time when it was committing gross human rights abuses.[9] International mediation led to the Arusha Accords, which in 1993 added the RPF to a coalition government under the sitting president, Juvénal Habyarimana. It also allotted 40 percent of the army to the RPF and provided for power sharing and future elections. Under this agreement, the ruling establishment lost power and hence sought to sabotage the accords. Some claim that the RPF was also preparing for a military victory.[10]

Starting in 1988, the military ruler of Burundi, Pierre Buyoya, had responded to international pressures by instituting a series of economic and political reforms. Structural adjustment guided by the World Bank was supposed to revive the economy. Political reforms aided by the United States Agency for International Development and others led to multiparty elections of both members of parliament and president in June 1993. Buyoya, a Tutsi who stood for president as candidate of UPRONA, the party with the most Tutsi support, lost to his Hutu challenger, Melchior Ndadaye, the candidate of FRODEBU, which defended the interests of the disenfranchised majority.[11]

Both of these reform efforts, however, broke down in successive and mutually reinforcing mass violence. In October 1993, Tutsi military officers murdered President Ndadaye and some of his senior advisers in a coup attempt. The military high command eventually halted the coup, but not before FRODEBU activists and others had killed thousands of Tutsis in reprisal for the murder of "our president," provoking, in turn, mass killings of Hutus by the army. In a few weeks, an estimated fifty thousand people were killed and tens of thousands displaced.

The international community that had supported and promoted the reforms now gingerly stepped further into this morass of fear, suspicion, and bloodshed. UN Secretary General Boutros Boutros-Ghali appointed Ahmedou Ould Abdallah, the former foreign minister of Mauritania, as his special representative to prevent further conflict in Burundi.

Ould Abdallah's mission had a fairly low profile until Burundi finally received a higher level of attention as a result of guilt and fear over the collective international failure to stop the Rwandan genocide.[12] Among the motives for the genocide was the feeling of the Rwandan Hutu extremists that the Arusha Accords, which they rejected, excluded them from power and their belief, reinforced by the events of October and November 1993 in Burundi, that power sharing with Tutsis would lead to the violent subjugation of Hutus. They propagated this view through mass media to create a base for the power they seized after a missile of as yet undetermined origin downed a plane carrying the Hutu presidents of both Rwanda and Burundi as it prepared to land in Kigali.

Despite very specific warnings, international actors took no preemptive action against the violence.[13] The UN Security Council responded by withdrawing most of the small peacekeeping force (ten Belgian members of which the *génocidaires* had killed) that had monitored implementation of the Arusha Accords. A Ghanaian contingent remained, doing what it could to save civilians. The U.S. administration reacted more to the domestic political fallout from the events in Somalia than to the situation in Rwanda. Interpreting the violence as tribal clashes in another "failed state" like Somalia (which resembles Rwanda as much as Sicily does Prussia), the Clinton administration not only declined to send U.S. forces but also blocked other attempts to act. A small, controversial French intervention force (Opération Turquoise), sent after most of the killing was over, was perceived by many in the region as protection for the remnants of the regime that had carried out the genocide, though it seems to have had more complex motives.

The RPF victory on July 19, 1994, sparked regional expansion of the conflict arena. More than 2 million Rwandan Hutus fled into North and South Kivu Provinces of eastern Zaire as well as into neighboring regions of Tanzania and Burundi. The international humanitarian effort to save them from a cholera epidemic in which thirty thousand died contrasted with the lack of response to the genocide that had preceded it. This operation established the "refugee" camps right on the border.

International actors are still struggling to deal with the legacy of this failure. The UN Security Council established an International Criminal

Tribunal for Rwanda in Arusha, Tanzania, sharing a prosecutor with the tribunal on the former Yugoslavia in The Hague. Major donor states, the UN, the Organization of African Unity (OAU), France, and Belgium carried out retrospective evaluations of their role in this failure.[14] Among major actors, only the United States and the Catholic Church have not examined their records in detail, though in March 1998, during a brief stopover at the Kigali airport, President Bill Clinton seemed to express regret to genocide survivors.[15]

International actors tried to compensate for their failure in Rwanda with escalation of "preventive" activity in Burundi. Ould Abdallah's mission attracted some attention in April 1994, when he rallied the fearful elements of Burundi's government to prevent the outbreak of another round of violence after the plane was shot down over Kigali, the second killing of a Burundian Hutu president in six months.[16] Ould Abdallah also helped to broker a power-sharing agreement. This Convention of Government aimed to combine the elected power of the FRODEBU (mainly Hutu) majority with security for the (Tutsi) minority to prepare the grounds for a "national debate" on the institutional reforms needed for long-term stability. The convention also called for an international investigation into the 1993 killings.

The international strategy for Burundi aimed to limit escalation of violence to make time and space available to strengthen legitimate, if fragile, democratic institutions and then institute more basic reforms.[17] Within this context of support for a legitimate government, international actors, Ould Abdallah argued, should support "moderates" and isolate "extremists." Scores of international agencies, governments, and nongovernmental organizations (NGOs) instituted programs of many types aimed at strengthening democracy, promoting conflict resolution, building civil society institutions such as independent media and human rights organizations, and much more.[18]

The CPA's Involvement: The Burundi Policy Forum

The CPA's involvement with Burundi dated to that time. At a November 1994 conference organized by the United States Institute of Peace in Washington, I spoke with John Marks and Susan Collin Marks, of Search for Common Ground, and Lionel Rosenblatt, of Refugees International. They had gone to Burundi to explore projects they might undertake. Ould Abdallah was trying to harness the power of such NGOs to leverage his own

effectiveness, not just in delivering humanitarian aid but also in conflict resolution and institution building. Their consultations with Ould Abdallah
also suggested a joint forum in Washington. Together with another NGO, the
African American Institute, we established the Burundi Policy Forum in
January 1995.[19]

After taking an inventory of conflict prevention activities in Burundi, the
forum noted a gap in the areas of security and justice. Few programs dealt
with the pervasive violence that underlay the apparent institutional framework of Burundian politics. Political assassinations targeted leaders who
were engaged in negotiations. Tutsi extremists paralyzed Bujumbura with
strikes. Dissident Hutu politicians fled abroad to initiate guerrilla warfare.
The aid for institutional reform might or might not have succeeded, but the
escalation of violence, leading to the coup d'état of July 29, 1996, rendered
success impossible at that time. International efforts failed to confront the
violence and instead concentrated on the easier but therefore futile task of
supporting reform.

The changed regional context facilitated not only vertical escalation but
horizontal escalation as well. To the long-standing Burundian Hutu resistance based among the 1972 refugees in Tanzania was added a stronger force
based in eastern Zaire, where the exiled Rwandan Hutu-power groups
assisted the Burundians under the patronage of Zairian president Mobutu
Sese Seko.[20]

Ould Abdallah tried to discourage violence by inviting international delegations, which he called "témoins gênants" (bothersome witnesses). Most
of the highest officials of the U.S. foreign policy establishment (including its
UN ambassador and national security adviser) visited Burundi during this
time, as did the UN secretary general, a Security Council delegation, a delegation of the European Union, and many others. The Organization of
African Unity sent a small military observer mission to monitor the army,
and the United States increased the amount of time that its regional military
attaché based in Cameroon spent in Burundi. Search for Common Ground
and Refugees International, which had lobbied for the latter measure, also
obtained some funding from the U.S. International Criminal Investigative
Training Assistance Program to train Burundian police. Individuals identified as extremists were placed on a list of those who should be denied visas
for travel abroad, an example of targeted sanctions.

Other proposals languished, however. Several organizations proposed
sending human rights or peace monitors. The UN high commissioner for
human rights established a monitoring mission, but funding problems always
prevented it from reaching full complement. The OAU could not obtain

funding for a modest expansion of its military observer mission. The UN commission of inquiry into the 1993 coup and "genocide" was repeatedly delayed and had no authority to make judicial referrals to either domestic or international courts, despite a provision in the Convention of Government asking for such referrals.[21] There were no programs for training or assistance for Burundi's Tutsi-dominated and overwhelmed judiciary or police.

In the spring of 1995, Human Rights Watch released its first report on arms flows to the region, including evidence that, despite a UN embargo, the Rwandan genocidal forces in eastern Zaire were rearming themselves from the world market and preparing to launch guerrilla attacks and, eventually, an invasion of Rwanda while being supported through the humanitarian assistance to the refugees.[22] The CPA initiated a series of meetings that led thirty-three organizations to issue a joint statement warning of the dangers of a broader regional war and advocating a regionwide initiative.[23] The group recommended measures to deal with the threat of violence, such as carrying out UN Security Council recommendations to deploy military monitors of arms flows in airports in eastern Zaire; imposing sanctions against visas and bank accounts of extremists; disabling radio stations inciting massacres; supporting the International Criminal Tribunal on Rwanda and expanding its mandate to include Burundi; seconding francophone officers to the police and judicial services as well as training those services in Burundi and Rwanda; and forming the International Commission of Inquiry into the 1993 coup and killings in Burundi that the Convention of Government had requested. These measures were supposed to buy time for the coalition's recommendations for longer-term efforts aimed at the structural sources of conflict, such as unblocking $600 million in funds for Rwanda and establishing a regional reconstruction fund.

The group also called for a regional framework for coordinated policy to be implemented by special envoys and missions of the United States, the UN, and the OAU. By September 6, President Clinton claimed in a letter to the CPA chair, General John W. Vessey, that a number of these measures had been taken, but no major power was willing to take the measures necessary to block the rearming of the militias in eastern Zaire and thereby halt the escalation of violence.

Escalation and Nonintervention

Burundi also became enmeshed in the internal politics of the UN. As the United States prepared to prevent Boutros-Ghali's reelection in 1996, and a number of scathing evaluations of the response to the Rwandan genocide were published, Boutros-Ghali took a number of steps. Ould Abdallah, whom Boutros-Ghali (accurately) perceived as campaigning for the post of secretary general, resigned (or was dismissed) in October 1995. Boutros-Ghali also issued a number of statements warning of the danger of "genocide" in Burundi. Ould Abdallah had opposed such public warnings on the ground that they risked increasing insecurity and hence violence on the ground.

Indeed, Ould Abdallah's fears seem to have been borne out by subsequent events: "early warnings," followed by empty threats of military action, seemed to escalate the conflict further, leading to the July coup. Throughout the winter and spring of 1995–96, Boutros-Ghali called for the deployment of a preventive force to Zaire that would be ready to intervene in Burundi if necessary "to avoid repetition of the tragic events in Rwanda."[24] The UN led a process of contingency planning for intervention in which the United States was actively engaged. France, badly burned by the response to Opéra-tion Turquoise, refused to participate and viewed the United States's role with suspicion, especially as the latter was increasingly engaged in military training and joint exercises with both Uganda and Rwanda, whose regimes France regarded with hostility. Boutros-Ghali wrote to twenty-one countries asking for troops but received positive responses from only three. Although the entire effort came to naught, everyone involved was able to blame the failure on someone else's incapacity or unwillingness.

In any case, the proposed intervention appeared to be based not on an accurate evaluation of the situation in Burundi but on a retroactive attempt to escape blame for "another Rwanda." There was never any danger of a "repetition of the tragic events in Rwanda" in Burundi. In the former case, a majority-based regime had exterminated opponents and the minority, while in the latter a minority-based regime faced resistance from the major-ity, creating a rough balance of terror. A force poised for future intervention would have done nothing to reduce the violence actually taking place and might, in fact, have aggravated it.

By spring 1996, East African states concluded that the broader interna-tional community would not take decisive action. Former U.S. president Jimmy Carter had convened some regional roundtables of heads of state. Carter involved some of his African associates as cochairs, including former Tanzanian president Julius Nyerere. The East African heads of state contin-ued this process, convening a meeting in March, at which the UN and the OAU jointly asked Nyerere to mediate a conflict that was now openly described as a civil war. Although Nyerere's prestige brought international attention to the negotiations, Tanzania's position as a haven for Hutu refugees and guerrillas created suspicions of partiality on the part of the Burundian government and Tutsi parties.

The East African states offered to send to Burundi a "security force," including troops from Uganda and Tanzania and police from Kenya, to protect key personnel and installations. Both the president (Hutu, FRODEBU) and the prime minister (Tutsi, UPRONA) supported the proposal at Arusha, but on their return to Bujumbura they turned out to have opposing interpretations of what the force would do. The president expected the force to monitor the army and rein in both its atrocities and violence by Tutsi extremists, whereas the prime minister expected the force to assist the army against the guerrillas. The army, Tutsi militias, and Hutu guerrillas all opposed the force. A two-person CPA mission in May 1996 returned from Burundi with the strong impression, shared by the East African leaders, that the failure to counter threats to security (assassinations, massacres) would doom efforts to prevent conflict through political negotiations and institution building.[25] The inconclusive international efforts to deploy a preventive or security force there, however, far from calming the situation, had aroused local opposition. The mission's analysis soon proved accurate, when, on July 29, 1996, the military overthrew the Hutu president (this time without harming him) and reinstalled Buyoya.

The dissolution of the parliament and elected government put an end to the years of democracy building. Burundi's East African neighbors imposed comprehensive economic sanctions on the country, though an exception was belatedly made for humanitarian supplies. Development aid had ceased in May as a result of increased violence, and trade was diverted to smuggling channels. Many states had qualms about the sanctions but did not want to contradict the efforts of the local actors. The UN Security Council "took note" of the sanctions without endorsing them. Major states abided by them, while traders in the regional states that had imposed sanctions profited from the smuggling that expanded to evade them.

Negotiations: Multiple Tracks

The international political effort now crossed the rather fuzzy boundary between prevention and peacemaking in an armed conflict. International strategy shifted from trying to marginalize extremists to trying to draw all parties into negotiations. The coup that overthrew the legitimate leadership, as well as the development of guerrilla warfare, led most actors to change their diagnosis and treat ending the violence as the primary goal. There was no clear repository of legitimacy. The conditions on the government of Burundi for lifting the sanctions thus included participating in externally based negotiations for, among other things, a cease-fire and restoring institutions such as the parliament.[26]

Three tracks of negotiation emerged: an initially secret, bilateral track between the government and the main guerrilla group (CNDD-FDD) under the patronage of the Community of Sant' Egidio in Rome; "all-party" talks convened by Nyerere in Arusha (which eventually absorbed the Sant' Egidio talks); and the government's negotiations with leaders of FRODEBU inside the country.[27] The Arusha talks, convened by Nyerere, took place under the patronage of the East African states with the assistance of the "special envoys club." The latter came to include envoys to the Great Lakes region from the United States, the European Union, the UN, the OAU, the Community of Sant' Egidio, Search for Common Ground, and others.

The sanctions were justified by the claim that African governments would no longer accept military governments and the suppression of democracy. The lack of a comparable response to the 1993 coup in Nigeria incited skepticism, but Burundi's transition also illustrated serious difficulties in the sequencing of reforms. The 1993 election had empowered the majority without either guaranteeing security to the minority or establishing adequate safeguards against those opposed to majority rule. In 1996, Buyoya displaced a constitutional president and parliament. Army abuses, including killings of civilians, continued. But it was arguably only the presence of a Tutsi military figure at the head of state that enabled the political authorities to reassert control over the security forces and open negotiations with Hutu guerrillas.

By the end of 1998, Buyoya had more than met the conditions for lifting the sanctions, and normal trade and travel resumed. The parliament had reopened with a Hutu FRODEBU leader as speaker, the government had signed a partnership agreement with the domestic opposition (which represented an electoral majority), and the government was fully engaged in the Arusha talks. Numerous NGOs still worked in both the capital and some of the more secure rural areas, and a number of Burundian interlocutors with whom I spoke during a September 1998 visit said that the work of conflict resolution and democracy-building NGOs had strengthened new ideas and more positive modes of interaction in local society and politics. Nonetheless, the sanctions on trade and the end of development assistance had taken a toll on the country's institutions. The sanctions that pressed Buyoya to make needed reforms also accentuated the deprivation that combined with the heritage of mass killing to make political and ethnic conflicts so violent.

The expansion of a regional war centered on the Democratic Republic of the Congo (the former Zaire), in which Burundi's Tutsi-dominated army and Hutu-led opposition guerrillas were allied with opposite sides, enmeshed the country in a wider web of conflict and conflict-related money-making activities. The flight of both Rwandan and Burundian refugees and guerrillas to Zaire's eastern region had linked the conflicts in these neighboring states. Although only eastern Zaire (North and South Kivu) belonged geographically and ethnically to the Great Lakes region, the impact of the conflicts there also began to dominate politics in Kinshasa, the capital city, and in the country's other regions.[28]

International Failure and Escalation

The outbreak of war in the Democratic Republic of the Congo, first in 1996 and then in 1998, was directly related to the international community's failure to take measures to prevent mass violence. The international relief effort for the Rwandan Hutu refugees also supported perpetrators of the genocide. Not only did guilty individuals receive aid, but the aid effort for the genuine refugees was largely administered by the transplanted organization of the Hutu-power regime, which used resources from that effort, as well as the central bank and treasury reserves transported from Kigali and income from smuggling and land grabs in Zaire, to rearm and train for another round of war. Humanitarian organizations have debated whether they should have stayed or withdrawn (as some NGOs did), but the principal responsibility among external actors falls on the political leaders, who found no way to separate the armed groups from the refugees, halt or limit the arms flows, or move the camps away from the border.

In August 1996, the Rwandan vice president and military strongman Paul Kagame traveled to the United States, where he warned that the situation could not remain as it was and hinted that he would act if others did not. An incident provoked by Zairian domestic politics soon provided the occasion for a joint Rwandan-Ugandan intervention in alliance with local rebels.

The incident that sparked the war derived from Mobutu's efforts to derail the democratization process. In eastern Zaire a long-standing issue concerned the citizenship of people of Rwandan origin, many Tutsis among them—the same issue that had stimulated the RPF's flight from Uganda in 1990.[29] Some had arrived centuries earlier, some as laborers during colonialism, and some as refugees from the Rwandan Hutu regime. Popular sentiment in Zaire considered these groups, known as Banyamulenge, as foreigners. Citizenship conferred few benefits in the failing state of Zaire, but the plans for elections required an electoral roll and hence raised the issue once again. In October 1996, Mobutu's governor of South Kivu announced that Banyamulenge would be considered foreigners and required to leave the country.

The response was a preplanned "revolt" whose military leaders were Rwandan-trained Banyamulenge supported by Rwandan and Ugandan forces. Among the military targets in eastern Zaire were the "refugee" camps and military facilities of the Rwandan Hutus. Many were killed in attacks on the camps. Most streamed back to Rwanda. Those in Burundi and Tanzania also returned, under pressure from host governments. A disputed number, but certainly at least two hundred thousand, fled into the jungle, where Rwandan commando squads appear to have hunted them down and killed them.[30] The vast numbers unaccounted for led to the establishment of a UN Commission of Inquiry that has still been unable to conduct an investigation. The relatively weak response to these massacres appeared to show that the 1994 genocide was being used to establish impunity for even immense crimes committed by those who claimed to represent its victims.

The missing refugees and fugitives sparked yet another failed attempt at international intervention. The UN Security Council authorized a force to protect the refugees, and Canada agreed to lead it. The contradictory goals espoused by the force's various supporters, however, guaranteed that local opposition would doom the effort. Canada and some others saw the force as a purely humanitarian force to protect refugees. France saw it as humanitarian cover for interposing an international presence between the rebels and Mobutu's crumbling forces. The United States appeared to support it on humanitarian grounds but, in fact, prevented it from occurring, as Washington supported the war aims of Rwanda and Uganda, which it saw as the core of a set of African regimes friendly to U.S. interests. The United States minimized the number of missing refugees or stigmatized them as *génocidaires* to reduce pressure for the so-called Multi-National Force. None of the potential international contributors wanted the mission to disarm the militias, whose presence constituted Rwanda's ostensible reason for the war. As the contradictions multiplied, the war advanced, the refugees and fugitives disappeared, and the force was canceled.

Instead, not for the first time, war took an unexpected turn. To provide the rebellion with a more Congolese, non-Tutsi public face, the Ugandan authorities had dug up an old anti-Mobutu leftist from the 1960s, Laurent-

Désiré Kabila. Kabila was made spokesman for the rebel movement, named the AFDL (Alliance des Forces Démocratiques pour la Libération du Congo-Zaire [Alliance of Democratic Forces for the Liberation of Congo-Zaire]). After the AFDL-Rwandan-Ugandan forces had taken the Kivu provinces, they laid siege to the important northern city of Kisangani, defended by, among others, Serbian mercenaries imported to Zaire by French intelligence.[31] Kisangani fell, Mobutu's army and regime crumbled, and the AFDL-Rwandan forces marched across the country they decided to rename as the Democratic Republic of the Congo (DRC), eventually installing Kabila as president—an outcome no one (save possibly Kabila himself) had foreseen or intended.

In early March 1997, as the AFDL-Rwandan-Ugandan forces laid siege to Kisangani, the Center for Preventive Action organized a consultation for Mohamed Sahnoun, an Algerian diplomat who had been named special envoy to the Great Lakes by the UN and the OAU. The CPA worked with the Carter Center and a Geneva-based African NGO, Synergies Africa, to convene experts and diplomats from the United States, Europe, and Africa, who spent several days in New York analyzing the interrelated conflicts of that region.[32] The recently passed UN Security Council Resolution 1097, which dealt with both the immediate violence and longer-term issues, helped frame the discussion around three topics: immediate concerns, such as ending the war and providing humanitarian aid; the political future of Zaire; and a long-term, regional solution to be developed by an international conference on peace, security, and development in the Great Lakes region.

The participants considered several different scenarios, including a negotiated settlement and the collapse of the Mobutu regime. Whereas some favored the Multi-National Force, others concluded that its internal contradictions, as well as the realities on the ground, would make its mission impossible. They suggested instead the dispatch of human rights and peace monitors to protect the civilian population. During the pause created, Zaire (as it was still called) could form a new government based on the decisions of the Sovereign National Conference, a national forum that had drafted plans for a democratic transition that enjoyed broad support. The group also argued for support for the civil society that had grown up in the vacuum left by the collapse of the Zairian administration. Discussions converged on ideas for an eventual regional conference and a comprehensive approach to the entire Great Lakes region, though some dissented. France had come to be a major sponsor of these ideas—a fact that Rwanda, in particular, looked upon with suspicion.

These recommendations were largely overtaken by fast-moving events. The "international community" lacked the consensus and capacity to carry out any such plans, as was evident to those on the ground, who were determined to solve their problems in their own way. Rwanda and Uganda had launched the Banyamulenge "revolt" to solve the security problems posed by the *génocidaires* and other insurgents and by the inability and unwillingness of Mobutu to serve as a partner in regional security. International mining companies, which coveted the wealth of the Congo, helped bankroll Kabila's march on Kinshasa, in the hope of future contracts.[33] As the Rwandan-supported forces moved west and south, Angola also played a key role. It sent the descendants of the Katangan gendarmerie back to diamond-rich Shaba (formerly Katanga) Province and intervened directly near Kinshasa to help overthrow Mobutu. Long before he had provided refuge for the Hutu-power regime of Rwanda, the Zairian president had provided Luanda's enemy, the UNITA (National Union for the Total Independence of Angola) guerrilla organization, with access to assistance—during the cold war from the United States and South Africa and thereafter from the international diamond market.

A period of Africa optimism followed Kabila's victory and Mobutu's departure, mediated by the United States. Media and U.S. official statements depicted Kagame, Museveni, Kabila, and others (including the presidents of Ethiopia and Eritrea, both of whom also came to power through guerrilla struggles ended by a United States–brokered deal) as a new generation of African leadership that took responsibility for its own affairs, supported market economics, would eventually establish democratic governance, and would be partners with the United States in creating an "African Renaissance."[34]

President Clinton traveled to Africa in the spring of 1998. He indirectly expressed regret for his inaction during the Rwandan genocide and held a summit with the "new" leaders in Uganda. The administration accelerated its campaign for passage of the Africa Growth and Opportunity Act to allow African exports better access to the U.S. market. It also increased military engagement with Uganda, Rwanda, and other African governments, especially those that agreed to participate in the Africa Crisis Response Initiative. The latter program, one of the U.S. responses to its failure in the Rwandan genocide, was intended to help African states prepare an indigenous military capability for peacekeeping and humanitarian intervention. Secretary of State Madeleine Albright also announced a $30 million "justice initiative" for central Africa, designed to address the problem of impunity in the region through aid to local courts, police, and other institutions.

Kabila's DRC remained outside these initiatives, as the new leader continued to block a UN inquiry into the killings during the war that had brought him to power. He showed scant inclination to allow democratic freedoms, protect human rights, or engage with either civil society or the political parties that had sprung up during the period of the Sovereign National Conference. He also reneged on promises on mining concessions, angering corporations that had backed him. Kabila's behavior sparked a policy debate in Washington, reflected in discussions at the Great Lakes Policy Forum. Human rights advocates argued for keeping a distance from Kabila until he met human rights benchmarks. Others, including development organizations and some in the U.S. government, argued for engagement to help build up basic infrastructure in the country. Most interested parties supported aid to civil society, but Kabila opposed it, seeing it (correctly, in fact) as support for his opposition. All agreed that the mass violence in the region was connected to predatory or ineffective state structures and the endemic poverty that deprived people of basic livelihoods and pitted them against one another. But organizations with different mandates disagreed on whether to use diplomatic and other means (such as sanctions) first, to end or limit the violence and thereby create conditions to address institutional and economic problems, or to address the "root causes" directly, even as the violence continued, in the hope that it would abate.

As the debates proceeded, the man who was supposed to be a pliant figurehead for the Congo's neighbors proved to be a shrewd politician himself. To increase his own autonomy and build support by playing on nationalism, Kabila denounced international actors, including the UN, the United States, and, increasingly, the states that had brought him to power. He started to distance himself from his Rwandan Tutsi backers, who dominated his military. He allowed the Rwandan Hutu militias on his territory to continue their war inside Rwanda.

By August 1998, an increasingly assertive Kabila responded to Rwandan pressure over these issues by dismissing his Tutsi bodyguard and military commanders. Rwanda and Uganda, both recipients of U.S. military aid and training, responded by launching another revolt in the east and north of the country. This revolt took place under a new political leadership, organized initially in the RCD (Rassemblement Congolais pour la Démocratie [Congolese Rally for Democracy]). The rebels attempted to seize Kinshasa through a quick coup de main, dispatching commandos by aircraft, but the breakup of their alliance with Kabila translated as well into a breakup of the regional coalition that had come together against Mobutu: the RCD-

Rwandan-Ugandan commandos were stopped by the swift intervention of Angolan troops, who sided with Kabila against "foreign aggression," as Kabila also inspired a wave of anti-Tutsi attacks in Kinshasa. Zimbabwe and Namibia soon engaged as well to assist Kabila on other fronts.

The war turned into a disastrous stalemate. The increasingly unpopular rebel coalition fragmented into three parts. The Rwandan government succeeded in pushing Rwandan Hutu militias away from the border, thereby increasing domestic security. Kabila, aided not only by Zimbabwe, Angola, and Namibia but also by the Rwandan Hutu forces, an eastern militia called the Mai-Mai, and others, held on to Kinshasa and the diamond-rich cities of Lubumbashi and Mbuji Mayi. Kabila now mobilized and armed Hutu fighters from both Rwanda and Burundi, despite the fact that the forces that had brought him to power (against whom he was now fighting) had slaughtered Rwandan Hutus in 1996–97.

If the war's military and political results were ambiguous, however, many benefited from it economically. Even more than the 1996 Congo war, this one revolved around control of the country's diamond, gold, coltan, and other resources. Ugandan generals enriched themselves, as did the entourage around President Robert Mugabe in Zimbabwe, while the Rwandan army exploited the resources in a typically disciplined way to pay for the war.[35]

The results for Congolese society were disastrous. Epidemiologists funded by the International Rescue Committee estimate that by May 2001, 2.5 million people (out of an estimated population of 18 million) had lost their lives in eastern Congo as a result of the war, some through direct violence, others as the result of displacement, unchecked disease, and starvation.[36] Ethnic hatred, especially of Tutsis in eastern Zaire, rose to the point that many warned of another genocide. Reconciliation projects between Tutsis and other Congolese, organized by local NGOs with little foreign support, were swept away. In northern Zaire, where Ugandan troops guarded the routes of gold smuggling, a vicious war broke out between the Hema and Lendu ethnic groups. The Hema had gained large tracts of grazing land in the preceding decades by supporting Mobutu. They now paid Ugandan soldiers to push the Lendu off yet more land. Thousands died in the resultant fighting, as well as many others from more mundane causes such as measles. The insecurity in the region caused the few international humanitarian groups to withdraw, leaving disease, like overt violence, to spread unchecked. All of this unfolded with little external hindrance, even as NATO claimed to elaborate a doctrine of humanitarian intervention based on the alliance's actions in Kosovo.

African diplomatic activity, mostly led by Zambia with important assistance from South Africa and meetings in a variety of capitals and supported by key members of the "special envoys club," led eventually to the Lusaka Accords of August 1999. These complex accords provided for a cease-fire to be monitored by both a Joint Military Commission of the belligerent states and a UN observer mission; the disarmament of unofficial militias, including the Rwandan Hutus; the withdrawal of all foreign troops; and a national dialogue in Congo leading to a representative democracy.

In February 2000, the UN Security Council passed a U.S.-drafted resolution to send 500 observers and 5,037 troops to provide for their logistics and security to monitor a cease-fire in a country of 905,063 square miles—roughly the size of western Europe—with virtually no roads. Meanwhile, 40,000 NATO troops were hardly able to provide security in Kosovo, a province of 4,203 square miles. This resolution was passed just months after the submission to the secretary general of two scathing reports on Rwanda and Srebrenica, detailing how sending too small a force with too weak a mission into a conflict situation led to the worst disasters in the history of the UN.[37] The observer mission would in any case not be sent unless security conditions improved, and it had as yet no cease-fire to monitor. It had no mandate to protect the population, which nonetheless expected the UN—in whatever guise—to bring peace and save it from the war.[38] In 2001, after Kabila was assassinated and replaced by his more cooperative son, Joseph, the UN decided to scale down the mission and deploy even fewer observers.[39]

This war affected all of Africa, from Sudan to South Africa, from Eritrea to Angola. It damaged U.S. prestige, as the same leaders whom Washington had supported, strengthened militarily, and held out as examples now turned on one another. Many in the region had come to see Rwanda and Uganda, with their effective U.S.-aided militaries, as Washington's agents, and the U.S. government seemingly knew in advance or approved of their actions in 1996, if not in 1998. Hence many interpreted these wars as grabs by Washington for control of the mineral resources of the Congo.

The wars in the DRC had contradictory effects on Rwanda and Burundi. Rwanda's internal security situation improved, as the Hutu militias fought for Kabila far from home. The government, which held more than 125,000 genocide suspects in overcrowded prisons, began to develop a system of village-level courts. Some hoped that this system might eventually address an explosive problem that otherwise would require either blanket amnesty or centuries of trials, but others cited many flaws. The regime, torn by conflicts among the Tutsi returnees, the internal genocide survivors, and various factions of the Hutu majority, seemed to grow ever narrower in its base, as symbolized in the forced resignation of the Hutu president Pasteur Bizimungu in March 2000 and his replacement by Paul Kagame.[40] But nowhere else were genocide's perpetrators and survivors supposed to live together in peace in a common political unit.

The DRC war helped escalate Burundi's civil war, as Kabila had provided new bases and equipment for Hutu groups. The Arusha negotiations continued, and Nelson Mandela accepted the mantle of facilitator after the death of Julius Nyerere, the former president of Tanzania who had served as the first mediator, in October 1999. By the end of 2001, implementation of the agreement had started. A South African peacekeeping force had entered the country, and donors had pledged $700 million in support of the new dispensation. The assassination of Laurent Kabila by a bodyguard and his succession by his son, Joseph, seemed to open previously closed doors to the national dialogue in the DRC and the implementation of other aspects of the Lusaka Accords. Several leaders, under increasing domestic and international pressure, seemed to be seeking a way to withdraw their troops, including both Museveni and Mugabe of Zimbabwe. But as a precarious cease-fire seemingly took hold in the DRC, Hutu guerrillas moved back to Rwanda and Burundi, raising the level of violence in the core of the conflict region. Outside actors, in any case, could claim little credit for any progress in a region that had experienced more than its share of crimes and tragedy and less than its share of effective human solidarity.

4

The South Balkans:
Landscape Painted with Blood

> Behind this invisible barrier, Belgrade is not Belgrade anymore, and the
> Danube is not a river. A bird, flying overhead in its yearning for freedom,
> banged against this barrier, the way birds trapped in a room bang against
> and break the window of the glass of a painting depicting a landscape
> painted with tea. The bird in Razin's painting had banged against this
> invisible barrier, broken and flown through it. But it is not known whether
> the bird found freedom, because it emerged on the other side stained
> with blood, and its blood trickled down the other, eternal side of the bar-
> rier, as if down a pane of glass, while it flapped its torn wings, trying to
> catch the wind from the other side.
>
> —MILORAD PAVIC, *Landscape Painted with Tea*, 1990

The conflicts resulting from the breakup of Yugoslavia have largely dominated debate in the United States and Europe about post–cold-war
conflict. Kabul, the "Dresden of post–Cold War conflict" according to
Michael Ignatieff,[1] may be more devastated than Sarajevo; Rwanda may have
a stronger claim than Bosnia to having experienced genocide; the landscapes
of Angola, Mozambique, Cambodia, and Afghanistan may be strewn with
more landmines than anywhere in southeastern Europe; victims of war
crimes in the Democratic Republic of the Congo or Sudan may outnumber
those in Bosnia or Kosovo; but until the attacks of September 11, 2001,
transformed the international scene, the wars in the former Yugoslavia
largely shaped the debate in the United States and Europe on post-cold-war
conflict.

This chapter draws heavily on contributions by Steven L. Burg to Barnett R. Rubin, ed.,
Toward Comprehensive Peace in Southeast Europe: Conflict Prevention in the South Balkans,
more than can conveniently be acknowledged in the notes. It has also benefited from extensive comments by Victor Friedman.

55

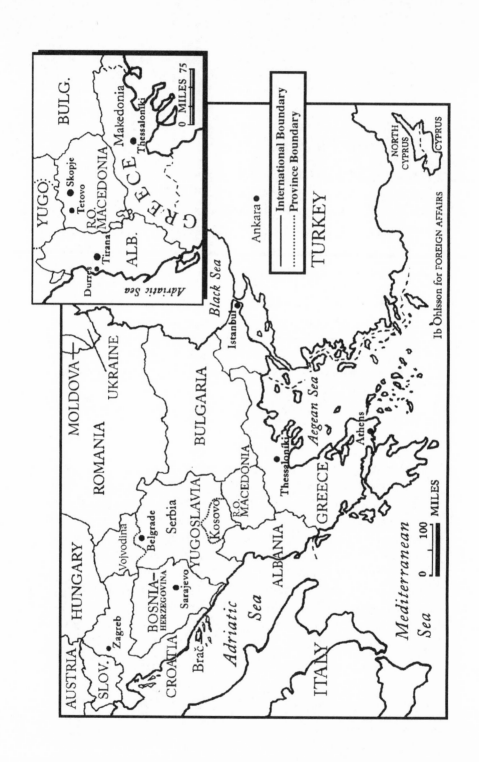

AUSTRIA

HUNGARY

SLOV.

Zagreb

CROATIA

BOSNIA–
HERZEGOVINA

Sarajevo

Brač

Adriatic

Sea

ITALY

Mediterranean

Sea

ROMANIA

MOLDOVA

UKRAINE

Vojvodina

Belgrade

Serbia

YUGOSLAVIA

Kosovo

R.O.
MACEDONIA

ALBANIA

GREECE

Thessaloníki

Aegean Sea

Athens

BULGARIA

Black Sea

Istanbul

Ankara

TURKEY

NORTH
CYPRUS

CYPRUS

International Boundary

Province Boundary

Ib Öhlsson for FOREIGN AFFAIRS

0   100
MILES

YUGO.

BULG.

Skopje

Tetovo

R.O.
MACEDONIA

Tirana

ALB.

Durrës

Adriatic Sea

G R E E C E

Makedonia

Thessaloníki

0   MILES 75

That debate has focused on dilemmas of "humanitarian intervention," defined as international military action to halt ongoing crimes and bloodshed and the possible trade-offs between indicting war criminals and negotiating with them.[2] The ability of NATO to threaten Slobodan Milosevic with air strikes with less delay after the outbreak of hostilities in Kosovo than in Bosnia showed a significant change in Euro-Atlantic strategic doctrine. The need suddenly to assemble a response to the conflict in Kosovo after the Drenica massacre in February–March 1998, however, showed that NATO and its members had adopted no effective doctrine to prevent such conflicts.

The Center for Preventive Action was founded in part to help transcend debates about intervention by testing more proactive strategies. By the time the CPA decided to work on the Balkans, in the summer of 1995, the first round of post-Yugoslav wars was approaching its climax as the military prelude to the Dayton Accords unfolded in Croatia and Bosnia. The CPA turned its attention to other conflicts in the same region, ones that had not yet led to massive, overt violence. A poll of the CPA's advisory board put both Kosovo and Macedonia at the top of our agenda.[3] Several years before Richard Holbrooke used the phrase to refer to Kijevo, where the Kosovo Liberation Army and Serbian forces battled in June 1998, the board clearly saw the South Balkans as "the most dangerous place in Europe."[4]

That meeting showed that "early warning" in any simple sense—the knowledge that an area risked major violence—was not the principal obstacle to prevention of war in the South Balkans. The CPA never found an analyst, decisionmaker, or activist who did not believe these situations might well lead to war. However, in the absence of political pressure to tackle the potential conflict in Kosovo, a feasible and effective strategy for doing so, and an international consensus among major states on the definition of the problem, it was easier to drift and hope for the best.

Background

So identified has the region of the "Balkans" become with the clash of rigid ethnic identities that it is easy to forget that this was once in many ways the most intermixed region in Europe. The very violence and assertion of difference that has accompanied the past centuries of nationalist struggle attest to the obstacles to homogenization posed by the interrelationships among peoples, religions, and languages there. The historian Ivo Banac has compared the political movements of the past two centuries to a "forest fire" burning through the region's ethnic rain forests and leaving in its charred wake nothing but sterile nationalism.[5] As in the Great Lakes region, the politically motivated simplification of identities cleared the undergrowth that resisted conflagrations.

Nationalism developed in these regions as the dominant ideology in the struggle against the Ottoman and Austro-Hungarian Empires. Discrete identities were carved out of a complex of interrelated factors, mostly language and religion.[6] Nationalist territorial claims overlapped. The first Yugoslavia, founded after World War I, incorporated Serbia, to which the 1912 Treaty of London had awarded control of the Albanian-majority province of Kosovo. Most of today's Republic of Macedonia was incorporated into that state as South Serbia, and ethnic Macedonians classified as southern Serbs. Albania also emerged as an independent state, but without the Albanian-majority areas that remained under Yugoslav rule, in both Kosovo and South Serbia (Macedonia). Albanians, depicted by Serbs as allies of the Turkish foe, were massacred and expelled from several areas. Greek, Bulgarian, Albanian, Serbian, and Turkish nationalism all claimed either territory or people in Macedonia. Albanian and Serbian nationalism largely defined themselves through conflict with the other. The Serbian national myth centers on the 1389 battle of Kosovo Polje ("field of blackbirds"), where the Serbian prince Lazar died in battle with an Ottoman Turkish army, though some of Lazar's allies were Albanian and the Ottoman allies included Lazar's Serb rivals.

Albanian identity, too, changed over time. Most Albanians became Muslim, although there were also Orthodox and Catholic minorities. Whereas affiliation with the Serbian Orthodox Church largely defined Serbian identity, Albanian nationalism is multiconfessional, based on a highly distinctive language and culture. As the saying there goes, "The religion of Albanians is Albanianism."

Albanian nationalism defined itself in resistance to Serbian and other Slavic and Greek nationalist claims, and its founding symbolic event also occurred in Kosovo. In 1878, Albanian intellectuals convened the League of Prizren, the first Albanian nationalist organization, named for the Kosovo town where it first met. The league contested Serb claims to Kosovo and other territories and asked the "Great Powers" (today known as "the West") to support an Albanian state, which gained recognition in 1913, though without Kosovo or the Albanian-majority areas in Macedonia. Over the centuries differential birthrates and migrations created an Albanian majority in Kosovo, estimated at 68.5 percent in 1948, 77.4 percent in the 1981 Yugoslav census, and well over 80 percent by the late 1990s.[7]

Macedonians, a people speaking a southern Slavic language between Serbian and Bulgarian, developed a national movement after their neighbors.[8] When Josip Brod Tito, founder of the Socialist Federal Republic of Yugoslavia (SFRY), recognized a separate titular republic for Macedonians in 1943, he created the first political unit recognizing Macedonian as a nationality.

The 1963 Yugoslav constitution recognized five "nations" (Serbs, Croats, Slovenes, Montenegrins, and Macedonians) as constituting the state; the 1974 constitution added Muslims (now often called Bosniaks). Each of the five groups had its own titular republic. The sixth republic, Bosnia-Herzegovina, was eventually defined as having three constituent nations: Serbs, Croats, and Muslims. Albanians, who outnumbered Montenegrins and whose share of the population in Yugoslavia was comparable to that of Macedonians, resented the second-class status this implied.

Yugoslavia's local and regional leaders used the system of "workers' self-management" to build local power bases. Yugoslavia depended heavily on foreign trade, international credit, and labor migration. Many workers, especially those from the poorer region, many Kosovars among them, found work in Western Europe, where their diaspora supported banned nationalist movements. The Communist Party, held together by Tito, provided a centralizing counterweight to the centripetal forces. Tito's break with Stalin in 1948 constituted the first breach in the expanding socialist camp. As a result, the country benefited from extensive aid that enabled it to maintain a large military and postpone economic reform.

Both global and local events dismantled every element of this system in the 1980s. Tito died in 1980, leaving behind only a regionalized Communist Party. The debt crisis hit Yugoslavia just as the end of the cold war deprived it of its strategic importance, and Western states were unwilling to bail it out. Unemployment mounted, surpassing 50 percent in the poorest regions, notably Kosovo. Global and local forces interacted, as the structure of the state cast virtually every painful decision demanded by creditors in terms of distributional conflicts among national republics.[9] The decisions of some leaders to exploit ethnic resentments and fears—notably, through control of mass media—escalated the dangers. Encouraged by allies abroad, the richer, largely Catholic republics of the northwest (Slovenia and Croatia) sought to withdraw, hoping to join the European Union (EU); the Serbian leadership under Slobodan Milosevic (which also controlled Montenegro) sought to reconstitute the federation under its domination; and Bosnia-Herzegovina and Macedonia sought to stave off a dissolution that they feared would be fatal for them. The latter finally opted for independence over staying in a federation dominated by an ever more aggressive Serbia without the counterweight of the western republics.

The Albanians of Yugoslavia found themselves deprived of a voice in most of these events. In several waves of demonstrations beginning in 1968, they had raised demands from greater autonomy to secession and merger with Albania. The 1974 constitution met some of these demands by making Kosovo (along with Vojvodina, with its Hungarian minority) a socialist autonomous province within Serbia.[10] Although Kosovo was "part" of Serbia, the collective presidency of the SFRY included eight members with equal rights, including six representatives of the federal republics and two of the autonomous provinces, including Kosovo, which gained a panoply of self-governing and educational institutions conducted in the Albanian language and controlled by Albanians. Kosovo functioned like an Albanian-controlled republic. Like the republics, its policies favored the predominant nationality. Serbs were sometimes harassed and subjected to discrimination and even some violence. Many emigrated, though their flight was also motivated by the search for jobs, increasingly scarce in Yugoslavia's poorest province.

Within a year of Tito's death, massive demonstrations by Kosovar Albanians in 1981 raised nationalist demands again. Violent repression of these demonstrations set off a process of escalation. Starting in 1989, Serbia under Milosevic enacted a series of constitutional changes that deprived Kosovo of all substantive autonomy, eliminated the Albanian language from public life and education, and effectively placed the province under the military and police control of Belgrade. Albanians were fired from jobs in state institutions, and Albanian parents and students boycotted the official schools, in which Serbian (as the government now called it, rather than Serbo-Croatian) was the language of instruction.[11]

The Albanian members of the provincial parliament reacted by declaring an independent Republic of Kosova, validated by a September 1991 referendum. The Democratic League of Kosova, led by Ibrahim Rugova, the president of the Writers' Association, emerged as the leading political force. The new Kosovar Albanian leadership established a network of parallel social institutions outside of Serbian control, funded by "taxes" collected from the Kosovar diaspora.[12]

Rugova, who articulated an ethic of nonviolent resistance, reigned as president of the "Republic of Kosova" from his home in Pristina. He frequently traveled abroad, where grateful Western leaders lavishly praised the policy of nonviolence that enabled them to postpone doing anything about Kosovo. Rugova's strategy was to avoid provoking Serbian repression while publicizing his people's claims and suffering, which he hoped would convince the West to place Kosovo under an interim UN administration as a step toward independence. In effect, this is what eventually happened, though the Kosovo Liberation Army (KLA or UCK, after its initials in Albanian) understood that only violence, not principles, would force the West to act.[13]

Kosovar Albanians staked their legal claim to independence on arguments about the Yugoslav succession. They acknowledged the principle, reaffirmed in the Helsinki Accords, forbidding forcible changes in international borders. According to Kosovar Albanian political leaders, however, Yugoslavia legally ceased to exist when the International Conference on the Former Yugoslavia (ICFY), convened in London by the EU, recognized the federation's internal borders as international ones—a decision affirmed by a Security Council resolution. The sovereignty that had belonged to the federation then devolved to the federating units, of which, they claim, the socialist autonomous province of Kosovo was one under the 1974 constitution, as shown by its representation in the collective presidency.[14]

The ICFY commission set up to adjudicate such claims, chaired by Robert Badinter, rejected the Kosovar claim to independence on the ground that only the six federal republics, and not the autonomous provinces, constituted units with the right to independence, though that rejection was met with some skepticism. The Badinter Commission also judged in 1991 that Macedonia, but not Croatia, had met criteria for recognition—notably, protection for minority rights. Germany nonetheless recognized the latter, dragging the rest of the West behind it, while Greece blocked recognition of the former. International principles were imposed only on those too weak to violate them with impunity.

Albanians from Macedonia who had flocked to Pristina, and especially its university, returned home in the wake of Milosevic's repression with a higher level of militancy.[15] This rising tension formed the context in which Macedonians voted for independence in September 1991. The new constitution defined the state as "the national state of the Macedonian people" while guaranteeing "full equality as citizens" to Albanians, Turks, Vlahs, Romanies (Gypsies), and other nationalities. The constitution also affirmed concern for "persons belonging to the Macedonian people" in neighboring countries.[16]

These provisions set off domestic conflict, especially with ethnic Albanians, and international conflict with Greece. Greece refused to recognize

Macedonia's independence and imposed a blockade that lasted for more than three years, claiming that the name "Macedonia," certain symbols, and the constitutional provision regarding ethnic Macedonians abroad implied revanchist intentions.[17] The political representatives of the ethnic Albanians of Macedonia, who form a majority in two districts contiguous to Albania and Kosovo, demanded recognition as a "constituent nation" equal to the Macedonians, claiming that, contrary to the official figures placing the Albanian population at about 22 percent, they constituted about 40 percent of the population.[18] Failing that, they demanded autonomy for the Albanian-majority areas of the country. Ethnic Macedonians, already rendered insecure by the Greek blockade and Greece's continuing refusal to recognize the Republic of Macedonia under its constitutional name, feared such demands as the starting point for "parallel institutions" and separatism, as occurred in Kosovo.

Though leaders articulate demands in the ethnonationalist discourse that dominates Balkan politics, they also express concerns about concrete issues such as access to education, employment, and government services. Ethnic Macedonians dominate the stagnating state sector of the economy. The constitution requires that all government offices use the Macedonian language. Education, however, has proved to be the most explosive topic. Although Macedonia, unlike Serbia in Kosovo, provides primary and secondary education in Albanian (as well as in other minority languages), all higher education has been in the Macedonian language.[19] Especially after the suppression of Pristina University, demand grew for higher education in the Albanian language. Professors, including nationalist activists who had returned from Kosovo, established an unofficial Albanian-language university in Tetovo. The inauguration of this university in February 1995, featuring a demonstration with nationalist speeches and violent rhetoric, sparked police repression and demonstrations in which one Albanian student was killed. The university has been tolerated, though not recognized, by the authorities. In January 2001, thanks to the efforts of Max van der Stoel, the former Dutch foreign minister and the high commissioner on national minorities of the Organization for Security and Cooperation in Europe (OSCE), Tetovo saw the start of work to establish a private, predominantly Albanian-language (though multilingual) Southeast Europe University as a way to resolve the crisis.

Despite these grievances, Albanians in Macedonia, unlike those in Kosovo, recognized the legitimacy of the state and participated in politics. In addition, the Macedonian government accepted the political role of Albanians. Every government of independent Macedonia, whether led by the Socialist (formerly Communist) Party or the supposedly more nationalist Internal Macedonian Revolutionary Organization–Democratic Macedonian Party of National Unity (VMRO-DMPNE), has included Albanian nationalist parties as coalition partners.

Preventive Efforts before the CPA Mission

As the CPA was preparing for its December 1995 mission to the region, preventive efforts were already under way in Macedonia. President Kiro Gligorov welcomed an international presence for "conflict prevention" as a kind of recognition that Greece's opposition otherwise denied the new state. The UN Security Council authorized its first preventive deployment in Macedonia. Originally part of the UN Protection Force, which included deployments elsewhere in the former Yugoslavia, the Macedonia contingent later gained a separate status as the UN Preventive Deployment Force (UNPREDEP). Comprising two battalions, including one from the United States, UNPREDEP ostensibly dealt with the cross-border threat, but it also helped stabilize the country internally by signaling that an independent Macedonian state enjoyed international legitimacy.[20]

To deal with the dispute with Greece, the UN fielded a mediation team of two Americans, Cyrus Vance and Herbert S. Okun. Vance and Okun worked with a U.S. special envoy, Matthew Nimetz. Decisive intervention by Richard Holbrooke, assistant secretary of state for European and Canadian affairs, brought these envoys' work to a partial conclusion in September 1995, as Greece, in response to Macedonian concessions, ended the trade embargo and its opposition to Macedonia's membership in international organizations.[21]

Europe's dense network of international organizations invested much effort in Macedonia. The OSCE established a mission to monitor respect for human rights and other Helsinki Accord principles.[22] Max van der Stoel, one of the few officials with an explicit mandate for preventive diplomacy, consulted with the government and other key actors about education, language, and other interethnic issues. The chair of the working group on minorities of the ICFY worked there, as did his successor, working for the Office of the High Commissioner on the Former Yugoslavia. The Council of Europe organized a group of experts to settle disputes over ethnic counting in the census.

The EU had a large aid mission, and the prospect of eventual membership provided a powerful incentive for peaceful behavior. Macedonia joined NATO's Partnership for Peace.[23]

Numerous private and semiofficial organizations set up conflict resolution and democracy-building projects in Macedonia. Search for Common Ground organized an interethnic project on journalism, to counter the way that media in the region had escalated conflict; together with several European organizations and a newly established program at Skopje University, the NGO also sponsored peace education and conflict resolution training. The National Democratic Institute for International Affairs advised the government on electoral reform, seeking to devise ways to reconcile majority rule with minority participation and representation. Catholic Relief Services sponsored village projects (building schools through interethnic associations of parents and teachers) to strengthen interethnic social capital at the grassroots level. George Soros provided the government with a bridge loan that prevented its financial collapse soon after independence, and his local foundation sponsored many civil society programs, including subsidizing the independent press when it lost government support.[24] These are only a sample of a panoply of programs that rivaled Burundi in number and probably surpassed it in funding.

From the breakup of Yugoslavia to the Dayton Accords there were few international efforts to prevent conflict in Kosovo. The Kosovar Albanians' adamant insistence that Kosovo was an international issue was fully matched by Milosevic's insistence that it was an internal issue of Serbia and could not be "internationalized."

International actors focused on the repression and violation of human rights in Kosovo as potentially destabilizing factors. But the contradiction between the international approach and that of actors on the ground eventually doomed the former. Kosovar Albanians interpreted condemnation of the Serbian authorities as support for their goal, which was not observance of human rights in Kosovo but the independence of Kosovo from Serbian authorities.

Milosevic's policy precluded an international presence to monitor or deter abuses. Exceptionally, in 1992, the prime minister of the Federal Republic of Yugoslavia (FRY), Milan Panic, a Serbian American businessman, permitted the OSCE to establish a mission of long duration in the three areas of Kosovo, Sandjak (an area spanning Serbia and Montenegro with a two-thirds Muslim majority), and Vojvodina. The Macedonia mission, considered a "Kosovo spillover" mission, was established under the same resolution. The OSCE mission's mandate included both encouraging dialogue and reporting on human rights conditions. After ousting Panic, however, Milosevic terminated the mission in July 1993.[25]

High Commissioner van der Stoel tried to become involved only after 1997. Milosevic refused him a visa, and the Kosovar Albanians objected to meeting with someone responsible for "national minorities," as they viewed themselves as the majority in the independent Republic of Kosova. In deference to Kosovar Albanian sensitivities, van der Stoel was granted an additional title (representative of the OSCE chairman-in-office for Kosovo) and held one meeting among experts from both sides in Austria.[26]

Nongovernmental organizations, too, made relatively few efforts to engage the parties before the Dayton agreement. Those trying to do so included the Sweden-based Transnational Foundation; the Catholic peace group Pax Christi-Flanders, which organized dialogues among Serbian and Albanian youth; and the Project on Ethnic Relations, based in Princeton, New Jersey, which held a June 1995 roundtable in Belgrade on ethnic relations in the FRY. After the CPA mission, the Project on Ethnic Relations convened a Serbian-Kosovar Albanian dialogue in New York, which several members of the working group attended.[27] The Community of Sant' Egidio also began consultations with Serbs, Kosovar Albanians, and neighboring countries in 1993.

Thus on the eve of the CPA's mission to the region, Macedonia had become, together with Burundi, one of the poster children for preventive diplomacy, including the first UN preventive deployment. Kosovo, however, had fallen out of public attention. The decision by Albanian leaders to use peaceful protest, rather than creating a "security risk" through violence, enabled the great powers dealing with the Yugoslav question to ignore them.

The Kosovar Albanians were excluded from the negotiations at Dayton. As part of the implementation of the Dayton agreement, the UN lifted the sanctions against Serbia and Montenegro. Most European states recognized the FRY and sent ambassadors to Belgrade. The United States, however, announced it would retain an "outer wall of sanctions," consisting of withholding full recognition and continued exclusion or suspension of FRY membership in international organizations and financial institutions, until four conditions were met: full compliance with the Dayton agreement; settlement of claims on the state succession of the former Yugoslavia; cooperation with the international war crimes tribunal; and improvement of respect for human rights in Kosovo. It again treated this issue primarily as a human rights question, to avoid appearing to support independence.

The CPA Mission to the South Balkans

The Center for Preventive Action sent a delegation to the South Balkans in December 1995. When the CPA started planning this project, we had no way of knowing that, when we arrived in Belgrade, the United States would have led NATO in bombing raids that ostensibly helped a Croatian-Bosnian offensive turn the tide in the war; that the main protagonists in the central contest of the breakup of Yugoslavia would have reached a tenuous agreement after weeks of discussion at an army base in Dayton, Ohio; nor that we would arrive in a limnal time, between the signing and the implementation of the Dayton Accords, when expectations were fluid and all eyes were turned to the United States.

Our discussions confirmed the vast differences among groups, especially over Kosovo. But we thought we detected a chance for movement. The predominant perception, that the Dayton Accords signified high-level U.S. engagement with the problems of the region backed up by military force, including NATO, raised expectations.

Kosovar Albanians saw that nonviolent resistance and appeals to principle had left them outside the perimeters of Dayton. The Republika Srpska, an entity with no previous legal existence led by indicted war criminals, had received more concessions than the Republic of Kosova, led by a peace-loving French-speaking intellectual garlanded with encomiums in all the capitals of the West. Militant Kosovar opposition to Rugova was on the rise.

Our group proposed a strategy composed of several interrelated elements:
—general principles;
—a concept of leadership as well as roles for different actors;
—specific actions regarding Kosovo, Macedonia, and, to a lesser extent, Albania.

Our decision on general principles evolved during a dinner in Skopje. During any such visit, local actors appeal selectively to international standards, whether the inviolability of borders or human rights. We argued that any settlement should be based on the whole package of Helsinki principles as they had evolved since the end of the cold war. Underlying this approach, however, was an analysis that went beyond the assertion of principles. Nationalism permeated all political discourse in the region. Politics largely revolved around political entities claiming to represent nations fighting for states or territories to control. Hence, we argued, just as the rest of Europe had transformed nationhood through integration, so the peoples of the Balkans also needed to envision a future in which citizenship was based on rights, not group membership, and borders were "channels of communication and exchange, not . . . mechanisms of exclusion."[28] Although we opposed the repressive, exclusionist nationalism practiced by Serbia in Kosovo, we hoped for a solution other than another Albanian state practicing its own version of exclusionary nationalism. In Macedonia, we argued, the path to a solution should be toward finding ways to meet common human needs, rather than granting Albanians constituent nation status or territorial autonomy, so that nationality could gradually become less rather than more important.[29]

In Burundi and the Great Lakes region as a whole, no single actor was willing or able to lead a preventive effort.[30] In the former Yugoslavia until mid-1995, "Europe" was supposed to be in charge, but in the summer of 1995, the United States took over the role and cemented it with the Dayton Accords. During our mission, it was clear that all actors in the region looked to the United States, whether with hope, fear, or confusion. We therefore urged the United States to exercise leadership in seeking ways to prevent violent conflict in the South Balkans by eventually appointing a senior official with responsibility for coordinating a regional approach to Kosovo, Macedonia, and Albania.

The elevated importance of the United States was confirmed during our interview with Slobodan Milosevic. One member of the delegation (David Phillips) asked the Serbian president if he would agree to a long-standing request to allow a U.S. Information Agency library in Pristina. To our surprise, Milosevic responded, "You can build your library wherever you want." U.S. diplomats followed up on this response, leading to the opening of the library the following spring—the first long-term international diplomatic presence in Kosovo since the closure of the OSCE mission in 1993.

Nonetheless, neither the U.S. government nor any other actor could carry out all the tasks needed. We argued that only international NGOs could break the initial deadlock over modalities of negotiation over Kosovo. We also advocated the expansion of existing NGO and international organization activities within Macedonia and their extension, when possible, to Kosovo.

Despite some differences within both sides, the distance between virtually all Serb and all Albanian positions was so great that an immediate direct negotiation on the political status of the province could not lead to a settlement.

Some on both sides, however, agreed that a solution could be "gradual." We therefore picked up on an idea suggested by some of our interlocutors for a multistage process.

To overcome the difference on modalities, we suggested that an international NGO could meet both the Kosovar Albanian demand for an international mediator and the Serbian official demand not to compromise sovereignty. The goal of initial talks would be to reach an "interim settlement" under which neither side would renounce its views on the final status of Kosovo but which would provide for confidence-building measures, dialogue, and negotiation.

Among the confidence-building measures we recommended were the reopening of the state schools to Albanian children and reaffirmation of the commitment to nonviolence by the Kosovar Albanians. We noted that the Albanians would be unlikely to continue nonviolent tactics unless they gained concrete benefits. Building on suggestions from Serbian moderates in Belgrade and ambiguous hints from some Kosovar Albanian political leaders, we expressed the hope that Kosovar Albanians would respond to these measures by participating in the 1997 Yugoslav elections, though we recognized they would not participate in Serbian elections.

This difficult process would require official international support. We recommended maintaining the outer wall of sanctions on the Milosevic government to pressure it to "normalize" life in Kosovo. We also noted the importance of human rights in central Serbia and called for the reversal of the bans imposed after our mission on independent media and the Fund for an Open Society–Yugoslavia (of the Soros Foundations Network), which had supported efforts at Serb-Albanian dialogue.

We left ambiguous our view on the future of the political regime in Belgrade. So soon after the Dayton talks, in which Milosevic had been a partner, we focused on pressuring Milosevic into negotiations and some internal democratization, not on measures to replace him. At the same time, an unarticulated hope behind the idea of the interim settlement and the participation of Kosovars in Yugoslav institutions was that the political situation in Serbia and Montenegro itself would change.

Underlying the strategy of postponing political demands while implementing measures to meet human needs (security, education) was also a central tenet of conflict resolution theory. According to this analysis, the demands made by conflict protagonists are attempts to realize basic human needs, even if through oppressive means. Over dinner in Skopje, two women, an ethnic Macedonian and an Albanian, who were working together with

Search for Common Ground on conflict resolution training, presented us with the same idea, that the process of conflict resolution or "transformation" is one of creating an atmosphere of sufficient confidence that the parties can exercise their creativity and develop alternative ways to meet needs that will not lead to intergroup conflict. One of Macedonia's leading politicians also emphasized to us the need to transform the electoral and political system so that officials would concentrate on meeting constituents' needs for water and power, quality education, and economic opportunity rather than on symbolic ethnic demands.

The single most important action the United States could take in Macedonia, we argued, was to support that country's security by reconfirming its participation in UNPREDEP. We also argued against recognizing Albanians as a constituent nation in favor of policies that reduced rather than increased the salience of ethnonational identity in politics in favor of common citizenship and meeting common needs.[31] In this vein, we advocated measures to transform the debate on education from one about language to one about quality. Tetovo University, we argued, should be made a legal, private institution; in the future, a regional consortium could organize higher education in the Albanian language throughout the South Balkans. Macedonian-language education should also receive international support. International involvement should increasingly include professionals in education rather than in ethnic conflict. We noted that although Albanians were underrepresented in the public sector, they were active in the private sector, where Macedonia's economic future lay. International assistance should nurture entrepreneurship in all ethnic groups. We also suggested measures for strengthening local government and reforming the electoral system to make elected officials more accountable to constituencies, both to improve governance and to encourage a shift in politics toward more concrete issues.

"Success" in Macedonia, Failure in Kosovo

It is difficult to say which might be more instructive: the apparent success, until 2001, at preventing violent conflict in Macedonia or the total failure in Kosovo. Skeptics on Macedonia always argued, "Just wait!" It was not yet the end of history there (or anywhere else, for that matter), but conflict prevention does not promise eternal peace without end, whatever may happen. Beating the odds for a while is also an achievement; and for a while, Macedonia beat the odds. Much of the nightmare scenario of Macedonian destabilization actually came to pass. War broke out in Kosovo. A mass of Albanian refugees, mixed with guerrillas, flooded across the border. The Kosovo Liberation Army established covert military bases on Macedonian territory. Albanians from Macedonia joined the KLA, just as Tutsis from Zaire joined the Rwandan Patriotic Front. All of this happened, as well, after the ethnonationalist Macedonian party, the VMRO, came to power and made a decision that deprived the country of UNPREDEP. The VMRO government recognized the Republic of China (Taiwan) in return for a promise of $2 billion in badly needed assistance. China consequently vetoed further UN deployments; nor did the money arrive.

Yet Albanians by and large continued to pursue their goals peacefully through the country's political process. The supposedly more extreme of the two major ethnonationalist Albanian parties joined a government coalition with the ethnic Macedonian nationalist VMRO-DMPNE. The government had de facto tolerated the university in Tetovo and enacted legislation on private educational institutions that could legalize it. Rather than provide support to that institution, a focus for Albanian nationalists who had returned from Kosovo, Max van der Stoel supported the establishment of a new Southeast Europe University designed to provide quality education in several languages.

By always participating in the government, Albanians gained some of the benefits of "constituent nation" status, but through practical politics rather than by institutionalizing a nationalist principle. When fighting broke out in the hills above Tetovo in March 2001, a solid show of opposition to the guerrillas and support for Macedonia by the international community pressed the government to form an even broader coalition. If Macedonia succumbs to violence, it will result as much from contagion within the Balkan regional conflict formation than from the internal weaknesses of Macedonia itself.

Macedonia might have avoided violent conflict for years even without international efforts because the disputes were inherently less threatening than those in Kosovo.[32] International projects may well have had misconceived ideas, lack of coordination, turf wars, misunderstandings, and so on.[33] As in any other area of human endeavor, if conflict prevention can work only if no mistakes are made, we may as well give up now. But the multiple international activities on the ground, as much as their content, signaled an international commitment that encouraged peaceful coping and discouraged escalation and outbidding. As Michael Lund has argued, Macedonia shows that even moderately successful conflict prevention must be open ended and evolve from crisis response to support for nation building.[34] As the experience of Kosovo shows, such commitments are much less expensive and more effective than high-profile crisis response.

Perceptions of Kosovo are now limited both by what actually happened and by how events were portrayed by the media, which turned their magnifying and distorting lens on the area only after blood had started to flow. Nonetheless, for some time after our mission there seemed to be some potential for progress. A few Serbian-Albanian dialogues mediated by NGOs proceeded. The Community of Sant' Egidio even mediated an agreement between Milosevic and Rugova to reopen the schools in Kosovo to Albanian children, one of our principal recommendations. Serbian opposition to Milosevic grew, culminating in mass demonstrations from December 1996 to January 1997.

Among the dialogue processes that proceeded after the Dayton Accords and the CPA report were the meeting organized by van der Stoel in Austria; a further dialogue organized by the Project on Ethnic Relations; a series of meetings, leading to the production of joint written proposals, sponsored by the German Bertelsmann Science Foundation; the confidential negotiations organized by the Community of Sant' Egidio, which led to the education agreement of September 1, 1996; meetings in Belgrade, organized by the British ambassador, among Serbian and Kosovar intellectuals; and a series of Serbian-Albanian roundtables organized by the Belgrade and Pristina Helsinki Committees for the Defense of Human Rights, one of which (in Ulcinj, Montenegro, in June 1997) the CPA cosponsored. By the spring of 1998, when the guerrilla war launched by the KLA increasingly dominated the scene, these unofficial efforts, some of which continued, were nonetheless largely displaced by official efforts at crisis management.

Sant' Egidio sponsored a second-track negotiation, which started with broad consultations in 1993 and culminated in secret talks in Rome in 1996.[35] Part of the reason for their success, in Sant' Egidio's own estimation, was that it had built up relations of trust with both sides through years of humanitarian effort. Although its international reputation derives from its work on conflicts, Sant' Egidio, an association of lay Catholics, is the largest private source of food and other benefits for the poor and homeless in Italy, and it came to know Albanians, including Kosovars, through its work among refugees and asylum seekers there. Its relations with Serbs grew through the participation of some of its key leaders (notably, Father Vincenzo Paglia, the principal mediator on Kosovo, now a bishop) in efforts to promote reconciliation between the Catholic and Serbian Orthodox Churches.

Sant' Egidio had been holding quiet discussions on Kosovo since 1993. In 1995 it mediated an agreement between Albanian president Sali Berisha and Milosevic to open three new border crossing points, thereby reducing Kosovo's isolation. By mid-1996, both Milosevic and Rugova had sent high-level negotiators to Rome. As our working group had recommended (though not for that reason), the discussions focused first on humanitarian issues—in particular, the opening of the schools. As we had observed during our mission, Albanian children were being taught in unofficial classrooms, often in overcrowded, unsafe, unheated buildings, and without adequate equipment or textbooks.

The agreement was signed on September 1, 1996, by "President of the Republic of Serbia Slobodan Milosevic" in Belgrade and, in Pristina, by "Dr. Ibrahim Rugova."[36] It provided for the "normalization of the educational system of Kosovo for the Albanian children and youth," foreseeing the "return of the Albanian students and teachers back to schools." A joint committee (the so-called three-plus-three group) would oversee implementation.

The agreement was more a statement of principles than a professional diplomatic document. The English translation distributed in Belgrade was only about 220 words long. It included not even a notional timetable for implementation. It avoided all the political questions raised by schools, such as who employs the teachers, issues diplomas, or sets the curriculum. But it was understood in Pristina and Belgrade as a significant political document. For the first time, Serbia and "Kosova" had negotiated, in the presence of an international, though private, mediator. Milosevic effectively recognized Rugova as the leader of his people. Rugova had agreed to discuss an issue of immediate practical importance, not simply the independence of Kosova. Serbian nationalists attacked Milosevic's compromise with Albanian separatists, while Pristina hard-liners attacked Rugova's recognition of Serbia's de facto control.

Both leaders had solid political reasons to seek such an accommodation, or at least appear to do so. Rugova, who was fast losing ground to more militant challengers both within and outside of the Democratic League of Kosova, needed to show that his policy of peaceful resistance could provide his people with concrete benefits. Milosevic needed to show the United States and other international actors that he was making an effort to improve the situation in Kosovo if he hoped to have the "outer wall" of sanctions lifted—in particular, those barring the FRY from membership in international financial institutions. International loans could help him deliver to his constituency.

The parties delayed appointment of the members of the three-plus-three group: Rugova would not name his representatives until the Serbian side agreed to an international chair. The deadlock was broken when international pressure led Milosevic to accept the chairmanship of Sant' Egidio's Father Paglia. As with the agreement to send a "security force" to Burundi in May 1996 (and other hasty "agreements" cobbled together under pressure of time), it turned out that the two sides had different notions of what the document meant: the Serbian negotiators thought that the Albanian classes might be held in the official buildings for part of the day, while the Kosovar side thought the agreement would give the Republic of Kosova control over the buildings; the two sides disagreed (and the original Serbian text diverged from the Albanian translation) as to whether Pristina University and university students were included.[37]

Milosevic may well have signed the agreement to test how little he needed to do to have the sanctions lifted. This was, therefore, the precise moment at which a unified, coordinated international stand in favor of both implementation of the accords and a mediated political negotiation with the Kosovar leadership might have been effective. Unfortunately, in a replay of the disarray shown by the West over Bosnia, this short-lived opportunity was squandered.

The mass media, as usual, failed to call public attention to an event that was not yet violent and did not involve American troops. Neither the *New York Times* nor the *Washington Post* deemed the Milosevic-Rugova agreement worthy of coverage.[38] Despite the lack of public attention, the United States, several international organizations, and a number of other states made efforts to press mainly Milosevic, but also the Kosovar Albanians, to implement the agreement. Nonetheless, the overall context was one of disarray. Milosevic maneuvered to evade pressure on Kosovo through his role in Bosnia. Although U.S. diplomats claim, presumably truthfully, that they raised Kosovo in every discussion, they had a long list of matters to discuss with Milosevic—primarily the implementation of the Dayton Accords in Bosnia, where U.S. troops were deployed under conditions of security that compared favorably with a county fair in Arkansas. After Somalia, they hoped to keep it that way, and they needed Milosevic's cooperation on that goal, even if they could not get it on others, such as turning over indicted war criminals to the tribunal in The Hague, implementing the education agreement, or offering meaningful political negotiations to Kosovar Albanian leaders.

Still, the United States did more than European countries to press Milosevic on this issue. Most European countries fully upgraded their representation in Belgrade after the Dayton Accords or when the Federal Republic of Yugoslavia finally recognized Macedonia in September 1996. In December 1997, as violence was gathering, a frustrated European official of the OSCE commented acerbically that the United States was mainly concerned with ensuring the safety of its troops in Bosnia, France wanted to show it was a European power by playing on its good relations with Serbia, and Germany's Christian Democratic government was mainly interested in seeking votes (in an election it lost anyway) by repatriating asylum seekers from the former Yugoslavia. These included an estimated 140,000 Kosovars, mostly young men, whose forced return to a life of unemployment under martial law seemed unlikely to stabilize the province.

The European Union itself had received a report on Kosovo from its newly formed Conflict Prevention Network. Established as a result of an initiative of former French prime minister Michel Rocard, a member of the European Parliament, the Conflict Prevention Network was a network of researchers coordinated by the German Stiftung Wissenschaft und Politik to provide the European Commission with confidential analyses and policy recommendations on potential conflicts. The Kosovo report advocated a "three-step approach" for increasing EU activity over Kosovo. As analyst Stefan Troebst observes, however, when the report was submitted on June 30, 1997, it "neither triggered off immediate action by the EU nor did it have a visible impact on Brussels."[39] When the EU finally did take a common position, in the Cardiff Declaration of June 1998, after the war had started, it could agree on no common actions other than stating general principles and banning direct flights to Belgrade.

The disarray over Kosovo prevented it from even being put on the agenda of the Contact Group—one of several ad hoc forums that states have created to deal with common problems, like the grouping of East African states that sponsor the Burundi negotiations. When it was founded in April 1994, the Contact Group was made up of the UN Security Council permanent members directly interested in the former Yugoslavia (the United States, Russia, the United Kingdom, and France), but it expanded in May 1996 to include Germany and Italy. Only the student demonstrations of September 1997 placed Kosovo on its agenda, leading to an expression of concern. In January 1998, the Contact Group named Kosovo "a matter of high priority," but by then the war was only a month away.[40]

The three-plus-three group, the only existing body with authorized representatives of both the Republic of Kosova and Serbia, might, eventually, have evolved into a forum for political discussions. It proceeded at the pace usual in discussions between opposing groups who distrust each other deeply. The slow pace of the negotiations and the state of Serbian and FRY politics meant that no concrete benefits or confidence-building measures were implemented that might have given Kosovars an incentive to participate in the FRY elections that took place in September 1997, as the Kosovar students were preparing protest demonstrations to demand implementation of the agreement. When the education agreement was partially implemented under international pressure in March 1998, after the first round of assassinations and massacres, rioting Serbian students first gutted and stripped the university buildings turned over to Kosovar Albanian control. The turnover became not a confidence-building measure but an attempt to humiliate the opponent in a violent confrontation.

The progress of Serbian and Yugoslav politics in 1996–97 also brought a false dawn that soon dimmed. The three more-or-less democratic parties of the Zajedno ("together") coalition won municipal elections in December 1996 and organized mass demonstrations when Milosevic tried to keep them from office. Though they eventually won control of the major municipalities, their unity collapsed, and the largest and most nationalist of the three (the Serbian Renewal Movement of Vuk Draskovic) joined Milosevic in a coalition government.

Most decisive, however, was the collapse of Albania under Sali Berisha, which constituted a trigger that provoked both horizontal and vertical escalation. The Albanian crisis was itself triggered by a crisis of financial institutions in Albania's new capital markets—an example of how flaws in economic institutions can spark conflict.

Conflicting regional imperatives also helped generate the political crisis in Albania. Berisha, who allowed U.S. and NATO aircraft to use Albanian airfields for missions over Bosnia and agreed verbally to moderate statements on Kosovo, enjoyed largely uncritical Western backing until he rigged parliamentary elections in May 1996, leading to demonstrations in Tirana. Attempts by the U.S. government and European organizations to pressure Berisha led to a defiant reaction, and he was slowly losing his grip. Meanwhile, the impoverished population was attracted to numerous get-rich-quick schemes, the largest of which also funneled money to the ruling party. The funds turned increasingly to outbidding one another with pyramid schemes and finally crashed in March 1997.

The people of Albania took to the streets in panic. Before Italy agreed to lead a peacekeeping force to restore order, at least in the major towns (and to keep a huge wave of Albanian refugees from Italian shores), the army and police had deserted, and the country's armories had been looted. Even before the crisis, Albania was known as one of the cheapest markets for black-market war materiel.[41] After the raiding of the armories, however, Kalashnikov automatic rifles were sold in the market for $5 (compared with the average price in Africa of $25 and the list price of more than $1,000), and heavier weapons were easily available as well.[42]

The sudden surge onto the market of cheap weapons finally enabled the Kosovo Liberation Army to field a militarily significant force. Much has been made by some authors of the KLA's antecedents in Stalinist or fascist projects of Greater Albania[43] (and others in the growing business of terrorism analysis link it to Osama bin Laden, global Islamic fundamentalism, and the international drug trade). The KLA was, above all, the expression of a new generation of post-Yugoslav militants among Kosovo's youthful population. Having largely grown up with and been educated by the Republic of Kosova, this generation had little or no memory of an autonomous Kosovo within Serbia or Yugoslavia, did not know the Serbian (let alone the Serbo-Croatian) language, and had no contact with Serbs except as oppressors. Its appeals drew support from much of the Kosovar diaspora, who contributed funds as well as volunteers.

The CPA started hearing of isolated assassinations claimed by the Kosovo Liberation Army soon after our return from the mission.[44] By early 1998, KLA military operations regularly killed Serb policemen and other officials, and several areas were under its de facto control, at least at night. The decision by Belgrade to take back control of one of these areas led to the first major massacre of the war, that of the Jashari clan in Drenica in an operation extending from February 28 to March 5, 1998.[45]

Both the KLA and the Serbian authorities rendered impossible a solution based on "international principles." The KLA was fighting for a Kosovo free of Serbia and Yugoslavia. Unless defeated by an opposing force, the KLA would make Kosovo de facto independent. Although a defeat of the KLA by Belgrade, maintaining the state's territorial integrity without committing war crimes, did not entail a logical contradiction, it was impossible in practice, given the Serbian and Albanian societies as they actually were. Hence every expression of support for the territorial integrity of Yugoslavia and Serbia or denunciation of KLA terrorism de facto supported Serbian repression, whereas every expression of outrage at the Serbian atrocities de facto supported the independence of Kosovo, independently of the intentions of those making the statements.[46]

Such seemingly theoretical considerations go to the heart of the practical dilemmas of conflict prevention. There is always more than one way simply to avoid violence, but preventive action does not aim indiscriminately at avoiding overt violence, as through repression. Internationally accepted normative principles should inform the goals of preventive action. Yet normative principles are not always mutually consistent in practice. Both the multiplicity of possible outcomes consistent with preventing or reducing violence and the contradictions among principles allow, even require, plenty of room for purely political decisionmaking. When major states or institutions make such political decisions, however, they inevitably act out of institutional imperatives or self-interest.

The practical measures demanded by the United States and its allies illustrate these and other conundrums. In September 1998, the reactivated Richard Holbrooke, acting as a special envoy on Kosovo (but in crisis management rather than preventive mode, as our working group had proposed), used the threat of NATO bombing to coerce Milosevic into an agreement. Under the agreement, Milosevic was to withdraw from Kosovo most of the police and paramilitary units that were committing war crimes. The OSCE was to send two thousand unarmed observers to prevent violence. In the event, the OSCE never managed to field the full complement, as there were no standing bodies of peace monitors, even small ones, as there are standing armies.

Without significant efforts to stop KLA infiltration and fund-raising, however, demands to withdraw Serbian military and police effectively furthered the KLA's war aims. Supported by the local Albanian population, the KLA easily moved into the vacuum created by the departure of Serb forces. Of course, these measures were supposed to be only temporary, pending a political settlement that would reconcile the logically compatible but practically contradictory principles at stake.

Meanwhile, the remaining Serb forces responded to the continuing attacks of the KLA as before. When the American head of the OSCE's Kosovo Verification Mission immediately visited the site of one such reported massacre, he charged the Yugoslav authorities with responsibility. Unlike many much larger and even more indiscriminate massacres in the Great Lakes region (or Sudan, or Angola, or Afghanistan, or many other places) images of this site in Raçak, located in Europe and visited by American and western European officials, were broadcast around the world.

The shock induced by this apparent massacre led to a change in policy. Unlike in Rwanda, however, where hundreds of thousands of people committed genocide under the nose of a UN peacekeeping force, the decision was not to withdraw international forces. Unlike in Burundi, where massacres larger than Raçak had occurred in dozens if not hundreds of places, the decision was not first to send a UN special representative and later, when fighting escalated, to discuss a proposal to send a preventive force to a nearby country in case the situation became worse—and then fail to do it. Unlike in the Congo, where murder, rape, and torture were far more widespread than in Kosovo at that time, the decision was not to wait until all the belligerents signed an agreement and then consider sending a ludicrously small UN force to observe implementation of part of the agreement, as long as the force's security could be guaranteed. The decision, rather, was to escalate coercive diplomacy by the United States and NATO by tying the threat of air strikes to agreement by Belgrade to a comprehensive solution in accordance with the international principles enunciated in various documents.

By now the United States clearly was the lead actor on Kosovo. Furthermore, the specter of immediate violence and of another European disaster like Bosnia galvanized a much more united front of the European states behind U.S. leadership. Russia, too, while articulating its opposition to moves that violated Yugoslav sovereignty, ultimately played a supportive role in reaching the accord and in passing Security Council Resolution 1244, under which the UN administered Kosovo.

The shuttle diplomacy shifted to a chateau in Rambouillet, France, where Kosovar Albanian and Serbian delegations gathered to consider documents largely prepared by the United States. These documents included a proposal that superficially resembled both the CPA's and a number of other proposals: an interim period during which Kosovo would be placed under international tutelage, its final status to be determined after three years. The interim regime, however, was to be run by NATO in partnership with the OSCE, to marginalize Russia (and China), with their vetoes in the UN Security Council, as well as to reinforce the overall strategy of NATO expansion as the framework for European security.

The United States and its allies, however, decided to engage in high-stakes coercive diplomacy—namely, threatening one party (Belgrade) with swift, severe, and sustained violence if it did not agree.[47] The United States insisted that NATO alone, not the UN, as some in Belgrade seemed to favor, would be in charge of Kosovo. Annex B of the Rambouillet draft also provided that the NATO troops could move freely anywhere in Yugoslavia, not only in

Kosovo. This curious provision seems almost designed to force a war, if it did not simply result from careless drafting.

The threat against Belgrade would be activated, however, only if the Kosovar Albanians agreed to sign. Key members of the Kosovar delegation (notably, Hashim Thaçi of the KLA, who chaired it) at first resisted signing, because the agreement promised neither the independence of Kosovo nor a binding referendum. The Serbian delegation did not negotiate at all, because all decisions were made by Milosevic in Belgrade. The only sanction against the Albanians was the war itself: if they did not sign, Serbia would not be bombed, and the war would continue with its attendant atrocities. No one ever offered a credible threat to attempt to close off infiltration from Albania or to embargo KLA funding or recruitment abroad if the Kosovar Albanians did not sign—indicating that by this time the United States was using the KLA as leverage against Milosevic. Under pressure from both the United States and Kosovar public opinion, which wanted to avoid yet more violence, Thaçi agreed to the accord.

When the bombing started, the Serbian regime responded with massive deportations of Albanians, including summary executions—mostly of adult males—accompanied by rape, looting, and the destruction of Albanian settlements. Milosevic held out longer than expected and was indicted for war crimes on May 27, two months after the start of the war. Finally, when threatened with a ground war and pressed by Russia to sign, he agreed to withdraw his forces from Kosovo, though only after the United States had climbed down from its objection to a UN mandate and withdrawn the offending part of Annex B.

The war did force Belgrade to withdraw its forces from Kosovo and allow the return of all refugees. Of course, the Rwandan and Burundian refugee camps in Congo, Tanzania, and elsewhere housed even more terrorized people, suffering in addition from hunger, malnutrition, and epidemics, including HIV/AIDS, and served as bases for warfare and even genocide that undermined the precarious stability of the host countries. The South Balkans is on the southeastern flank of NATO, however, not in the middle of Africa, and the humanitarian issue was also, therefore, a strategic one for powerful states.

Could a better preventive strategy have prevented the war and refugee flow? Many political pressures, among them the West's failures in Bosnia, militated against negotiating while atrocities in Europe were shown on television. The West did not want to celebrate the fiftieth anniversary of NATO at a grand Washington gala while massacres and war crimes were taking place in Europe. Still, a few months later the United States did not hesitate to press the government of Sierra Leone to accept an amnesty for the limb-hackers of the Revolutionary United Front and to accept its leader, Foday Sankoh, as official trustee of the country's diamond mines.

The NATO celebration made the deadline too brief, but at this point we still lack enough evidence (though there are plenty of inferences and charges) to be sure of Milosevic's motives and whether he might have been induced to agree through a longer, more flexible negotiation process. Madeleine Albright expressed a political reality when she said in Bonn, on May 6, 1999, that "the end of the twentieth century cannot allow ethnic cleansing to succeed and aggression to pay dividends in the heart of Europe."[48]

That fact, however, if it is a fact (and there was no such reaction when U.S.-supported Croatian forces drove Serbs from the Krajina in Yugoslavia's single largest act of ethnic cleansing), is far more ambiguous, morally and politically, than the triumphalist rhetoric surrounding its claims. Although Secretary Albright, speaking on German soil, evoked through her words the heritage of the Holocaust and the imperative of "never again," the geo-graphical qualification communicates a troubling hidden message: apparently, the end of the twentieth century (and the start of the twenty-first) can allow such crimes elsewhere—not only in Africa but also a few hundred miles to the east, in Chechnya. The consolidation of a hegemony based on democratic ideology in the "heart of Europe" corresponds to the erection of a doctrine of humanitarian discrimination, in which human rights are identified with an ideologically defined "Europe."

One response to this challenge is to protest that the better must not be the enemy of the good. Neither the United States nor NATO nor anyone else (certainly not the UN in its current role as an underfunded repository for lost causes) can intervene in every civil and criminal war. Nor can one crit-icize the tardy, and therefore overly militarized, response to Kosovo while simultaneously deploring the lack of such actions in Africa without recall-ing the restaurant patron who complained that the food was terrible and the portions were too small.

If there is a solution to this problem, it lies in improving international resources for early, targeted, and largely nonmilitary action. Such methods are difficult to use and require training different from that of traditional diplomats, but they are far less expensive than military deployments and do not compete as much with other security requirements. The United States defines its national security priorities in other ways and therefore spends billions defending itself against international terrorism or hypothetical missiles from rogue states and very little on creating appropriate civil, political, and economic (as well as more appropriate types of military) capabilities to prevent or end murderous conflicts in distant countries. In Kosovo, where a humanitarian concern turned into a strategic challenge, the billions of dollars spent on the war contrast strangely with the paltry efforts at prevention. From the Dayton Accords to the NATO bombing there may have been ten Serbian-Albanian dialogues at a cost of about $100,000 each (probably an overestimate), totaling about the same as a single cruise missile. What if there had been a hundred such dialogues? What if the OSCE had been able to deploy twenty thousand peace observers, rather than fail to deploy two thousand?

The final puzzle of Kosovo, however, is that this was the tragedy of a war foretold. No one involved doubted it would occur, sooner or later, without serious international action. Not until European victims appeared on TV screens, however, did major powers make any effort to resolve their differences and coordinate action. The Albanians of Kosovo tried for almost ten years to win over world opinion through nonviolent resistance; in the end, they were taught the bitter lesson that only the willingness to kill and die can mobilize international action. The Albanians of Macedonia learned the same lesson. Conflict avoidance is not conflict prevention. Warning alone—early or not so early—failed to galvanize action, in Kosovo as in central Africa. Is this a correctable flaw, or are the definitions of only violence as threat, and of security only as response to direct threat to the powerful, too deeply encoded in our international system?

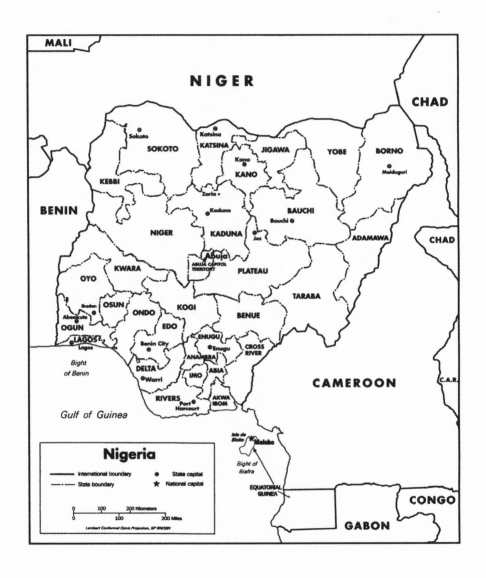

5

Nigeria: The Mirror of Oil

> History records that the cruelest of the governors of the Sudan was Yaqub the Afflicted, who abandoned his nation to the iniquities of Egyptian tax collectors and died in a chamber of the palace on the fourteenth day of the month of Barmajat in the year 1842. There are those who insinuate that the sorcerer Abdusalam al-Masmudi (whose name might be translated "The Servant of Peace") murdered him with a dagger or with poison, but a natural death is more likely—especially as he was known as "The Afflicted."
>
> —JORGE LUIS BORGES, *"The Mirror of Ink," in*
> *A Universal History of Iniquity*

"We need preventive diplomacy very much. Otherwise we are sleep-walking to disaster." In January 1997, during a hot afternoon of the Ramadan fast, these words from a prominent scholar at Bayero University of Kano in northern Nigeria impressed our CPA delegation with their frankness and intensity. A man with close relations both to the military regime of General Sani Abacha and to those most opposed to it, he urged on us the need for engagement with Nigeria. Its leaders, he argued, did not understand the dangers they were courting or the international reaction their deeds were eliciting.

International actors, too, may not have understood the dangers of the situation in Nigeria. Not only did the "international community" fail to respond coherently to the challenge of Sani Abacha's regime, but the U.S. government itself, which alone might have been able to coordinate other actors, engaged in a long "policy review" on Nigeria that had still not reached a conclusion when Abacha, the cruelest of Nigeria's rulers, died, reportedly of a heart attack, on June 8, 1998. Only death kept Abacha from following through on his plan to succeed himself as president. Not content merely to rig the elections, Abacha had also rigged the organization of parties and the parties' nomination processes. Had he thus imposed himself as an uncontested, superficially civilianized president, corruption and violence might have escalated to the extent that Nigeria could have become the world's most populous failed state.

Abacha's death and the subsequent democratic opening of politics prevented—or at least postponed—a major crisis. Yet except for the domination of the state by a corrupt and brutal dictator and his family, all the risks of conflict and collapse that the CPA identified in its report remain.[1] President Olusegun Obasanjo has refreshed Nigerian politics by openly identifying those problems and proposing to attack them. Nigeria's civil society can now monitor human rights, oppose corruption, empower women to resist violence and participate in public life, resolve local conflicts, and organize communities. These civil society groups' international colleagues can now support their work more openly. The structural obstacles to accountable governance, however, have barely been touched. These obstacles are deeply ingrained in the institutions of the Nigerian state, jerry-rigged by colonialism and funded by oil rents.[2] The end of the Abacha regime has made preventive efforts possible, not superfluous.

Background

The Nigerian crisis began when the military ruler Ibrahim Babangida stopped the counting of ballots and annulled the poll results from a presidential election held on June 12, 1993. After ten years of military rule and an eight-year "transition to democracy," the wrong person—of the wrong ethnic group—had won the election. Chief Boshurun Moshood Abiola, a Yoruba magnate, had for years cooperated with and profited from Nigeria's military rulers. Far from being an opposition radical, he was the candidate of one of two officially approved parties. Still, the élites of northern Nigeria were not ready to allow a Yoruba multimillionaire from Lagos, the country's business center and former capital, to add to his vast wealth command of the army and control of the oil revenue that funded both the state and virtually all imports. Such a result would have undermined their power, leaving them, as one northerner rather exaggeratedly said to the CPA delegation, like "slaves."

This event illustrates the principal contradiction of Nigeria—that between the need for ethnic accommodation and power sharing and the centralizing effect of an oil economy. Although for centuries rulers like Yaqub the Afflicted oppressed their people with predatory tax collectors, the international state system and market now provide rulers with different means to finance their activities—and enrich themselves. The oil revenues that funded 80 percent of the Nigerian government and 90 percent of the country's foreign exchange inflows accrued directly to the central government. Such effortless wealth depleted incentives for effective governance, undermined power sharing or decentralization, fed corruption, and oriented politics toward an increasingly high-stakes game of grabbing the bounty at the center. As each year about $10 billion of oil revenue flooded the Nigerian state and the élites that controlled it, the country's major institutions decayed. According to President Obasanjo, Abacha and his family looted about $ 4.3 billion during less than five years in power.[3]

With a population estimated at 110 million, Nigeria is Africa's most populous country.[4] It is also among the region's most diverse, with some 250 ethnic and linguistic groups and numerous religious communities. The population is estimated to be somewhat less than half Muslim and about 45 percent Christian. The largest economy in West Africa, Nigeria produces 80 percent of the total output within the sixteen-member Economic Community of West African States.

At the time it achieved independence, Nigeria consisted of three large provinces: the West, the East (together, generally, called the South) and the North. Each was dominated by one ethnic group—the Yoruba in the West, the Igbo in the East, and the Hausa-Fulani in the North. Together these groups account for about two-thirds of the country's population. Each region also contains other groups, known as "minorities" in a country with no ethnic majority.

In Nigeria's first republic the major political parties organized along regional-ethnic lines, though each region had its dissidents as well as a dominant party. Successive military coups in 1966 led to both the civil war and a prolonged military regime. Igbo officers declared federal Nigeria a unitary state; a few months later, northern and middle-belt officers overthrew them, as pogroms against Igbos in the north led to a remigration home and, soon thereafter, to the declaration of independence of Biafra. More than a million people died in the ensuing civil war. The decision of Yoruba political leaders to side with the north against their fellow southerners left a heritage of mistrust, but overall, Nigeria's leaders and people achieved a remarkable degree of reconciliation after such a bitter struggle. The experience increased the commitment of many to maintaining the otherwise arbitrarily created

Nigerian state. It also provided a rationale for the brutal suppression of opposition perceived—or labeled—as "separatist."

The arrival of oil wealth in the 1970s transformed politics. Governments began to create ever more administrative units both to fragment sectional coalitions and to provide more oil-funded patronage jobs. After General Murtala Muhammad, a northern Muslim, was killed in a failed coup in 1977, his successor, General Obasanjo, a Yoruba Christian, presided over a peaceful transition to an elected civilian regime in 1979, just as oil prices were rising to an all-time high under the impact of the Iranian revolution.[5]

Nigeria's second republic (1979–83) began in an oil bonanza and ended in an oil crash. Northern Muslim politicians dominated it, as they had the first. Although the first republic fell largely because of ethnic contention, the second succumbed to rampant corruption and illegality and, finally, the government's inability to manage the shortfall in resources it confronted when oil prices declined.[6] As in most oil states, politics revolved around patronage, government contracts, and other means of access to oil wealth.[7] Worn down by the spectacle of corruption and suffering from shortfalls caused by the collapse of oil prices in 1981, the public hardly protested when General Muhammadu Buhari, another northern Muslim, put an end to the democratic experiment in 1983.

In 1985, however, General Babangida, a middle-belt Muslim, took power and soon launched the "endless transition" to democracy. A constitutional commission devised an elaborate new setup designed to limit ethnic competition and weaken civilian politicians by creating new states, limiting political competition to two officially organized parties (one, supposedly, center right and the other center left), and requiring victorious candidates to obtain support in several regions. After a series of elections from local to national, the presidential election of June 12, 1993, was supposed to lead to a final transition in August of that year.

Turnout for the election was low (about 35 percent), but the polling proceeded without violence. Abiola, who chose a northern Muslim as his running mate, ran against Bashir Tofa, a relatively obscure northern Muslim politician with an Eastern Christian vice presidential candidate. The electoral results crossed ethnic lines, with Abiola winning even on Tofa's home ground, the city of Kano. The flamboyant business magnate created a patronage-based following by endowing Islamic institutions in the north as well as his home area.

As Abiola's victory became apparent, a celebratory mood spread through Yorubaland. Many Yoruba felt that, despite their intellectual, professional, and commercial achievements, Nigeria's dominant northern élites had deprived them of their rightful share of power. The rulers had moved the capital from the Yoruba city of Lagos and lavished vast sums on a new capital city, Abuja, in the middle belt. Now Nigeria had elected a Yoruba president, the first president the Yoruba considered truly theirs. The announcement of the "nullification" of the elections correspondingly unleashed deep resentments among Yoruba, expressed in demonstrations and strikes as well as the campaign that then unfolded, despite deepening repression, for implementation of the verdict of "June 12."[8] Just as notable, however, was the lack of such demonstrations elsewhere in the country. The question whether Abiola's cause was a democratic one or a Yoruba one posed obstacles to unifying opposition to the military dictatorship.

In August, Babangida vacated office in favor of a powerless acting president who was soon shoved aside by the military chief, General Sani Abacha, another northern Muslim. Abacha made himself head of state in November 1993. Two years later, on October 1, 1995, he announced yet another "transition."

Abiola had at first fled abroad, seeking support for the election verdict. Receiving little more than moral encouragement, he returned home and was arrested when he claimed the presidency a year after the election. Obasanjo, as well as his former deputy, Shehu Yar'Adua, were also arrested in the fall of 1995, charged with involvement in plotting a military coup. (Abacha did not, however, jail himself, despite his success in the same endeavor.) Yar'Adua, a former general from the north with a genuine political following in his home region, died mysteriously in prison on December 8, 1997. A member of a secret "hit squad" of Abacha is now on trial for murdering him by lethal injection. Abiola, too, died while still in custody, apparently of a heart attack, while meeting a U.S. diplomatic delegation on July 8, 1998. A death squad had gunned down his senior wife, Kudirat, who had led the campaign for his release, in the center of Lagos on June 4, 1996. Abacha's son and members of the "hit squad" were tried for that killing.

Other Abiola supporters and opposition figures or independent journalists were targets of assassination attempts—some of which were successful—and far more were arrested, most of them Yoruba. A number of bomb explosions took place, and the government charged the opposition with involvement in terrorism, leading to treason charges against a number of prominent individuals, mainly Yoruba, including the outspoken exiled Nobel laureate, Wole Soyinka. The government's allies circulated forged documents claiming there was a secret "Yoruba Agenda" to seize control of Nigeria.[9]

The national confrontation over democracy, military rule, and ethnic power, however, was not the only source of conflict and repression in the Abacha years. On November 10, 1995, the government hanged the prominent Ogoni writer Ken Saro-Wiwa and eight of his colleagues from the Movement for the Survival of the Ogoni People (MOSOP), who had been found guilty by a military tribunal of the murder of four pro-government Ogoni chiefs. The trial was riddled with flaws, the executions were carried out in haste, and the relatives of the victims were not even allowed to reclaim the bodies. Saro-Wiwa had organized his fellow Ogonis against the Shell Oil company and the Nigerian government, demanding a sharing of oil revenues with the impoverished local population and a cleanup of environmental damage from oil production in the Niger Delta. These hangings occurred during a meeting of the Commonwealth Heads of Government, who suspended Nigeria's membership as a result.

The government also created dissension among Muslim leaders and repressed a new Islamic movement in northern Nigeria, some of whose members had been involved in violent incidents. Abacha deposed Ibrahim Dasouki, the sultan of Sokoto, generally recognized as the leader of Islam in Nigeria. Dasouki had seemed overly sympathetic to Abiola.[10]

In previous decades populist and reform movements invoking one or another interpretation of Islam had developed in parts of northern Nigeria. One heterodox movement, the Maitatsine, had staged an armed revolt in Kano in the 1980s. A newer Islamist movement, modeled on the Muslim Brotherhood, arose among students and youth in the 1990s. The movement is popularly (though inaccurately) described as "Shiite," apparently because its main leader, Sheikh Ibrahim Zakzaky, received some support from Iran. Abacha detained Zakzaky and a number of his followers after they staged some protest demonstrations.[11]

Religion had long been a point of contention in Nigeria. The Nigerian constitution established government-funded *sharia* (Islamic law) courts in the north to deal with personal law and disputes among Muslims. It also provided generous subsidies for the annual pilgrimage *(hajj)* to Mecca. Babangida had also unilaterally decided to join the Organization of the Islamic Conference without public consultation. All of these made Christians feel like second-class citizens, while activist Muslims, mainly in the northern emirate areas, sought increased Islamization of public life.

Abacha's rule also sowed political and ethnic dissension in the military. Besides arresting Obasanjo, Yar'Adua, and others for an alleged coup plot in 1995, in December 1997 the government also announced the arrests of eleven officers, mainly Yoruba, on coup charges. Their condemnation to death (commuted after Abacha's death) led to Yoruba riots in April 1998.

Local conflicts were also endemic in many areas of this vast country.[12] Despite—or perhaps because of—the country's oil wealth, people were becoming more and more impoverished, and public services were failing, all of which put a premium on capturing whatever assets were available. Often arising from competition for land, employment, or other resources, many of these conflicts would have been the stuff of peaceful, everyday politics in a country with functioning institutions and a reasonably healthy economy. But Abacha had abolished all local and provincial governments elected under Babangida's transition program, and years of military rule and oil-fed corruption had prevented the colonial administration, courts, judiciary, police, and other institutions from evolving into legitimate institutions for the peaceful resolution of conflict. Inevitable disputes, therefore, risked escalation into violence, and few official measures existed to control the escalation other than lawless violence from the military government itself.

International Responses

The international response to the Nigerian regime developed gradually, almost reluctantly, in response to events. Nigeria's regime played a strong hand. As black Africa's largest country, Nigeria is a major spokesman for Africa in international forums. The Nigerian state in general, and President Babangida in particular, had given wholehearted support to the recently concluded struggle against apartheid. Nigeria's prominent role in Africa and in pan-African concerns meant that the African American community in the United States, which had been united in pressing for harsher measures against apartheid in South Africa, was somewhat divided over Nigeria, though a majority of the Congressional Black Caucus spoke out against the suppression of democracy.

Nigeria under Babangida had taken on a measure of responsibility, in Washington's and others' eyes, by dispatching its troops to form the bulk of a West African peacekeeping force in Liberia, an effort that was later expanded to include Sierra Leone. Nigeria was an influential African member of both the Organization of the Islamic Conference and the Organization of Petroleum Exporting Countries. It dominated the Economic Community of West African States, headquartered in Abuja, which sponsored the Liberia and Sierra Leone operations.

The world's ninth-largest oil exporter, Nigeria was a major trading partner of the United States, which purchased about 44 percent of Nigeria's oil, accounting for 8 percent of U.S. domestic consumption.[13] The Nigerian oil industry had been "indigenized" according to a formula that required all extraction to take place through joint ventures between transnational oil companies and the Nigerian National Petroleum Company, which held the majority of shares. Among foreign partners, the Anglo-Dutch company Shell had the largest allocation, nearly 50 percent. The U.S. firm Mobil was second, with many other companies involved as well, including Chevron and Texaco from the United States, France's Elf, and Italy's Agip.[14] The major European governments and the United States were committed to both the free flow of oil to their domestic consumers and the fortunes of their own companies abroad.

Arrayed against these assets was the damage inflicted by the deterioration of Nigerian institutions not only on its own people but also beyond its borders. Of course, the specter of violent conflict in such a vast country frightened many, first of all Nigeria's neighbors, who might face overwhelming refugee flows, arms trading, and the spillover of military operations. Nigeria had also become an important entrepôt for drug trafficking. Its financial institutions were used for scams so widespread and clever that even Amnesty International was the victim of one.[15] Murtala Muhammad International Airport was blacklisted as a security risk, and no U.S. airlines flew there. Following the election of the British Labour government in May 1997, British Airways flights to Nigeria were also suspended.

The United States, Europe, and the Commonwealth imposed a variety of measures against the Nigerian government in response to the election nullification, the execution of Saro-Wiwa and the other Ogoni prisoners, and Nigeria's involvement in drug trafficking. The United States prohibited visas for important officials of the military regime, restricted arms sales, and suspended bilateral economic and military aid as well as trade credits and guarantees. The decision to classify Nigeria as a noncooperating drug trafficking country in 1994 legally required the United States to vote against any International Monetary Fund or World Bank loans to the country not already precluded by the country's disastrous financial performance. Bills introduced in both the Senate and House would have written these measures into law and added new sanctions, prohibiting additional U.S. investment and freezing official Nigerian assets.

The Commonwealth enacted similar though nonbinding measures. It suspended Nigeria's membership following the Ogoni executions. The 1996

Commonwealth meeting then called on its members to end arms exports and military training, ban sporting links, downgrade diplomatic missions, and restrict visas for Nigerian leaders. The UN Human Rights Commission appointed a special rapporteur on Nigeria.[16]

In addition to these sanctions, the United States and the Commonwealth also tried to engage the Nigerian regime to convey their concerns. The United States appointed Ambassador Donald McHenry, a former U.S. permanent representative at the UN, as a special envoy and held confidential meetings in Geneva with emissaries of the regime. Representative Bill Richardson (D-N.M.), who had made forays to rogue regimes into a minor specialty, followed up with more visits. The Commonwealth sent high-level missions that became even more controversial when Nigeria tried to block the participation of Canada, which had emerged as one of the few states to press for vigorous measures, including an oil embargo. At least until the election of the Labour government, both Britain and France took passive roles, concerned primarily with maintaining access for their oil companies.

Abacha responded to these pressures by courting North Korea, Sudan, and Libya in addition to Louis Farrakhan and other pariah figures. In the U.S. government, some argued for a tougher line, some for more engagement. The new foreign policy team that took over the State Department in President Bill Clinton's second administration ordered a formal review of U.S. policy toward Nigeria, which proceeded through consultations with NGOs and experts followed by various interagency meetings—all in preparation for the "principals' meeting," which, after several postponements, had still not been held when Abacha died, seventeen months after the inauguration.

These official actions took place against a background of polarized political views in the United States. Unlike the subject of any other CPA project, U.S. policy toward Nigeria became a divisive domestic political issue. Some organizations that had campaigned for sanctions against apartheid in South Africa (notably, the Africa Fund) now campaigned for sanctions—specifically, an oil embargo—against military-ruled Nigeria. This campaign also enlisted activists to promote a boycott by consumers and state and local governments of companies that did business in Nigeria, including Shell, Mobil, and Chevron.

The oil companies responded in different ways. Besides denying wrongdoing, Shell also reviewed its business practices, consulted with NGOs, and adopted respect for human rights as one of its business principles. Human

Rights Watch noted that Shell was the only oil company to take such measures, though the adequate implementation of these decisions was still in question.[17] Led by Mobil Oil, however, U.S. corporations took a different tack. They had become alarmed at what they viewed as the proliferating use of economic sanctions as a tool of U.S. foreign policy. These corporations established a Nigeria project at the Corporate Council on Africa. They argued that the Abacha regime had a positive agenda of economic reform, to attack the poverty that lay at the root of Nigeria's problems; that existing U.S. sanctions were not effective in changing the regime but were driving it into more extreme positions and alliances with unsavory forces; and that a unilateral U.S. oil embargo would be particularly ineffective and would mainly disadvantage U.S. firms vis-à-vis their European competitors.

The other side argued that engagement would fail. The regime was corrupt and was kept in power only through oil money. The oil companies were complicit in repression, both by pumping the oil that funded the corrupt regime and state and, more directly, through their participation in the repression of protests against their operations in the Niger Delta. All of the half measures imposed by the United States and other governments, the activists argued, were hypocritical in the face of the fact that these same governments continued to fund and support the regime by permitting imports of Nigerian oil and even encouraging further investment in the country. Only a comprehensive oil embargo would press the Nigerian military to leave power by depriving it of the resources that both motivated it and enabled it to rule. The United States should not wait for international consensus to form around a multilateral embargo but should rather, as the purchaser of nearly half of Nigeria's oil, exercise leadership by starting with a unilateral embargo, if necessary, and working to extend it.

The NGOs engaged in this campaign did so in partnership with Nigerian human rights and pro-democracy groups that were operating under threat of repression in Nigeria. They formed what some analysts have termed a transnational "advocacy network." Their strategy exemplified the "boomerang pattern" described by Margaret Keck and Kathryn Sikkink, a strategy by which NGOs that find access to their own state blocked link up with foreign or transnational counterparts to bring pressure on their home government through third-party governments, international organizations, or corporations.[18]

Some international NGOs played another role. At least two organizations—the International Human Rights Law Group and the Gorée Institute, with support from the Soros Foundation—sponsored confidential meetings outside Nigeria to bring together disparate components of the democratic and human rights movement. The sponsors hoped that these meetings, in South Africa, in Ghana, and on the island of Gorée off the coast of Senegal, would help the opposition forge a more united front. No state with major resources, however, offered to support such efforts.

The CPA Project and Mission to Nigeria

The CPA did not undertake a project on Nigeria only because a military regime had suppressed democracy and violated human rights. At one advisory board meeting, Julia Taft, who was then the head of Interaction, the coordinating body for U.S. humanitarian NGOs, recounted a story she had heard from one of Interaction's affiliates.[19] Sometime in late 1994, humanitarian workers were unloading supplies for the Rwandan refugees in Goma, Zaire. One of the freelance pilots remarked that he and his fellows often found themselves delivering relief supplies to the very same places where they had previously been delivering weapons. A relief worker asked him where, then, he might be delivering relief supplies in the near future. "Nigeria," he answered.

Everyone on the CPA board agreed on the importance of Nigeria, but deciding what to do and how to do it took longer, and was more contentious, than it had been in any other project. A U.S.-based oil company with which we tried to open discussions crudely tried to pressure the Council on Foreign Relations to prevent the CPA working group from endorsing an oil embargo.[20]

A mission to Nigeria posed difficult political issues. The Nigerian government was as selective about issuing visas as any country we visited, and we did not want to compromise our independence. In Serbia, we had to contend with state television cameras showing our group meeting with President Milosevic, images that communicated the message that international visitors sought out and met with the president—regardless of what they might say. We did not want to appear on Nigerian television shaking hands with Abacha while Abiola, Obasanjo, and so many others were in jail, Wole Soyinka was accused of treason, Kudirat Abiola had been buried just months before, and the United States and other governments were trying, if inconsistently, to convince the regime that its behavior made it a pariah. At the same time, we wanted to establish contact with Nigerian civil society. We finally decided to send a small, entirely academic group, rather than the larger, somewhat higher-profile groups we sent elsewhere, and depict our mission as a purely academic investigation. We decided not to request any meetings with government officials in advance, though we met with some officials and others familiar with the regime's thinking in the country. We could not ask Abacha for the release of prisoners, as others had done without result, but at least we did not risk helping to legitimate their jailer.

This was not the first visit to Nigeria for any of the senior members of our group, but we still were not quite prepared to be halted by gun-wielding soldiers at a checkpoint on our way from the airport and threatened until we paid an adequate bribe (thanks to the funders for allowing this expense). The decay and pollution of the tropical lagoon city of Lagos, the dilapidation of the once outstanding university in Ibadan, all contrasted with the opulent buildings and well-tended (though largely empty) streets of Abuja, the show capital that sucked up so much of the country's oil money. The cultural and physical distance between tropical Yorubaland and sub-Saharan Kano, with its mud-walled palaces and mosques and its labyrinthine bazaar filled with products of the trans-Saharan trade, made visible the country's diversity. Places of worship of hundreds of sects seemingly on every street called our attention to the religiosity of many Nigerians and made us wonder if this institution, so often a force for division, could also be a force for change.

The intensity, anger, and determination of the country's democratic activists in their sweltering and crowded offices in Lagos contrasted with the comfort of élites gathered in the opulent, air-conditioned Sheraton Abuja at a government-sponsored conference called Vision 2010. Yet even here reality broke through, as participants voted in a preparatory meeting to name the end of military rule as the country's top priority. The Roman Catholic archbishop of Jos, in his opening invocation, expressed a common theme: "We thank God for a country rich in human and material resources. And we confess that we have wasted both. But God permits U-turns."[21]

The CPA's developing understanding of preventive action inspired the focus on civil society. Nearly all the international attention toward Nigeria focused on the annulled election and the Ogoni struggle. These problems, however, resulted not only from the destructive choices of some leaders but also from long-standing problems of governance and development in Nigeria. We decided to focus more on the longer-term, underlying problems, to complement the debate about the immediate crisis. The long-term problems could not be addressed without breaking through the immediate crisis that escalated violence and promoted corruption. At the same time, any strategy for dealing with the immediate crisis should take into account its impact on long-term problem solving. International action to push Abacha and the military from power should not devastate Nigerian society as a whole, intensify ethnic or religious conflict, or provoke violent reactions. This is an endemic problem in prevention, as I discuss further in the analytical chapters. Kosovo exemplified this dilemma, and we were spurred on to work on Nigeria as we saw time running out in the South Balkans.

As in the project on the South Balkans, we built on these general principles to develop a concept of appropriate leadership for the preventive effort and a recommended strategy with roles for different organizations. I cannot recall anyone suggesting, in any of our discussions about Nigeria, that any entity other than the U.S. government could play the principal role, though some suggested a greater role for the UN, South Africa, or the Commonwealth. U.S. leadership, of course, does not mean unilateral effort. In the South Balkans, while we argued for a principal role for the United States, we also argued for a more coherent European policy, appropriate roles for the UN, the OSCE, and the European Union, a central role for NGOs, and coordination mechanisms. In the Great Lakes region and, as will be seen in the following chapter, in Central Asia, the situation seemed to call for a less obtrusive U.S. role, given U.S. interests and capabilities as well as the role of other states and organizations in those regions. In the case of Nigeria, U.S. leadership had to be exercised in collaboration with the Commonwealth and, among the Commonwealth's members, the United Kingdom, Canada, and South Africa.

The strategy we proposed for such a coalition, together with private organizations, included sanctions and incentives designed to influence Nigeria's ruling élites and engagement with civil society in order to strengthen the society's capacity to govern itself and monitor its leaders, despite the pathologies of the oil state. The proposed sanctions were mostly aimed at promoting an exodus of the military from power to end the immediate crisis. In deciding what recommendations to make about sanctions, we had to consider three issues:

—what, if any, sanctions to recommend and, specifically, whether to recommend imposition of an oil embargo;

—whether to pair sanctions with incentives;

—what conditions to place on the sanctions.

At the time we were considering our recommendations on Nigeria, a number of research projects were proceeding on the effectiveness of sanctions.[22] The CPA brought together several of the major researchers in the area for a panel discussion at its December 1996 annual conference, held just before our departure for Nigeria.[23] Furthermore, we could observe the effect of the comprehensive embargo imposed by the UN Security Council on another oil state, Iraq, since 1990. Iraq, like Nigeria, had depended on oil revenues for about 90 percent of its foreign exchange, though by 1997 that figure for Nigeria had reached 98 percent.[24]

Sanctions, of course, is a broad term that includes political measures such as visa restrictions as well as measures that are better conceived of as ending benefits (for example, aid cutoffs). Most of the discussion, however, deals with economic sanctions against trade or capital flows. The literature on such economic sanctions gives no clear-cut results that could be translated directly into policy recommendations, but certain findings influenced our decision:

—Sanctions are not particularly effective, but they are at least as effective as some other policy instruments—notably, the use of force.

—Sanctions are more effective when targeted on well-specified goals. They are rarely effective in changing major policies.

—Financial sanctions, which tend to be targeted more directly at the authorities, are more effective than trade sanctions, which harm many innocent people.

—Sanctions are more effective when combined with incentives, just as incentives work better when combined with sanctions. Combining incentives with sanctions also avoids the moral hazard of seeming to reward wrongdoers for ending objectionable behavior.

—Sanctions are more effective when they are multilateral, enjoy the support of broad sections of the target nation, and are sustained over time.

The example of the sanctions against Iraq gave pause. Since 1990, the UN Security Council had imposed comprehensive economic sanctions (including an oil embargo) against Baghdad without succeeding in changing the regime or reversing its major policies. Furthermore, the sanctions (or the Iraqi government's failure to comply with efforts to implement humanitarian exceptions) deprived Iraqis of imports of food and medicine, leading to hundreds of thousands of preventable cases of disease and death. Supporters of an oil embargo against Nigeria sometimes said that only the élite would suffer, because the people received no services and had even become more impoverished as a result of the oil economy. Like other petrostates, however, Nigeria had neglected agriculture and basic industries and depended on imports of food and medicine. Only the foreign exchange earned by oil enabled Nigeria to import these items.

Of course, harmful unintended consequences would have been a danger only if the embargo were effectively enforced. Had the United States imposed such an embargo, the result might have been simply a reorientation of the market and an increase in corruption. As little appetite as the U.S. government had for an oil embargo on Nigeria, other governments had even less. Furthermore, the oil market was extremely decentralized. Many spot traders purchased Nigerian oil from the Nigerian National Petroleum Company and then wholesaled it abroad. Partnership with such traders, many of them from the Middle East, was a favorite form of corruption among Nigeria's rulers. One of Abacha's business partners, the ethnic Lebanese oil broker Gilbert Chagoury, was revealed to have contributed $460,000 to a Democratic Party voter registration campaign and to have met with officials at the National Security Council to discuss Nigeria. These same traders could have diverted the oil elsewhere, diluting the impact of unilateral sanctions and increasing, not decreasing, the corrupt income of Nigeria's rulers. In Yugoslavia we had seen how criminal elements linked to the regime and ethnic-cleansing militias had enriched themselves through sanctions busting.

It should have been up to an informed Nigerian public, of course, to decide whether they wanted to pay such costs. In South Africa, the African National Congress and its allied civil society organizations supported the call for sanctions. In Nigeria, many of the pro-Abiola, pro-democracy, pro-MOSOP, and human rights organizations did so. Nonetheless, in view of the poor track record of the internationally enforced oil embargo against Iraq and the general finding that trade sanctions were less effective and more harmful to innocents than other forms of response, our report did not endorse oil sanctions.

Nonetheless, our report did not propound any of these arguments against an oil embargo. The main flaw in U.S. and international policy toward Nigeria was not an overreliance on broad-gauge coercive measures like an oil embargo but rather insufficient pressure and the absence of a focused goal. The campaign for oil sanctions was mobilizing political pressure against the Nigerian dictatorship and pressing for a more forceful policy. Overall, therefore, rather than arguing against an unlikely oil embargo, our report presented an alternative proposal for a package of targeted financial sanctions, combined with incentives and direct support for and engagement with Nigerian civil society.

The most important element of any sanctions regime, of course, is the criterion for imposing and, ultimately, removing the sanctions. The CPA's report argued for three conditions: transition to civilian rule, release of political prisoners, and the lifting of barriers to free discussion and debate. These fell short of demanding "democracy" or of insisting on recognition of

Abiola as president. A fake transition to an Abacha presidency in an uncontested election with no free debate would not have constituted a transition to civilian rule. These minimal demands would have created the conditions for Nigerians to determine for themselves their means of self-government.

We recommended that sanctions be intensified if these conditions were not met and that the sanctions "should focus on financial measures against the regime and individuals who profit from it, including a ban on transactions by the regime and its key figures. . . . The intelligence, diplomatic, and legal work necessary to freeze these assets should begin immediately."[25] We included the latter sentence because U.S. officials claimed to have no information on where the Nigerian leaders kept the proceeds of their corruption and had not investigated what would be required, legally and politically, to freeze them. We heard repeatedly that the United States could not touch these assets, as they were all held in Europe or the Middle East. Senate hearings in 1999, however, proved this assertion false. In the wake of the revelation that the Bank of New York had been used for money laundering by corrupt Russian officials, the Senate Banking Committee held hearings on a significant loophole in American law: though the Money Laundering Control Act forbids banks to handle money for foreign clients engaging in drug trafficking, kidnapping, and foreign bank fraud, there is no such prohibition against accepting the proceeds of official corruption.

In the course of the hearings, it emerged that two of Abacha's sons (including Mohammad, later charged in the murder of Kudirat Abiola) had apparently kept enough money in Citibank accounts to withdraw $39 million "prematurely" in response to an investigation.[26] One of the lessons of this case, then, was the need for governments to monitor more closely the way the international financial system facilitates the looting of countries by predatory rulers.

We also recommended incentives linked to the same conditions. These incentives were directed at Nigeria and its population, not at the military rulers themselves. A number of our interlocutors had argued for guaranteeing a "soft landing" for Abacha and his clique. This issue recurs in most efforts to remove harmful rulers. Such efforts may help avoid violence by facilitating the peaceful departure of dictators, but they also create a moral hazard by rewarding people for malfeasance and reducing the deterrent effect of sanctions and other measures. We ultimately included no such recommendations. We focused, instead, on tying commitments to foreign assistance and investment to a clear change of direction in Nigeria toward "civilian rule, inclusion, and dialogue."[27] These included debt relief and restructuring, aid for creating institutions to manage and share the oil revenues, access to export markets, support for privatization and stabilization,[28] assistance in reconstruction of infrastructure, and support for investments beyond the energy sector.

We also proposed action by a broad range of private actors, not only different kinds of NGOs but also religious, business, trade union, and other groups, in support of their counterparts in Nigerian civil society. Of course, "civil society"—organizations representing views and interests independent of government—may do harm or good, promote or prevent conflict. But positive action by civil society is a necessary component of open, accountable governance—the principal element in preventing conflict. We had discussed civil society to some extent in our work on the South Balkans: work with NGOs and the media was a key part of preventive work in Macedonia. In Rwanda the legacy of the genocide, including the state's overriding concern for security, dominated political life to the detriment of private efforts, but in both Burundi and the Democratic Republic of the Congo, private organizations organized dialogues, monitored human rights, and provided social services. In the DRC, in particular, the civil society that had developed in the vacuum left by the decay of the Mobutist state formed the basic infrastructure for any democratic alternative that might develop.

On our brief trip to Nigeria we found that civil society, though embattled and beset, still maintained a level of activity and independence that provided a wellspring of hope for the future. Therefore we argued that, besides pressing the military to exit from power, "it is also vital to offer support for those domestic groups that can encourage a sustainable and legitimate basis for democratic politics."[29] We also warned, however, that such private activities could never substitute for public policy. Thinking in part of the failure of major states to follow up on Sant' Egidio's breakthrough with the education agreement in Kosovo, we noted that "if we have learned any lesson from the work of the Center for Preventive Action over the past few years, it is that these efforts by the private sector and nongovernmental organizations, while they are necessary, will not work without the leadership of committed states, most particularly the United States. NGOs and the private sector can undertake actions that governments cannot, but unless real power and resources are placed in the balance, the private efforts will not have the framework they need for success."[30]

God Permits U-Turns

These recommendations were still in press when the invocation of the archbishop of Jos took on a strange hue of prophecy as I sat in my hotel room in Islamabad on June 8, 1998, waiting for clearance to board a UN plane to Qandahar, Afghanistan. In January of that year, the CPA had held a conference on Nigeria attended by dozens of Nigerian participants, including leaders of NGOs, Nigerian Catholic and Islamic leaders, Shell Oil and Ogoni activists, all the U.S. organizations concerned with Nigeria (except one oil company, which continued its boycott), scholars, and Commonwealth diplomats, with a scheduled speech by U.S. Under Secretary of State Thomas Pickering.[31] That conference had clarified the impasse: activists called for an oil embargo; the U.S. government condemned the dictatorship but had no concrete policy to promote a transition; social disintegration and low-level violence continued; and oil companies (those that did not boycott) registered dismay but argued that promoting political change was not the role of corporations. Meanwhile, Abacha proceeded with his plans to win a presidential election while hardly ever leaving his palace. He insisted on gaining the nomination of each of the five fake parties his government had recognized. He seemed on the way to installing his kleptocracy as permanently as Mobutu had his.

I was consequently riveted to the screen in Islamabad when I heard on the BBC *World News* that soldiers had surrounded the presidential palace in Abuja. Over the next few days the report emerged that Abacha had died of a heart attack. Other stories and rumors filtered out—that the general's heart gave out after a Viagra-fueled orgy with three Indian or Lebanese prostitutes, that these women had been handsomely paid to feed the general poisoned fruit, that his wife was seized at the airport with thirty-eight suitcases filled with U.S. dollars. Abacha had rendered himself almost invulnerable to coups, immuring himself in an impregnable palace and recruiting a new Presidential Guard. Had he died of natural causes, or of corruption, or had some hand within the palace poisoned him? Unless the latter were the case, and those involved wanted to end Nigeria's pariah status rather than simply take their turn to loot, the movements against his rule could claim no credit for his ouster. But they did help shape the transition.

General Abdulsalami Abubakar, whose name might be translated "servant of peace," took over as transitional ruler and began another, more genuine transition. Crowds took to the street in many parts of Nigeria, especially, though not only, in the Yoruba areas, to celebrate the dictator's passing. Crowds returned to riot in the same places barely a month later following Abiola's death while still in detention, after he collapsed during a meeting with a U.S. delegation led by Pickering. Abiola's death virtually ended the major debate of the transition period: whether to hold new elections under the transitional military government or to install a civilian transitional government led by Abiola to preside over a national conference to draft a new constitution. The latter demand reflected not only dissatisfaction with Nigeria's military-drafted constitutions but also the Yoruba desire to reopen the question of the nature of the Nigerian federation. Always in the background were oil prices: they had been falling throughout 1997 and 1998. During the transition oil fell to $10 a barrel, the lowest price since the oil shock of 1973. No doubt such conditions encouraged the military to leave power.

During the political contests that followed, political parties emerged to define the contours of Nigeria's third republic. The presidential election—during which most of the CPA delegation of 1997 served on a joint monitoring team organized by the Carter Center and the National Democratic Institute for International Affairs—was marred by massive fraud in some areas, but Obasanjo had behind him both much of Nigeria's power élite and much of the international community, which had grown to venerate him during the sixteen years between his handover of power to an elected president and his arrest by Abacha. He had joined many international efforts to support democracy and human rights, oppose corruption, and raise the profile of Africa in international forums.

Obasanjo's presidency thus far demonstrates how deep-seated Nigeria's problems are. He has launched a campaign against corruption and established inquiries into past human rights violations. Members of Abacha's family and former high officials are on trial for political murders and official corruption. Obasanjo initiated a campaign for the return of Nigeria's looted wealth. He canceled questionable contracts and entered into a negotiation with the International Monetary Fund in the hope of obtaining forgiveness or rescheduling of Nigeria's debt. He permitted full foreign ownership of petroleum enterprises and tried to raise domestic fuel prices in order to attack Nigeria's fuel crisis. He visited the Niger Delta to hear the grievances, he said, of the people who had been struggling for a fair share of the oil wealth. As an ethnic Yoruba with long-standing ties to the military and northern élites who described himself as a nonethnic Nigerian, he is better positioned than anyone to heal the country's ethnic divides. He is a world-renowned leader whose personal prestige instantly restored much of Nigeria's lost international standing. And he has done all this (and more) as oil prices rebounded to their highest level since the mid-1980s.

Yet despite these efforts, violence seems to have increased in Nigeria. Obasanjo's decision to increase the retail prices of petroleum products led to massive strikes and public protests, but these subsided when, unlike previous rulers, he negotiated with the trade union leaders who led them and reached an agreement on a more moderate price increase.[32] Obasanjo's efforts to calm the situation in the Niger Delta have not succeeded, despite his sponsorship of a law to set up a local Development Authority there and to return 13 percent (up from 3 percent) of the oil revenues directly to the area. Clashes have continued to expand, leading to the killing of hundreds of people and the closure of yet more oil operations. Activists dismiss the president's proposals as inadequate, and, in any case, the Nigerian Congress has not passed them.

The fundamental tensions that had underlain the conflict over June 12 broke out in two different ways: interethnic riots between Yoruba and Hausa and interreligious riots between northern Muslims and Christians. Like ethnic riots in other parts of the world—notably, like those in Central Asia toward the end of the Soviet period—the Yoruba-Hausa riots broke out over seemingly small events but soon grew to crystallize broader grievances and may have been manipulated by political forces bent on undermining the authorities.

Yorubaland had been in a state of turmoil since June 12, 1993, and a number of organizations had come to champion Yoruba identity and even separatism. In July 1999, Yoruba traders claim to have caught a Hausa woman watching a Yoruba ritual closed to outsiders in the city of Sagumu. Attacks on Hausa by Yoruba street gangs left at least sixty dead; thousands fled. Reprisal attacks on Yoruba in Kano took more than a hundred lives.

If the interethnic riots appeared to be more or less spontaneous outbreaks of tension, the interreligious ones resulted from something even more dangerous: the political manipulation of religion. It led to what President Obasanjo called the "worst blood letting since the civil war."[33] During his poorly funded campaign for governor of Zamfara in northern Nigeria, Ahmed Sani Yerima Bakuru found that calls for *sharia* resonated with the public, which apparently saw the imposition of Islamic law as a way to attack crime and corruption. After he was elected, his opponents taunted him as a hypocrite until, in October 1999, he announced a plan to enact *sharia* as the law of the land.[34] Several other states followed suit. In Kaduna the announcement that the legislature would consider enacting *sharia* led to protests by local Christians, who were in turn attacked by Muslims. In the ensuing riots, mobs attacked southern Christians living in the north, killing hundreds. Many, mostly Igbo, fled back to their ethnic homelands, reenacting the events that preceded the civil war in the 1960s. Several hundred Hausa living in the southeast were then massacred in reprisal. Many argued that the *sharia* laws violated the federal constitutions, but Obasanjo hesitated to take firm action. As a Christian president he was caught in a political trap: opposing *sharia* would enable his enemies to portray him as a communalist, even as allowing it to be implemented undermined the legal order that provided the only basis for national unity.

With the crisis of military rule past, both Nigerians and a range of international institutions gained an opportunity to address the underlying problems that were aggravated by Abacha's dictatorship but were not eliminated by his passing. All of the fault lines we identified under Abacha have become even more active, and, except for the sanctions designed to force a transition, all of the recommendations remain relevant. Supporting governance in Nigeria is now a major focus of work for many international organizations, foreign aid missions, foundations, and NGOs. Furthermore, in doing so they are supporting, not opposing, the objective of the government in power.

Still, the major efforts Nigeria needs—forgiveness of debt concluded by illegitimate regimes and massive aid in restructuring the polity and economy—have not been forthcoming, although both the International Monetary Fund and the World Bank did resume financial and development assistance to Nigeria in 2000. Merely remedial work may fail. Nigeria was established by imperial Britain, forcing together radically different societies with no common institutions and, in some cases, a history of conflict. Transnational oil companies make much of its lopsided and distorted economy run. International banks enabled its rulers to loot the revenue from the oil economy. Post facto palliatives that do not touch this structure may leave behind little that is permanent. Conflict in Nigeria results in large measure from the way that international actors and institutions have shaped that society for decades, even centuries. Preventing further violence there will require changes not only in Nigeria but also in those international actors and institutions—the same actors and institutions, often enough, that failed to respond to Abacha's dictatorship with much more than belated verbal condemnations.

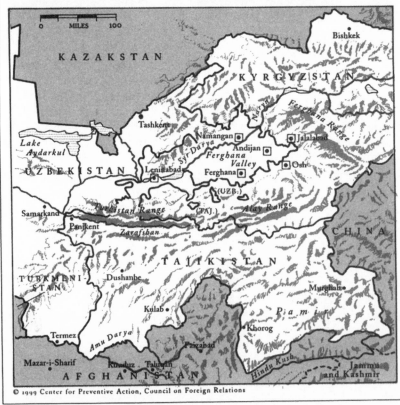

© 1999 Center for Preventive Action, Council on Foreign Relations

6

The Ferghana Valley: Festering Inner Wounds

> Lowborn and noble, poor and unfortunate, all opened their mouths with curses and raised their hands in supplication.
>
> Beware of festering inner wounds, for inner wounds surface in the end.
>
> Distress no one insofar as you are able, for one cry of anguish can upset the whole world.
>
> As a consequence of tyranny and vice, he ruled in Samarkand no more than five months.
>
> —ZAHIRUDDIN MUHAMMAD BABUR, *prince of Ferghana, king of Kabul, emperor of Hindustan, The Baburnama*

The Center for Preventive Action's first three projects dealt with conflicts at relatively advanced stages of development. Burundi had already passed through several waves of massacres. The South Balkans had not broken out in violence (at least not recently), but the resurgent conflicts between Albanians and their Slavic neighbors, linked to the violent disintegration of Yugoslavia, formed part of a network of nationalist disputes and wars. The crisis of democracy and governance in Nigeria poised that country on the brink of more turmoil, though the complexity and multiplicity of conflicts there made it harder to predict what form violence might take.

The CPA therefore sought a case in which we would confront the problems of long-term preventive action, focusing more on factors that increase the risk of conflict than on events and actions that trigger it, preferably in a different region. My own research background led me to Central Asia, and in particular the Ferghana Valley. The Ferghana Valley is in many ways the heart of Central Asia. Although it accounts for only 5 percent of the Central Asian land mass, nearly one-fifth of the region's population dwells there in several large cities and the densely populated, overexploited farmland between them.[1] Colleagues spoke about it as the tensest area of Central Asia, except for those parts of Tajikistan already devastated by civil war. Spanning the southern part of the Kyrgyz Republic, eastern Uzbekistan, and northern Tajikistan, the Ferghana Valley suffered from multiple social, economic, and political problems. The division of what was once an integrated, though ethnically diverse, region into three different nation-states with different policies and currencies had aggravated many of these problems.

The CPA's research documented those stresses. In Bishkek, the capital of the Kyrgyz Republic, we learned that the United Nations Development Program (UNDP), encouraged by the government, had identified the Ferghana Valley as a potential conflict zone and proposed a regional plan for "preventive development." Support for some such regional development program became a central tenet of our recommendations. Uzbekistan, however, rejected the idea as an unwarranted intrusion into its internal affairs.

As we prepared our report, however, the very crisis we had foreseen developed. During our March 1997 field mission, the male members of our delegation attended a funeral in the central mosque of Namangan, Uzbekistan. We thought that the invitation had been prompted only by a desire to show us a ritual exhibiting the area's deep Islamic culture. Our female colleagues, however, who had been speaking to people in the street, learned that the deceased had been a high police official, assassinated in the line of duty. We heard multiple tales about this killing, which the government of Uzbekistan seemed to want to hush up. By the end of the year, Tashkent openly charged that Islamic radicals from the Ferghana Valley based in Afghanistan and Tajikistan had carried out assassinations in Uzbekistan's part of the Valley. After a campaign of mass arrests, the government blamed the same groups for a spectacular terrorist bomb attack in the Uzbek capital, Tashkent, in February 1999. The following summer, Islamist guerrillas seeking to fight their way home to the Uzbekistan part of the Ferghana Valley crossed from Tajikistan into the Kyrgyz Republic, where they sparked an international crisis. They mounted attacks again, this time from several directions, in the summer of 2000. Most observers expected further attacks in 2001, but instead their leader, Juma Namangani, and many others perished in the battle for Kunduz, in northern Afghanistan. That war showed that the Central Asia crisis had dimensions that were not only local but regional and even global.

As had been the case in the Great Lakes region, it proved impossible to isolate one conflict area—whether Burundi or the Ferghana Valley—and treat it "preventively" in isolation from other conflicts in the same region. The tensions in the Ferghana Valley grew not only from the "root causes" of conflict there but also from the connections that developed with the wars in Afghanistan and Tajikistan and the links of those countries, in turn, to Pakistan, Iran, and international markets in drugs and guns. The support of Osama bin Laden, living in Afghanistan under the protection of the Taliban, for the Islamic Movement of Uzbekistan linked this problem to that of "international terrorism" and obscured its local roots. The annihilation of the parts of the movement based in Afghanistan with external support might mislead international actors into believing that the challenges to stability in Central Asia are over.

The framing of the problem solely as "terrorism" and the resultant support to the Central Asian regimes, especially to that of President Islam Karimov of Uzbekistan, risks aggravating the crisis. Protests against deteriorating economic conditions, government corruption, or political repression and state violence can all too easily be stigmatized as "fundamentalist." Military and coercive approaches to narrowly defined security interests threaten to overwhelm concern for more deeply rooted problems. As in Nigeria, a genuine preventive strategy would integrate measures to confront the immediate threat with those to address the underlying risk factors.

Background

For much of history, Central Asia's economy consisted of nomadic pastoralism on the arid steppes and agriculture and trade in the better-watered oases and river valleys. Cities grew up along the roads collectively known as the "Silk Route," which for thousands of years connected China to western Asia and the Mediterranean world. From the eighteenth century on, however, the area declined economically as land-based long-distance trade lost out to the European-dominated sea trade. Eventually Central Asia became part of the Russian and then Soviet empires, in which it supplied raw materials, largely cotton and oil and gas, to industries located elsewhere.

Russian and then Soviet rule had as far-reaching and deep effects on this region as colonial rule had in Africa. Here, too, some of the identities around which people now mobilize were formed from indigenous cultural elements as part of political projects. Among the most successful policies of the Soviet government was the creation of ethnonationalities and national republics among a population in which no single type of identity—religion, language, tribe or clan, political unit—had clearly predominated. The Soviets developed and taught an "all-Soviet" identity, expressed in the Russian language, but Moscow also divided Central Asia into five national republics, each defined as the historical homeland of a particular "nation" that had supposedly participated in the construction of socialism. These new national identities were designed to undermine pan-Turkic or pan-Islamic movements that might oppose Sovietization.

The four Turkic-speaking Central Asian nations—Uzbek, Kazak, Kyrgyz, and Turkmen —as well as the only one speaking an Iranian language—Tajik—were formed out of a political process of classifying local groups into supposedly more "scientific" categories. Currently about 62 percent of the Ferghana Valley's population is classified as Uzbek, including 27 percent of the people in the Tajik western part of the Valley and 31 percent in the eastern Kyrgyz part.[2]

Soviet language policy imposed national languages written in Cyrillic characters for each group, making it impossible for anyone but historical scholars to read any publication or manuscript from before the 1920s, when local languages were written in variations of the Perso-Arabic script. This linguistic legacy affects the Ferghana Valley today, as Uzbekistan is gradually introducing the Roman alphabet (as did Ataturk in the Turkish Republic), while Uzbeks in neighboring Tajikistan and Kyrgyzstan continue to use Soviet-Uzbek Cyrillic characters, making textbooks from Uzbekistan unusable.

Today the peoples of Central Asia have largely adopted these national identities, and the political élites of all the new nations have set themselves the task of turning former Soviet national republics, which Moscow designed as dependent mechanisms of control, into independent national states. Some of the difficulties encountered resemble those of African states trying to build national identities and institutions within boundaries arbitrarily drawn by colonial rulers for entirely different purposes.

Soviet economic and social policies also affected people's identities in unintended ways. Strong "territorial" identities developed around administrative and work units that, in this predominantly rural region, mostly consisted of collective and state farms (kolkhoz and sovkhoz).[3] These new institutions seemed largely to be based on previously existing villages or clans, and people organized society within them around familiar models of patron-client relations within localities (*mahallas*). The significant subsidies that the Soviet center gave to the social budgets of these republics (20–50 percent of the total by the end of the Brezhnev period), as well as the revenues from the sales of cotton, funded these patron-client relations. Local leaders, kolkhoz chairmen, cotton traders, party secretaries, kingpins of organized crime, and other "big men" emerged as quasi-autonomous leaders of communities, like the khans, beys, or *arbabs* of pre-Soviet times. These regional leaders became key politicians in the newly independent states. Loyalty to such local collectivities and leaders has often outweighed ethnic or ideological factors in conflicts such as the civil war in Tajikistan.

Although Central Asia was the poorest part of the Soviet Union, the subsidies provided by the center accustomed the people to a level of social welfare—universal education, basic health care, at least the pretense of employment, opportunities for women—far above that of most of the postcolonial world. The erosion of these benefits has been deeply felt.

The Ferghana Valley has been under particular pressure. Its population, denser than that in any other rural area in the Soviet Union, was organized into huge kolkhozes and sovkhozes that grew cotton for the country's textile industry by saturating the soil with pesticides, fertilizers, and poorly managed irrigation water. Irrigation diverted so much water that the Aral Sea dried up, creating an ecological and social crisis. The labor system of the kolkhozes disguised massive unemployment. As a result, the Central Asian governments face a dilemma: the kolkhozes, which provide an increasingly frayed social safety net and means of political control through local strong men, stand in the way of the development of a more efficient market economy. The erection of national borders and customs posts in order to assert control over the national economies and prevent the spread of the drug trade, gun trafficking, and militant Islam prevents the free circulation of goods and people necessary for social and economic development. In all these ways the logic of social control contradicts—and often trumps—the logic of development.

Personal interests also play a role: in Uzbekistan a few people with permits to purchase foreign currency at the official rate can accumulate huge profits simply by exploiting the difference between the market and official rates.[4] Making the currency convertible would eliminate this opportunity. As in Nigeria, financial corruption also blocks development and accountability.

Although the Soviets tried to control Islam, they did not eliminate it.[5] An official, pro-Soviet Islam coexisted with an unofficial Islam in the villages and kolkhozes. The Ferghana Valley remained the part of Central Asia with the highest level of Muslim observance. With independence, unofficial Islam grew, and the new governments, while espousing loyalty to their cultural heritage, still feared its challenge. In Tajikistan an Islamic party played an important role in the "opposition" movement during the civil war and today forms part of a shaky government of reconciliation. Uzbekistan has suppressed Islamic movements in the Ferghana Valley and also bred the largest group of violent Islamist opponents, formerly based in Tajikistan and Afghanistan. The Kyrgyz Republic has tolerated its local Islamist groups, largely of Uzbek ethnicity, but in 1999 and 2000 it faced a military challenge from Uzbek Islamists trying to fight their way into Uzbekistan from Tajikistan.

The breakup of the Soviet Union was accompanied by conflict in Central Asia, though less than in the Caucasus. Only Tajikistan, the poorest and most externally dependent of the Soviet republics, fell into civil war, partly stimulated by the availability of weapons and sanctuary in nearby Afghanistan. The élites from the Tajikistan part of the Ferghana Valley, who had long dominated the republic, were on the winning side, but they lost power to another regional faction (Kulabis), from southern Tajikistan.

In both the Uzbekistan and Kyrgyzstan parts of the Valley, the transition period was marked by pogroms and ethnic clashes between ethnic Uzbeks and their Turkic neighbors. In June 1989 a small clash over the price of strawberries in the town bazaar of Kuvasi (Ferghana district) exploded into violent attacks by Uzbeks against Meskhetian Turks, a small ethnic group whom Stalin had deported to Central Asia from Georgia. Uzbeks demonstrated for sovereignty, and Soviet militia fired on them. Hundreds, perhaps thousands, of people were killed. In June 1990 bloodshed broke out between Uzbeks and Kyrgyz in the Osh region of southern Kyrgyzstan. Uzbeks in Osh were demanding greater representation in government, while Kyrgyz were demanding more land and better housing. When local authorities agreed to make land from an Uzbek kolkhoz available for housing for Kyrgyz, confrontations escalated. Several hundreds were killed in rioting that was stopped only by Soviet airborne troops. Economic competition and ethnic aspirations formed an explosive mixture in the context of rising demands for national sovereignty.

Further conflict broke out in Namangan, one of the principal cities in the Uzbekistan part of the Valley, in December 1991. An Islamic group called Adolat ("justice") that had organized against crime occupied the local administrative headquarters and raised several demands for the Islamization of public life. Although President Islam Karimov temporarily compromised with the movement, he eventually arrested seventy-one of its members. The rest fled abroad, where they formed the core of the guerrillas who fought from bases in Tajikistan and Afghanistan until being defeated or dispersed in the U.S. offensive of October–November 2001. After years of calm, conflict also broke out in Khujand, the Tajikistan part of the Valley, in 1996.[6] Demonstrators demanded the removal of officials from Kulab. At least five were killed and thousands arrested. This took place against the background of a peace accord between the government and the Islamic opposition, both dominated by groups from southern Tajikistan. Uzbekistan supported the Khujandis, as it was competing for influence with Russia, the main backer of the Kulabis. Both these incidents and the indicators of conflict and social distress led us to conclude that the Ferghana Valley was the site of a number of potential conflicts, ones that could interact in unpredictable ways.

The CPA Mission to the Ferghana Valley

Toward the end of March 1997, the CPA's mission visited parts of the Ferghana Valley in both Uzbekistan and the Kyrgyz Republic.[7] During our short stay in Namangan we breakfasted with the deputy administrator, visited the bazaar and mosque (for the funeral described earlier in this chapter), and met with both dissidents and some ordinary citizens. Our drive to nearby Andijan the next evening encountered numerous police checkpoints, apparently in response to the assassination of the man whose funeral we had attended and other rather murky violent incidents. Andijan, like Namangan, presented an appearance of normality, but an evening meeting with the son of a charismatic Islamic preacher who had disappeared in the Tashkent airport revealed undercurrents of discontent. The next morning, however, the local deputy district administrator, an energetic and forceful woman, presented to us a full array of measures the government was taking to meet the citizens' needs.

The short drive across the border to Osh, in the Kyrgyz Republic, acquainted us firsthand with one of the newer problems in the Ferghana Valley. Uzbek border guards took our passports (all with valid visas) and halted us for no apparent reason. Half an hour later, they let us go, offering no explanation.

Once across the border the atmosphere changed. In Uzbekistan some in the group wondered if there really was a potential for conflict in the Ferghana Valley. In more open Kyrgyzstan many people, in the government, the parliament, and the nongovernmental sector, spoke openly about the heritage of the "Osh events" and the danger of future clashes. The domination of the government by northern Kyrgyz; the separation of the Uzbeks of Kyrgyzstan from Uzbekistan and its implications for access to media and education; conflicts with Uzbekistan over water, fuel, and power; problems of employment, education, and health; the corruption of the police and administration (as well as the Russian border guards) by drug trafficking coming from Afghanistan; ethnic competition over land, jobs, and places in the bazaar; increasing pressure on the press; the growth of Islamic movements among ethnic Uzbek youth; and more—all figured in our conversations as possible sources of conflict. By the same token, many in the government and civil society were actively working to prevent future violence in this more open atmosphere. Many people expressed their determination to learn the lessons of the past.

Still, the government of the Kyrgyz Republic was so concerned about the danger of violent conflict in the Ferghana Valley that it had argued to several international organizations that they should launch a cross-border program to ameliorate some of its potential causes. At a dinner with the U.S. ambassador in Bishkek, the Kyrgyz capital, an official of the UNDP described to us the project his program had proposed. Officials of the foreign ministry privately furnished us with the unofficial draft then in circulation.[8]

We had heard talk in New York of such a project. Our previous projects had followed upon others' efforts at conflict prevention, but there had been few such efforts in the Ferghana Valley. Max van der Stoel, the OSCE high commissioner on national minorities, had sponsored some interethnic roundtables in Kyrgyzstan. Both the UN and the OSCE had small missions in Khujand as part of the implementation of the Tajikistan peace accord. The UN high commissioner for refugees had established a listening post in Osh. Many agencies and donors were sponsoring programs in these countries to support humanitarian efforts, democratization, human rights, economic reform, and other items on the international agenda for Central Asia, but few of these efforts reached the Ferghana Valley. A few international corporations were present: in Namangan, Daewoo had established a van assembly plant, and Coca Cola a bottling plant. Both joint ventures had members of the president's family as local partners. These investments had as yet produced little employment, however.

Stepping into this vacuum, the UNDP proposed programs that would "pay equal attention to income generation and job creation, peace education, inter-ethnic and inter-country confidence building, promotion of trade (and related dialogue on the maintenance of open boundaries) and the improvement of security conditions."[9] It envisaged a joint regional framework for such activities including governments, international organizations, and civil society from all three countries. Some members of the CPA group (particularly this one, I must confess) may have been overly enthusiastic about this program, which seemed to embody virtually every item in the catechism of conflict prevention. The difficulties this proposal encountered taught some lessons about the politics of external benevolence insufficiently grounded in local realities.

Our group's recommendations concentrated on measures to reduce sources of conflict through targeted programs of governance, development, and institution building. Although assassinations and even terrorist bombings increased in the Ferghana Valley and then in Tashkent, even as we prepared the report, our group argued against what seemed to be the government of Uzbekistan's preferred solution: massive repression.

We also argued that the United States had an interest in preventing conflict in the Ferghana Valley, though we did not suggest that the United States take the lead, as in the South Balkans or Nigeria. The idea that the United States should make a war on terrorism in this region its top military objective never occurred to us or to any of our interlocutors. We were pleased enough when, in July 1997, Deputy Secretary of State Strobe Talbott made a speech emphasizing the importance to the United States of stability and reform in the Caucasus and Central Asia, arguing that conflict resolution should therefore be Washington's "Job One."[10] We argued for a more proactive policy, a policy of prevention.

The main principle we enunciated was the same as in Nigeria: "Accountable politics and dynamic economies provide the best institutional framework to channel strife into peaceful competition, a necessary condition for investment."[11] We argued, therefore—as had liberals about leftist insurgencies during the cold war—that the repression of suspected Islamist sympathizers by Uzbekistan, in which thousands of people passed through the hands of the police, would be counterproductive and would lead to more support for revolt. We argued instead that the Kyrgyz Republic's approach of tolerating nonviolent opposition, including Islamic activity, could incorporate dissident elements into the polity and create a basis for institutions of governance that would manage conflicts without violence.

We noted, citing the Great Lakes region and elsewhere, that conflict tended to spread throughout regions and that the Ferghana Valley contained closely linked parts of three countries. Furthermore, the immediate neighborhood included Tajikistan and Afghanistan, where conflict was already being spread through armed groups, drug trafficking, and weapons proliferation in addition to the intentional support of insurgency by governments and networks such as al-Qaida.

Perhaps paying inadequate attention to the broader regional threats, we emphasized the need for cooperation among states and civil societies in the Ferghana Valley itself. Economic development in the region would require open borders and convertible currencies, which would in turn require dialogue and cooperation among the regional states. The United States, we argued, along with other major states, should support a framework for regional cooperation similar to that proposed by the UNDP, even if that program were stymied by Tashkent. In the absence of any obvious lead organization for the effort, the UN appeared almost as the default option, but, as in other regions where UN action resulted mainly from the lack of interest or capacity of other actors, it did not prove effective.

As we had in Nigeria, we emphasized the importance of civil society, though the Soviet heritage had greatly sapped private initiative. We propounded the argument, developed while working on Nigeria, that strong civil society organizations that bridged communal boundaries and monitored government performance for conformity to standards of good governance were essential to accountability and hence to conflict prevention. We recommended cross-border partnerships in the Ferghana Valley among NGOs and other civil society organizations; a few NGOs were already working on such projects.[12]

We also explored the possible contribution of foreign direct investment to employment creation. We argued that convertible currency, more open borders, and incentives for cross-border cooperative ventures by international financial institutions could promote employment-creating investment. Daewoo, for instance, had proposed establishing a parts manufacturing plant in Osh to supply its assembly plant across the border in Namangan. The difficulties entailed in moving goods between Uzbekistan and Kyrgyzstan had prevented further exploration of this project.

Finally, because a number of our recommendations involved foreign assistance, we discussed its modalities. The United States Agency for International Development, like many donors, worked mainly bilaterally with partners in the capitals. This made it difficult both to fund multicountry regional programs and to target projects to vulnerable subregions like the Ferghana Valley. Technical personnel of some aid projects seemed to have little understanding of the political and social context, leading them to undertake possibly counterproductive measures. We suggested both that regional experts participate more fully in the aid process and that donors undertake a multidisciplinary "conflict impact assessment" of projects. Finally, even in Central Asia, where the field was a bit less crowded than some other places we had worked, donors and major actors needed to coordinate their efforts, perhaps by setting up a clearinghouse for information about donor activity.

Obstacles to Prevention: Political Resistance and Escalation

In the period following our mission, both the Kyrgyz Republic and Tajikistan agreed to participate in the UNDP program, which established headquarters in Osh and set up a website.[13] The UN revised the statement of purpose to take Uzbekistan's concerns into account. The new statement presented the program entirely in terms of development, not conflict prevention, and noted that the program would respect the sovereignty of all three countries, implement some programs on a national basis, and set up national offices in each part of the Ferghana Valley.

Uzbekistan still refused to participate. Indeed, when Uzbekistan's foreign minister, Abdulaziz Kamilov, spoke at the UN General Assembly in September 1999, he devoted a portion of his remarks to a criticism of the Ferghana Valley Development Program, which, he said, "interferes with the security of the region."[14] Without the cooperation of the state that controlled the majority of the Valley, the UN eventually closed the office in Osh.

Through its interagency framework for coordination (discussed in the final chapter of this book), the UN held several meetings to discuss the situation in the Ferghana Valley. Some took place in headquarters, and one was held in Almaty, Kazakstan, bringing together UN country teams from each of the concerned states. As part of this effort, the UN made a low-key approach, asking the Uzbek government to permit it to send a fact-finding mission to the Uzbekistan part of the Ferghana Valley, but Tashkent turned down this request as well.

The CPA attempted to create a network of supporters for preventive measures. Together with the Central Eurasia Project of the Open Society Institute (of the Soros Foundations Network), we convened a joint conference in Washington in November 1999 with the UNDP administrator, Mark Malloch-Brown, as the principal speaker. Because Uzbekistan opposed "conflict prevention," we entitled the conference "Toward Sustainable Development in the Ferghana Valley." An official from Tashkent who had initially agreed to speak withdrew at the last minute.

This conference assembled virtually all major donors, international financial institutions, international organizations, and NGOs with concerns in the Ferghana Valley. Thanks to the network established by the Open Society

Institute, the conference also benefited from the participation of scholars and NGO activists from the region itself, as had the CPA's conference on Nigeria. The discussion revealed that awareness of the risks presented by the situation in the Ferghana Valley had spread considerably since the start of the CPA's project. Every relevant major institution now included at least a few people who were thinking about the problem, and some donors were seeking ways to commit resources to it.

Nonetheless, the conference confronted the same problem as the UN's program: how could one conduct a program of conflict prevention in the Ferghana Valley without any cooperation from Uzbekistan? Some participants argued that Uzbekistan's objections had some valid basis. The Western model of development on which most proposed prevention projects were based had not proved itself in Central Asia or the rest of the former Soviet Union. On the contrary, Uzbekistan's economic performance since independence was on the whole better (or less bad) than that of Kyrgyzstan, which had adopted a more Western model.[15]

Uzbekistan's major objections to regional cooperation for conflict prevention were connected to political issues that outsiders too often ignored. Though the Ferghana Valley Development Program and the CPA's recommendations were presented in neutral language, they were nonetheless, like all programs for conflict prevention, political documents that took stands on issues. These proposals advocated the development of civil society, the growth of private enterprise, transparency of borders, and other goals that contradicted policies and interests of the leadership of Uzbekistan.

Of course, in Nigeria under the Abacha regime or in Kosovo under Milosevic, the CPA and others had recommended or undertaken preventive efforts with little or no cooperation from the government in power. In both cases, sanctions and other coercive measures designed to change government behavior formed an important part of the strategy. Human rights organizations had documented the repressive activities of the Central Asian governments, including the repression of Islamist opposition in the Uzbek part of the Valley and of Khujandi regionalist opposition to Kulabi domination of northern Tajikistan.[16] The International Crisis Group, partly spurred by the CPA's report and links to our partners in the Soros Foundations Network, began to monitor the region. Its initial report in August 2000 advocated a focus on conflict prevention, including internationally assisted regional development, security measures that did not interfere with needed regional interchanges, and greater openness rather than repression as the response to Islamic opposition, which it characterized as having "legitimate political interests."[17]

No major organization or movement, however, advocated a campaign of sanctions or stigmatization against Uzbekistan. Karimov pursued a forceful and at times overweening policy of regional influence, but he gave no signs of pursuit of a "Greater Uzbekistan" and had in fact told ethnic Uzbek politicians in Kyrgyzstan to take their problems to Bishkek, not Tashkent. Although Karimov suppressed opposition and distorted democratic procedures, he had not seized power by force, halted a legitimate election, or deposed an elected leader. Furthermore, major powers were preoccupied, above all, with stability in Central Asia, a potentially oil-rich region bordering some of the world's most volatile zones, including Taliban-ruled Afghanistan.

The effects of the region's proximity to these volatile zones contributed to our redefining the issue of prevention of conflict there. The year of the CPA's mission marked the start of a rise in overt violence in Uzbekistan's part of the Ferghana Valley and an increase in regional tensions. The conflict broadened in ways reminiscent of the spread of war in central Africa by the involvement of so many nations in the Democratic Republic of the Congo, even if the violence in Central Asia had not yet attained the same scale or intensity.

Even before September 11, 2001, major events that occurred after our mission changed the regional situation in ways that ultimately spread violence to new areas and increased the interrelationships among conflicts in the region:

—In June 1997, the Russian-supported, Kulabi-dominated government of Tajikistan signed a peace agreement with the opposition. Under this agreement, the Islamic Resistance Movement's troops and leaders returned to Tajikistan to be integrated into the government and armed forces.

—The Islamic Movement of Taliban (Islamic students) had captured control of the Afghan capital, Kabul, in September 1996, and in August 1998 it took control of most of northern Afghanistan, including the border with Uzbekistan. Ethnic Tajik commander Ahmad Shah Massoud remained the only significant force in the field against them.

—Al-Qaida cells operating in East Africa succeeded in simultaneously bombing the U.S. embassies in Kenya and Tanzania on August 7, 1998, one day before the Taliban captured Mazar-i Sharif. This incident focused the attention of the Clinton administration more than previously on the terrorist threat emanating from networks based in Afghanistan.

The Tajik civil war had pitted two coalitions of regional forces, cemented by different ideologies, against each other.[18] The main military force of the

Tajik opposition, under Islamist leadership, had found refuge in northern Afghanistan, largely controlled by Massoud. The advance of the Taliban changed the stakes of major powers in Tajikistan. Russia, Uzbekistan, Iran, and Massoud all opposed the Taliban advance, but the first two opposed the last two in Tajikistan. After the Taliban capture of Kabul in September 1996, these powers decided that a settlement of the Tajik civil war was necessary to ensure a consolidated rearguard against the Pakistani-supported fundamentalist group.

As a result, by June 1997 the parties to the war in Tajikistan had signed a peace agreement, and the repatriation of opposition leaders and fighters had begun. In return for his cooperation, Massoud received access to an air base in Kulab, Tajikistan, which he used for repair and logistics. Access to Central Asia eased his supply lines from Iran.

The Khujandis, supported by Uzbekistan, remained excluded from power in Tajikistan, however. Tashkent was concerned that the agreement brought together two ethnic Tajik nationalist factions from southern Tajikistan, brought the Afghan war onto Central Asian soil by giving Massoud a base, and consolidated the Russian presence. Tashkent continued to support a dissident ethnic Uzbek military commander in Tajikistan, Mahmud Khudaiberdiyev. Khudaiberdiyev, a Soviet Afghan veteran, staged an uprising in Dushanbe in August 1997 and then fled to Uzbekistan and territory in Afghanistan controlled by the ethnic Uzbek warlord Abdul Rashid Dostum. After Dostum's defeat in August 1998, Khudaiberdiyev staged another uprising, this time in Khujand in November, together with some of Dostum's men. The pattern of defeated but not disbanded militias participating in a variety of conflicts throughout a region is, of course, reminiscent of Central Africa.

The remnants of the Islamic movement Adolat from Namangan had reassembled in bases and camps together with the Tajik Islamists in both Tajikistan and Afghanistan. Their leader, Tahir Yuldash, remained in Kabul and Qandahar, while the military commander, Juma Namangani, moved back and forth between Tajikistan and Afghanistan. Although Massoud had given this group refuge, the victory of the Taliban provided them with a new level of support, as well as bases in the north of Afghanistan, close to Uzbekistan. Al-Qaida, led by Osama bin Laden, also supported the Uzbek fighters, who reorganized under the name Islamic Movement of Uzbekistan (IMU). The IMU became closely integrated with both al-Qaida and the Taliban armed forces. The need for U.S. military access to Uzbekistan led President George Bush to name the IMU explicitly—the only organization other than al-Qaida so singled out—in his speech to a joint session of Congress on September 20, 2001. Within Central Asia, in Uzbekistan, Tajikistan, Kyrgyzstan, and Kazakstan, leaflets had also begun appearing from a hitherto unknown group, the Hizb-ut-Tahrir, or Liberation Party. This transnational group, founded by Palestinians in the 1960s, advocated revival of the Caliphate and appeared to enjoy growing support, especially among ethnic Uzbeks, in Uzbekistan, Tajikistan, Kyrgyzstan, and even Kazakstan.[19]

Tashkent had accused members of Hizb-ut-Tahrir of assassinating officials in the Ferghana Valley in 1997 and 1998. In response to these assassinations, the government undertook mass arrests in the Ferghana Valley, pushing refugees into Tajikistan, where some joined the IMU guerrillas. Repression increased in the wake of a spectacular terrorist attack in Tashkent on February 16, 1999. Coordinated car bomb explosions killed 13 and injured 128 people, though they missed President Karimov, the apparent principal target.

That summer, open war broke out for the first time. A group of armed Uzbek Islamists crossed from Tajikistan into southern Kyrgyzstan in an attempt to fight their way back to the Uzbekistan part of the Ferghana Valley. Many of those fighting were reported to be Ferghana youths making war out of desperation in response to political repression and lack of economic opportunity. The group took Kyrgyz officials and then Japanese geologists as hostages, reportedly gaining a sizable ransom for freeing the latter. In response, Uzbekistan bombed areas of Kyrgyzstan and Tajikistan, and accusations flew among Central Asian states. Uzbekistan suspected Tajikistan of harboring the Uzbek Islamists in response to Uzbekistan's continued sponsorship of Khudaiberdiyev. Privately, Uzbek diplomats accused Russia of supporting the IMU to pressure Uzbekistan into joining Russia-dominated security arrangements.

These battles occurred as the United States, Russia, and China were reorienting their policies. The United States had started to focus more on the region, originally because of its oil and gas resources and then because of the presence of bin Laden. Russia was facing a renewed insurgency in Chechnya, which it claimed was receiving assistance from the Taliban. Under President Vladimir Putin, Moscow was seeking to reestablish its predominance in the security of Central Asia. China, facing a small but growing insurgency (mainly a few acts of terrorism) among Muslims in Xinjiang Province, where the Turkic Uighurs were inspired by the independence of their former-Soviet neighbors to the west, also opposed the expansion of Taliban influence. These factors converged in the formation of the Shanghai Cooperation Group, a consortium of countries concerned about the security of

Central Asia, and led to much closer military cooperation between Russia and the Central Asian states.

The United States, Russia, China, and the increasingly authoritarian rulers of Central Asia largely agreed to define the problem in the region as "terrorism." All but China (which abstained) supported UN Security Council sanctions against the Taliban designed to force them to hand over bin Laden to the United States for trial for the embassy bombings. The fighting in 2000 was at a higher intensity than it had been the year before, as was the reaction by the region's governments, which showed a greater level of preparedness and coordination.

After the September 11, 2001, attacks on the Pentagon and the World Trade Center, the Central Asian states, and particularly Uzbekistan, became key parts of the coalition against al-Qaida. In President George Bush's speech to the U.S. Congress on September 20, the only "terrorist" organization mentioned by name, other than al-Qaida and the Taliban, was the Islamic Movement of Uzbekistan. President Karimov granted basing rights in Uzbekistan to the U.S. military units engaged in the battles in Afghanistan.

Certainly much of the world has awoken to the danger of conflict in the Ferghana Valley and the states and region of which it forms a part. Many also understand that this conflict includes both indigenous and international elements and is linked to a set of conflicts in the region. The CPA initially set out to establish the severity of a set of problems that could lead to more intense conflict and to highlight indicators of incipient trouble. The danger now, however, is the opposite of that when the CPA started this project. When we started, few took seriously the prospect of conflict in the region. Now, security establishments may repeat the kind of errors the United States often made during the cold war. The United States has defined the "war against terrorism" as a global struggle in which nations must choose sides. But leaders choose to ally with the United States as much for local reasons as because they share Washington's global agenda. President Karimov, like Mobutu and others before him, is counting on a free pass on both economic reform and human rights in return for his cooperation with the United States's immediate military needs. The United States risks becoming allied with an increasingly fragile regime whose opposition is largely homegrown.

As in other cases, the evolution of perceptions of Central Asia illustrates both a lateness to respond to warning signs and a tendency to overemphasize intervention to halt escalation of violence and underemphasize programs to strengthen fundamental factors that prevent conflict, such as governance and equitable development. Furthermore, the stigmatization of

Islamic movements as terrorist, strongly supported by Russia and more ambiguously by the United States, prevented any attempt at dialogue or negotiation with the Uzbekistan Islamic movement before its involvement with al-Qaida ruled out such an approach.

In Tajikistan's difficult peace process, a government that had originally stigmatized the opposition as criminal eventually sat down with its opponents. Both a second-track dialogue process sponsored by a joint U.S.-Russian team and changes in regional geopolitics played a role in bringing the sides together.[20] Uzbekistan's problems were not identical to Tajikistan's. The IMU never enjoyed anything like the degree of support and legitimacy that the Tajik opposition had. Nonetheless, ultimately opening some dialogue, negotiation, or at least communication with internal dissident groups could have been part of a solution.

It is now obvious that the problems of Central Asia cannot be treated separately from those of Afghanistan. The disintegration of this hyperarmed, impoverished, and devastated country posed dangers to all its neighbors, though above all to its own people. The drug trade, gem trade, and smuggling that sustained its people and its war also supported insurgencies and undermined economies from Pakistan to the Persian Gulf and in Central Asia as well.[21] The Taliban's extremism was in part a reaction to the country's extreme situation. Pakistan's support for the Taliban, in turn, derived from that country's precarious position and insecurity, which also pushed it to develop nuclear weapons. As much as in the Balkans, the political and military problems of the region are unlikely to be solved simply in their own terms; they will require a massive, internationally assisted effort at reconstruction and regional security that transforms the conditions under which conflicts occur.[22] That is what conflict prevention has required, in Central Asia, Central Africa, the South Balkans, West Africa, and elsewhere. Unfortunately, only the devastation of September 11 created the determination to rebuild Afghanistan, and the continued disparity between the huge expenditure on the military effort and the much smaller and delayed spending on reconstruction shows that the U.S. government and many others have still not learned this lesson.

Preventing Violent Conflicts: Analytical Framework and Strategies

7

Prevention: Concept and Scope

It is vulgar to speak like a dentist when one isn't a dentist. It creates a false impression.

—OSCAR WILDE, *The Importance of Being Earnest*

Although no human effort will ever achieve the prophetic vision of beating all swords into plowshares and spears into pruning hooks, it is possible to reduce violence in politics. The peaceful change of political control over states through processes involving little or no violence, as happens in stable democracies, is an immense achievement that results from legitimate processes of governance. Those engaged in prevention should seek to strengthen such governance processes. They should not seek an end state in which conflict will never emerge, whether one calls that end state justice, democracy, security, freedom, respect for internationally recognized human rights, the Day of Judgment, or the Rapture. The quest for some such fixed state, whether the classless society of Marx's communism or the free-market democracy of Fukuyama's "end of history," lends itself too easily to programs of social engineering that try to impose simple, principled, generalized solutions on complex and unique realities. When such terrible simplifications encounter refractory reality, they too often generate disaster, whether in the realm of city planning, forestry, or social development, as

125

shown by the colonial reading of Hutu and Tutsi identities and the effects of one-dimensional nationalism in the Balkans.[1]

The main locus of legitimate governance in the modern world is the nation-state, and strengthening national and local capacities for peaceful self-government constitutes the ultimate goal of conflict prevention.[2] But transnational governance processes through international NGOs, international organizations, or foreign governments are now permanent parts of the governance process to a greater or lesser extent everywhere. The globalization of economics and communication has diffused the locus of governance. For instance, NGOs that monitor labor practices by transnational corporations distribute to consumers information about conditions in the country of production. The resulting pressures may enable workers to obtain more concessions than they could solely within the national arena of the producing country. *Conflict prevention* and allied terms, as applied to international or transnational action to prevent violent conflicts other than interstate wars, provide a conceptual umbrella and a form of legitimation for such transnational governance processes; and, like other governance processes, preventive action is not technical but political.

Politics and Prevention

Over the past few years of working on preventing violent conflict, as I presented the agenda of the CPA and the field of conflict prevention to a variety of audiences in both the United States and abroad—including the countries on whose conflicts we were working—I repeatedly encountered a few annoying questions: What are you trying to prevent? Isn't conflict sometimes necessary? I eventually concluded that these deceptively simple questions captured some often hidden aspects of the problem of conflict prevention. All pointed to the conceptual and, as we discovered in our projects, practical difficulties of taking a humanitarian approach to political problems.

Humanitarian organizations have learned that even the most seemingly innocent acts, such as providing food or medical care to those fleeing violence, can inadvertently fuel violence or empower its perpetrators. Although the late François Jean of Médecins sans Frontières documented these dilemmas in Ethiopia in the mid-1980s, Somalia brought them home in the post–cold-war era. Although the first Bush administration in its last days sent troops to protect food deliveries to the starving, U.S. forces eventually clashed with the major warlord, Muhammad Farah Aideed, losing eighteen Army Rangers and killing hundreds of Somalis. The role of humanitarian organizations in calling for the initial intervention in Somalia incited the first major attack on "humanitarianism unbound," as Africa Rights called it.[3] The experiences of Bosnia and Rwanda added new weight to the argument against a purely humanitarian approach to political problems.

Some of the same lessons apply to many attempts to prevent conflict. A humanitarian problem—hunger and violence—developed from a struggle over power and resources. Foreigners intervened with a simplified view of the situation and without consultation with or accountability to those directly affected. The general good the interveners thought they were supplying, food, turned out to be a key resource for power. Somalis included strategic actors, not just undifferentiated victims. When things went wrong, the foreigners could fly home.

To understand the origin of these conundrums, we can go back to my annoying questioners. To the query "What are you trying to prevent?" I (and my colleagues in the field) generally replied, "Violent or deadly conflict." We recognized, of course, that conflict per se is an inevitable and sometimes positive part of human affairs.[4] This response sometimes led to the second question: "Isn't even violent conflict sometimes inevitable or justified?" One questioner at a conference asked, for instance, if those in the field would have tried to prevent the U.S. Civil War by brokering a compromise settlement.

These questioners saw that defining one's goal as prevention of conflict or even prevention of deadly conflict focuses attention on the process by which the dispute is pursued rather than the content of what is at stake. It depoliticizes the problem. Such a view has an affinity with the perception that conflict, like famine, earthquake, or plague, manifests the spread of chaos. If preventive action saves victims from such evils, the key question for those concerned to stop the violence is a technical one: what tools work best to prevent or stop the killing? The actors who carry out the goal are humanitarian technicians who know how to deliver the goods, whether Meals Ready to Eat or the transformation of ethnic conflict.[5]

Anyone can recognize the fallacy of such a depiction thus caricatured. The basically apolitical view it embodies, however, pervades discussion of the field, as in the common comparison of prevention of violent conflict to health care provision. Prevention of conflict, however, is not simply a public good, to be enjoyed by all, and the obstacles to its provision are not simply problems of collective action, coordination, or will.[6] Whereas health care harms only vermin and microbes (who benefit from disease processes), provision of conflict prevention provides negative externalities to human beings who would otherwise pursue goals through violence. Comparing those engaged in (usually self-defined) prevention of violent conflict to physicians (or dentists) can lead to a dangerous hubris, a blindness to the risky and above all political nature of the task. To evaluate prevention of violence, one must ask whose violence one is seeking to prevent and what conditions would prevail without violence; one must seek not merely to prevent it but to address the problems that provoke it. Otherwise, the seemingly innocuous goal of peace may camouflage the noxious goal of maintaining existing power relations. Some Kosovar Albanians resisted discussions of confidence-building measures even with relatively liberal Serbs unless the discussion accepted the eventual independence of Kosovo as the framework for any such measures.[7] The Rwandan government resists "dialogue" with those whose program includes genocide, though it can also manipulate this standard to avoid speaking with a broader range of opponents.

Debates and struggles over strategies in different cases derive more from such political differences than from divergent causal analyses. The goal of prevention of deadly conflict alone rarely leads to a unique strategy. Most Western analysts trace the crisis in Kosovo back to the suspension of that province's autonomy in 1989. Such an analysis led to the conclusion that the fundamental requisite for prevention of conflict was restoration of some form of autonomy. Russian analysts of early warning, however, traced the crisis back to the declaration of independence from Serbia by the Democratic League of Kosova and therefore argued that the fundamental requisite for prevention of conflict was revocation by the Albanians of their goal of independence for Kosovo.[8] Arguing that one or the other factor is "fundamental" justified quite different strategies for "preventing conflict," but the difference between the two arguments could not be settled solely by reference to "facts." Because this conflict involved a clash among different values and interests, a course of action depended on political choices. Neither Russia nor the United States nor European states were simply external interveners with different understandings of conflict prevention. They sought solutions that served their interests and thus became parties to the conflict. Indeed, a motto for all those who involve themselves in others' conflicts might be, "If you're part of the solution, you're part of the problem."

In an attempt to balance the goal of violence prevention with respect for the claims at stake, the Carnegie Commission on Preventing Deadly Conflict proposed terms such as "principled preventive action" or "prevention with justice."[9] "Principled" prevention aims not simply to stop escalation of overt violence (including that of the state) but also to accept that violence may in part be a response to a real threat or injustice, especially when few nonviolent responses are available. As in Uzbekistan, violent governments may be responding to real fear; violent rebels may be responding to real injustice or deprivation; and either governments or rebels may employ violence to pursue selfish interests. Prevention "with justice" would not support repression of symptoms of "structural violence," such as revolts, but would seek to remove or transform the causes.

The difficulty with this response, at least in the bald way I have stated it here, is that it proposes too utopian a goal and is too general to guide practice in specific situations. The principles that should guide prevention—human rights, security, respect for boundaries, human development, reconciliation—are numerous and at times contradictory, and each is difficult, if not impossible, to realize fully. Sir Isaiah Berlin reminded us that not all good things are compatible. Valued goals such as justice and peace, development and stability, no less than the classic pair, equality and freedom, may contradict each other. If "prevention with justice" means prevention of conflict by establishing a just social order, that, too, overreaches the goal. Hence, again, prevention must ultimately focus on supporting political processes of governance rather than any end state.

The CPA encountered the problem of defining the goal in all its projects. Our mandate to promote "prevention of deadly conflict" led us to emphasize different elements of these situations than did others who viewed them through different lenses, whether human rights, promotion of democracy, or U.S. strategic interest. Working on Kosovo in late 1995, for instance, we framed the problem as a conflict between nationalist projects, those of the Serbian state and of Kosovar Albanians. Although we recognized that the Serbian state under Milosevic had deprived Albanians of rights and subjected them to police terror, we nonetheless depicted the situation differently than did others who approached it looking not for "conflict" but for abuses of human rights, suppression of national rights, or threats to U.S. national security. We rejected arguments for self-determination in an independent state advanced by Kosovar nationalists, in part because we thought that a Kosovar Albanian state could spark further conflict. The recommendations may or may not have been right at the time—they are certainly outdated now—but our argument for them, based on estimating their effect on the prospect for violent conflict, differed from those of the parties to the conflict and partisans abroad, who focused on the rightness of their cause, not the consequences of their actions.

The CPA's project on Nigeria encountered similar difficulties. Our report rejected the idea of engaging with Abacha. A dictator making millions if not billions of dollars from corrupt oil deals, whose power rested on human rights violations, was inherently incapable of implementing needed reforms. At the same time, we did not support an oil embargo or the demand that Abiola be made president. The CPA's report, perhaps because of the definition of its mission as conflict prevention, gave greater weight than did human rights or democracy advocacy organizations to the ethnic divide that had opened over Abiola. In part because the question of Abiola's presidency had become an ethnic as well as democratic issue, we were prepared to accept a longer and more circuitous transition to democracy, one in which the removal of the military from power and oil revenue sharing could be negotiated in a pacted transition that would reduce the risk of violence. Perhaps the CPA's consideration of multiple goals and values alongside democracy and human rights made us more averse to risk in their pursuit. As usual, the seemingly clear distinction between empirical analysis and value judgments became clouded in practice. Interests and values affect evaluation of causal relations, especially when analysis consists mainly of estimates of risk and uncertainty.

"Conflict prevention" can thus provide a flag of convenience for a variety of political goals, leading some in societies that are objects of such activity to express suspicion about its real agenda. Do outsiders aim to provide support for and solidarity with those struggling for democracy, or to ensure stability so that foreign corporations can operate freely, or so that the U.S. government will not have to take risky decisions about opposing authoritarian regimes or stopping atrocities? Our colleagues in Nigeria posed such pointed questions.

The weakness of accountability for transnational preventive action reinforces the suspicions of many that it provides a cover for other political goals. Much work on prevention focuses on adherence to abstract principles or accurate causal analyses, but the legitimacy of domestic governance in a sovereign state lies not in these but in a process that makes those in power accountable to the subjects of governance. The absence of institutionalized accountability leads organizations in this field to justify their actions by some international legal principle by pledging accountability to local partners or "civil society."[10] The involvement and empowerment of local actors with local knowledge is vital not only because of their practical knowledge of local complexities but also because they are more likely to be accountable to the society in which they live than are international actors.[11] Choosing partners, however, is also a political act.

Hence the gap between the goal of preventing violent conflict and the implementation of effective policies to do so is not merely lack of knowledge of what works or lack of political will to implement it. The concept of "political will" derives from the humanitarian concept of preventive action. It presents the choice as one between doing something (preventing conflict) or doing nothing, rather than as a political conflict about setting priorities among various goals and deciding among various strategies, with different implications for interests, values, and ideologies. Such political differences cannot be resolved by appeals to principles, analysis of causal relations, or the formation of partnerships. All prevention is political.

The Scope of Prevention

There is no need to strain overmuch to define prevention or cordon it off from other sorts of interventions. Preventive action in practice is as likely to transgress analytical as political boundaries. Like the conflicts they aim to prevent, preventive interventions bear at best a family resemblance to one another. They always overlap with other forms of intervention: conflict resolution may be a form of prevention, and postconflict peace building largely consists of preventing the reemergence of past conflict. Efforts at prevention have to take into account the different levels of political organization that generate violent conflict and their relation to different frameworks of time and space. The notion that prevention consists of "outside" intervention in a particular "conflict" at an early "stage" of development itself does violence to the complexity of the challenge such efforts face.

Multiple Levels of Prevention

Just as the sources of conflict can be decomposed into global, structural, and escalatory factors, so prevention can be similarly categorized in corresponding types of action:[12]

—*Systemic prevention* promotes policies that counteract ways that global institutions promote or facilitate violence.

—*Structural prevention* reduces the risk of violent conflict in countries or regions by transforming social, economic, cultural, or political sources of conflict; it can consist of general policies applied "blindly" (without regard for risk assessment) to all countries, such as policies in support of account-able governance, or it can be targeted to countries at risk.

—*Operational prevention* seeks to contain or reverse escalation sparked by leadership strategies or crises that act as accelerators or triggers of violence.

Prevention over Time: Early or Proactive Action?

In *An Agenda for Peace,* UN Secretary General Boutros Boutros-Ghali defines preventive diplomacy in terms of phases of a conflict, as actions "to prevent disputes from arising between parties, to prevent existing disputes from escalating into conflicts and to limit the spread of the latter when they occur." He distinguishes preventive diplomacy, in the preconflict phase, from other forms of peace operations in other phases. Conflict resolution or peace-making attempts to move combatants to an agreement under which they will lay down arms. Peacekeeping operations monitor and enforce such agree-ments. Peacekeeping forms a transition to postconflict peace building, which creates institutions to ensure that peace is permanent and—completing the circle—prevent violent conflict from breaking out again.[13]

Defining prevention using a notion of stages of conflict served as a rea-sonable starting point for the choice of cases for the CPA, but these cases eventually alerted us to the definition's limitations. Our work on Central Asia initially dealt with preventing disputes from emerging out of social, economic, and institutional grievances that had not yet generated sustained violence. We saw the project as focusing on long-term, structural prevention through regional development. In the interval between our mission and publication of the final report, however, a dangerous regional environment helped spark vio-lence. The Islamic Movement of Uzbekistan could resort to arms because of its links to armed groups and drug traders in Afghanistan and Tajikistan. Hence we could not ignore the need to limit escalation and to address regional problems that promoted both vertical and horizontal escalation.

The project on Nigeria was motivated by signs of escalation in response to the suppression of democratic institutions and repression of ethnically based protests. But our working group also foresaw that in this charged envi-ronment new disputes could emerge, as later happened in the Niger Delta, where protests spread beyond the Ogoni and became more violent. We also saw that the underlying clash between the two largest ethnic groups, the Hausa and the Yoruba, as well as that between Muslims and Christians, could escalate to violence, as has happened in several incidents since 1998.

The project on the South Balkans formulated the challenge as a classic example of the need to prevent the escalation and spread of existing disputes, including those between Kosovar Albanians and Serbia-Yugoslavia, among the various ethnic groups in Macedonia, between ethnic Albanians and the Macedonian state, and between Macedonia and Greece. None of these disputes had recently provoked sustained, open violence (though they certainly had at various times over the past century), and we suggested a combination of deterrence, confidence building, and negotiation to head off confrontation and buy time for longer-term approaches.

The CPA's first project, on Burundi, was more difficult to classify. When the CPA and its partners began to discuss this project in the fall of 1994, we defined involvement in Burundi as an attempt to prevent a recurrence of the genocide in Rwanda, which was the dominant, though misleading, concept defining the goal of international intervention there. But was this action early in a conflict life cycle? A death toll of more than fifty thousand in the aftermath of the October 1993 coup attempt does not seem to qualify as a "limited armed conflict." Some called the Burundi killings genocide.

Nor does the model of a conflict life cycle fit Burundi. Since independence, that country had been marked by repeated revolts and massacres. When the 1993 violence occurred, Burundian Hutu refugees were already cultivating memories of atrocity during a twenty-year exile in Tanzania.[14] Burundi, then, suffers not from an acute but from a chronic ailment. The conflict among politicized identity groups over access to state power and resources had developed in a series of confrontations since the late colonial period. Any period of conflict could be the prelude to worse, and whether any period of relative calm is postconflict or preconflict is not a fact but a contingency, depending on the decisions of political actors. Because every period of Burundian history was simultaneously preconflict, a time of conflict, and postconflict, "prevention" required a comprehensive approach to the country's problems.

Burundi's situation supports the contention of Janie Leatherman and her colleagues that action at every stage of conflict should include a preventive component oriented toward the future, a peacemaking component oriented toward the present, and a peace-building component oriented toward overcoming the past.[15] Overlooking the cyclical nature of conflicts, the authors point out, may lead to costly errors of diagnosis: in 1994 the UN thought it was in Rwanda to implement a peace agreement, not to prevent a genocide. The Arusha negotiations on Burundi initially convened by the former Tanzanian president, Julius Nyerere, and continued under the leadership of Nelson Mandela, took this comprehensive approach. Different working groups dealt with the causes of the conflict in the past, the means to achieve a cease-fire and political and institutional reforms in the present, and reconstruction for the future.

Prevention over Space: Regional Conflict Formations

The CPA encountered an additional complication in dealing with the Great Lakes region: relations among conflicts throughout regional conflict formations. The potential for regional contagion and mutual reinforcement of conflict presented dilemmas in most of our projects—as it does, indeed, in most contemporary conflict situations.

The CPA initially took a more bounded view of prevention. To focus on prevention of future violent conflict rather than settlement of active civil wars or past conflict, we chose to work on Burundi, not Rwanda. We considered Mobutu's Zaire as a possible case separately from Burundi. For similar reasons, in the Balkans we studied Kosovo and Macedonia, not the entire Yugoslav or Balkans question. We recognized that the Albanian question linked all the countries of the South Balkans in a common problem, and so we chose at least a limited regional focus. In Central Asia we concentrated on the Ferghana Valley rather than Afghanistan or Tajikistan. Even this choice linked three countries with a common problem, but it attempted to isolate that future problem from the ongoing or terminating wars in neighboring countries. In West Africa we chose to work on Nigeria rather than on the ongoing wars in Liberia and Sierra Leone, in both of which Nigeria was involved, ostensibly as a peacekeeper.

Each of these situations turned out to be embedded in a regional conflict formation. In the course of analyzing and monitoring these conflicts, we found that the longer the conflicts persisted or escalated the more each became linked to others in its region:

—Both the Burundian government and the Hutu guerrillas participated in the 1996–97 and 1998–99 wars in the Democratic Republic of the Congo. Those wars were largely set off by refugees and fugitives from Rwanda, including perpetrators of the 1994 genocide, who had continued their activities on Zairian-Congolese soil. The genocide was the culmination of the crisis that erupted when Rwandan Tutsi refugees in Uganda lost their rights to land and hence sought to return home by force, launching their 1990 war against Rwanda's Hutu-power regime. President Mobutu of Zaire used his role as host of the Rwandan Hutu refugees to rehabilitate himself internationally. His revocation of citizenship rights of the Banyamulenge, however, triggered the 1996 war. By 1998 the war in the Democratic Republic of the Congo—combined with concerns of Uganda, Rwanda, Burundi, Angola,

Zimbabwe, and Namibia as well as with the quest to control that country's mineral wealth—included multiple indigenous armed groups as well as both official and unofficial forces from at least six foreign countries, with several others indirectly involved. Smuggling networks for gold, diamonds, coltan, and other minerals funded and motivated much of the fighting.

—The recognition of the Republika Srpska of Bosnia-Herzegovina in the Dayton Accords convinced many Kosovar Albanians that they could gain international recognition only through violence, and the collapse of Albania led to the looting of armories, providing Kosovar fighters with weapons. President Milosevic used his role as an implementing partner of the Dayton Accords in Bosnia to escape pressure over Kosovo. The resulting crisis led to pressures on Albania and Macedonia, pushed Serbia and Montenegro toward separation, and fostered insurgencies by Albanians in both the Presevo Valley of southern Serbia and in Macedonia.

—The division of the Ferghana Valley into three states weakened its political clout in all three and helped send it into steep economic decline. Members of an Islamic group there fled to Afghanistan and Tajikistan in 1992 when the government of Uzbekistan sought to arrest them. By 1998, their leaders, under the protection of Islamic groups in both Tajikistan and Afghanistan, had formed a group of militants from various ethnic groups and countries. In August 1999 these guerrillas sought to fight their way from Tajikistan to Uzbekistan across southern Kyrgyzstan, taking hostages and setting off an international crisis. They attacked again, on more fronts, in 2000 and fought alongside the Taliban and al-Qaida in 2001. Some of their fighters also received training in the same Pakistani *madrasa*s (Islamic seminaries) that nurtured the Taliban. Their activities were reportedly supported by the drug trade centered in Afghanistan that flows outward in all directions but increasingly northward, through Central Asia and Russia.[16] They seem to have been destroyed or dispersed in the U.S. offensive that destroyed their sanctuaries in northern Afghanistan in the fall of 2001.

—Nigeria's dictatorship seemed to spread military rule to some of its neighbors (Niger, for instance). Although the military government provided peacekeeping forces in neighboring countries (even fighting for the restoration of an elected president in Sierra Leone), it seemed incapable of actually stabilizing these neighbors. It blamed some for allegedly supporting the Nigerian opposition and threatened neighboring rulers if they undermined Nigeria's international position. General Abacha, like Presidents Milosevic and Mobutu, also manipulated his involvement in some nearby conflicts to escape pressure over other issues. A conflict formation continued to evolve in West Africa as Liberia's president, the former anti-Nigerian guerrilla Charles Taylor, fostered disorder and illicit diamond and arms trading in both Sierra Leone and Guinea-Conakry, and the previously stable Ivory Coast risked civil war as politicians manipulated the north-south ethnic divide in their quest for power.[17]

A regional conflict formation is thus a set of conflicts in contiguous or nearby areas or states that may have different origins and internal dynamics but become linked in a mutually reinforcing process. The following processes and mechanisms of linkage occurred in all or some of the regions the CPA studied:

—State institutions may collapse, decline, or fall into political crisis. Borders then become more porous (Afghanistan-Pakistan), citizenship may become more contested (Banyarwanda in Uganda and eastern Zaire), or administrative capacity may weaken (collapse of Albania).

—States may support armed groups in a nearby country for strategic, economic, ethnic, or ideological reasons.

—Repressive or outlaw rulers can manipulate the international community by playing off their roles in several conflicts against one another. Milosevic, Mobutu, and Abacha all obtained greater freedom to maneuver through their roles in neighboring states, even as their policies destabilized the countries they ruled.

—Social networks that cross borders (ethnic, religious, economic) may sustain transnational political actors. Such networks facilitate flows of people, trade, and arms. Refugees from one country may become political actors in another. Armed groups fleeing in defeat or advancing in victory, sometimes accompanied by refugees or other civilians, may become actors in more than one country.

—The weakening of borders and administrative capacity combined with the mobilization of transnational networks and armed groups creates ideal conditions for the growth of a contraband war economy based on looting, smuggling, or trafficking in drugs, arms, or human beings. These economic activities create interests in perpetuating the network of weak states and conflicts that creates opportunities for profit.[18]

Hence prevention of conflict in one country may require resolution of an ongoing armed conflict in one part of the larger region and successful post-conflict peace building in another part.[19] Rather than singling out only potential conflicts—or portions of conflicts—that are not yet violent or that might escalate, a preventive approach to conflict requires strategies for entire regions that address links among conflicts at different stages of evolution.

Complicating the notion of prevention by introducing the problems of repeating cycles of violence and regional networks of conflict does not negate the still useful notion of stages of a conflict. The intensity of conflicts and violence changes over time, and different forms of preventive action are more appropriate at a given moment, depending on, among other things, the level and history of violence. Because conflicts are likely to be chronic, however, and periods of calm and violence are likely to succeed each other unpredictably, prevention means more than merely acting early: it means integrating proactive, forward-looking measures into actions at every stage and remaining alert to the dangers of escalation even as peace agreements are being implemented. Because conflicts are likely to be linked through regional networks, effective prevention requires coordination among actions in a variety of interlinked conflicts. Finally, because the global environment affects all conflicts, preventive action should target portions of that environment that provoke or facilitate conflict, or its sources, such as corruption or state disintegration. Conflict prevention must be global as well.

8

Warning: Risk Assessment and Monitoring

He cerrado mi balcón
porque no quiero oír el llanto,
pero por detrás de los grises muros
no se oye otra cosa que el llanto.

I have shut my balcony
for I do not want to hear the weeping,
but beyond the gray walls
nothing is heard but the weeping.
— FEDERICO GARCÍA LORCA, *"Casida II: Del Llanto,"*
from Diván del Tamarit

Before the attacks of September 11, 2001, perhaps no event in the previous decade had provoked more retroactive analysis and attempts to learn the lessons of failed warning than the 1994 genocide in Rwanda.[1] No special efforts were required to determine whether Rwanda was at risk of conflict. A UN peacekeeping mission was on the ground monitoring implementation of the Arusha Accords. The genocide was triggered by an unforeseeable event—the downing of the plane carrying the presidents of Rwanda and Burundi—but it was also preceded by a systematic campaign by Hutu extremists fomenting murderous hatred of both Tutsis and Hutu "traitors." Furthermore, in January 1994, three months before the start of the genocide, a defector from within the regime revealed to the UN force commander, Canadian general Romeo Dallaire, secret plans for massacring Tutsis. Dallaire, in turn, reported the information (using the word "genocide") to the UN Department of Peacekeeping Operations in New York. The

Comments from Susanne Schmeidl were of great help in revising this chapter.

UN denied Dallaire authorization to undertake actions he thought might prevent the killings.

The failure at UN headquarters was matched by uncertainty on the ground. Rwandan human rights activist Monique Mujawamariya, who barely escaped from her house when soldiers came to kill her, recounted how only a few days earlier she had hesitated before faxing her New York colleagues to warn them, unsure whether the situation was really as bad as she feared. She also warned some of her colleagues, who bought international airline tickets to escape from the country. Three were slaughtered with the unused tickets still in their pockets.[2]

These events warn of the limits of warning. To the Hitlerian technique of the Big Lie we must add that of the Horrendous Truth—a truth so awful that one can hardly credit it. Furthermore, the UN officials who received Dallaire's fax knew that the members of the Security Council—notably, the United States, whose troops had been killed and humiliated in Mogadishu just a few months earlier—did not want to hear such warnings and were unwilling to act on them. In the absence of a framework for response elaborated by political leadership, the highest officials of the UN failed to turn intelligence into warning. This extreme case shows that effective warning is not just information that something bad will happen. It consists of strategic analysis focused on questions needed for action and linked to a framework for response. The framework for response is inherently political, and the task of advocacy for such response cannot be separated from the analytic tasks of warning.

Warning, Response, and Big Questions

In December 1998, the CPA organized one session of its annual conference on the failure of early warning in Kosovo.[3] One speaker argued that there was no failure of warning: everyone concerned with the issue knew years in advance that a conflict was inevitable. Another speaker countered that mere knowledge of a potential danger did not constitute warning: if the analysis, however accurate its forecast, does not identify strategic options, it fails as warning.

This debate addressed common arguments about warning. Some argue that warning of conflict is usually available to any observer who wants to know,[4] as in the oft-heard remark, "The problem is not lack of early warning. It is lack of political will."[5] But citing only actual, predicted conflicts that occurred in the absence of significant preventive efforts neglects the numerous predicted conflicts that never happened. Governments or organizations with global tasks are sensitive to the risks of squandering resources where they may not be needed. For instance, U.S. intelligence warned of the ethnic breakup of Ukraine in 1993. Fortunately, no major program was launched to halt this nonevent.[6] Others argue that policymakers are unwilling to spend resources on problems they do not know how to solve: the problem is lack of knowledge of policy options.[7]

Howard Adelman, coauthor of the most influential report on early warning of the Rwandan genocide, addresses these arguments by defining early warning as "the communication of information on a crisis area, analysis of that information, and development of potential, timely, strategic response options to the crisis."[8] This approach to early warning parallels the conclusions of intelligence professionals, who define successful warning not as correct analysis or prediction but as analysis that results in action.

Although intelligence and early warning differ to some extent in goals and methods (for example, predicting humanitarian crises versus threats to a state, use of open versus confidential sources), both engage in collection and analysis of information, scenario building, and recommending options to decisionmakers. A consensus of intelligence professionals holds that warning takes analysis a step beyond analysis, and the U.S. National Intelligence Council includes a national intelligence officer for warning. Indeed, the current U.S. intelligence apparatus originated in the problem of warning and prevention: how to prevent another Pearl Harbor by obtaining early warning of such a threat.[9] Warning, roughly speaking, consists of intelligence linked to a framework for response, and success in warning is defined not just as an accurate analysis but also by the ability to galvanize response. Because U.S. intelligence's warning apparatus during the cold war focused on threats of nuclear or conventional attacks on U.S. and NATO forces, the link to national interest and organizational mandate was clear, unlike most warning of humanitarian emergencies.[10]

The problem of early warning, however, involves more than whether information is available or linked to response. Linkage to response is mainly a political question. The changes in the international system since 1989 have stimulated thinking about intelligence that is particularly relevant to early warning of the types of crises that are of concern here. No longer focused on one big threat except to the extent that "terrorism" has supplanted the Soviet threat, U.S. intelligence spends more resources defining problems, not just analyzing data relevant to problems that are given.

Some intelligence analysts recognize different levels of problems that require different types of approaches. The bread-and-butter work that consumes most intelligence resources consists of the collection of "secrets"— data known to others but not to the collector—that can help answer well-defined questions. The next-higher level consists of analysis of trends and changes in the basic components of a given situation. Above that, however, are "big changes" in the international environment that generate changes not just in answers but also in the questions that need to be asked. The latter questions require, besides the collection of more data, analytical frameworks for and insight into what some students of intelligence call "mysteries" and "obscurities." At this point, "intelligence" merges with political debates about how international trends affect the goals and interests of actors.[11]

The major warning problem for the United States and other international actors consists of such mysteries and obscurities, not just estimating in what "hot spots" violence may break out. President George Bush and his advisers, supported by a commission headed by Donald Rumsfeld, now secretary of defense, argued that the Clinton administration overreacted to "humanitarian" crises and did not do enough to protect the United States from missiles from outlaw states or terrorists.[12] The United States Commission on National Security in the Twenty-first Century concluded that threats to Americans (as it defined its terms of reference) include the poorly understood effects of failed states and civil conflicts.[13] It turns out, as has become evident since September 11, that failure to prevent or cope with failed states and civil conflicts promotes terrorism. The dominant conception about national security failed to connect these two important phenomena. According to one intelligence official, whereas 80 percent of U.S. intelligence assets are devoted to the "hard targets" of top priority, more than half of recent crises, even before September 11, stemmed from supposedly lower-priority problems. Developing a clearer appreciation of the risks posed by more diffuse and systemic challenges—mysteries and obscurities—constitutes the fundamental warning problem.

If the analytical problems of intelligence and early warning are similar, however, the response problems differ. If early warning is more open and decentralized than intelligence, that is partly because the response framework is also more open and decentralized. Preventive action requires galvanizing and coordinating a range of organizations. Precisely because the major obstacle to action is not just failure of warning about particular conflicts but also failure of warning about a particular type of event, organizations that assign themselves the task of warning about civil wars, genocides, and failed states engage in political advocacy, not just in advising policymakers. Far from being insulated from the policymaking process, as intelligence agencies are supposed to be, advocates of conflict prevention leap headlong into it, spending a great deal of their time doing something hardly discussed in the early-warning literature: making the case that the interest, duty, or values of some actor requires the response they recommend. The main issue is not simply which real or potential humanitarian emergency is more pressing but also what distribution of resources among different types of problems—preventing humanitarian crises, stopping terrorism, building an antimissile defense—better serves an actor's interests, values, or mandate.

Levels of Early Warning and Organizational Roles

Analysts of "early warning" have applied the term to two different problems: comparative risk assessment (over space) among potential conflict situations and the monitoring (over time) of real or potential given conflict situations. These correspond to different levels of analysis and types of prevention.[14] Comparing the risk of conflict across various units (states, groups, regions) corresponds to structural prevention. Monitoring societies for signs of escalation corresponds to operational prevention. Global analysis of trends in conflict should also be considered a type of warning information, linked to systemic prevention.

Global Early Warning for Systemic Prevention

Information on changes in the frequency and type of armed conflict, state failures, and humanitarian emergencies constitute components of global early warning. Global sources of conflict affect the overall level, type, and intensity of violence. Moving from documentation of global trends in conflict to global early warning of conflict would require research that shows more clearly how global factors affect both structural risk of conflict in different situations and opportunities for escalation.

Global warning—of trends in conflict and their causes—answers to the needs of those responsible for establishing, leading, and modifying major global institutions and regimes. This includes the top leadership of the UN, regional organizations, and major states but also global social movements that seek to influence those actors' behavior. A major task of warning in this area is to link issues not usually connected to conflict. As noted in the previous discussion of global sources of conflict, there are a number of such possible factors: the international trade, licit and illicit, in small arms and light weapons makes it easier for those in conflict to intensify or spread violence; international banking and finance practices that facilitate money laundering of corrupt or criminal incomes may do the same and also cosset leaders and regimes that loot states and undermine institutions; the international criminality of the drug trade helps finance weapons flows and corruption; changes in flows of aid and political support as a result of strategic realignments undermine the capacities of some states; changing practices regarding state sovereignty, such as the degree of international tolerance for the breakup of existing states, affect incentives to political leaders, often encouraging them to fight for sovereignty rather than more limited goals; and the expansion and globalization of trade, capital flows, and information flows both diffuse wealth to some and, left unregulated, increase the insecurity and poverty of others.

Contrary to a common impression, no clear evidence shows that violence or "chaos" increased from the end of the cold war to September 11, 2001.[15] Different studies have counted or measured the number or intensity of wars or armed conflicts, humanitarian emergencies, ethnopolitical conflicts, and failed states. According to one prominent set of studies, the number of both wars and less intense armed conflicts, as well as the intensity of violence, had leveled off and decreased by about 1992. The decline in war, and especially interstate war, led the trend. This trend continued until 1998, which saw a slight increase again, with several wars in Africa and in Kosovo.[16] Other studies show a more consistent though slight increase. The trend is sensitive to definitions and sources of information, and, whether it is rising or falling, it does not inundate the data. The world is not being overwhelmed by unprecedented waves of violence, though the nature and meaning of that violence is changing.

Comparative Risk Assessment: Structural Prevention and Allocation Decisions

Comparative assessment of the risk of conflict over space at a given time answers the question, Where on the globe at a given time is the risk of violent conflict greater? Assessing the risk of conflict over time in a given place seeks to answer the question, When is conflict likely to break out, and along what lines? The questions are clearly related. In principle, one way to answer the former would be to collect lots of answers to the latter: scan the press, diplomatic traffic, or whatever other information sources are available to see where there appear to be dangers of conflict. Then, using that data and some criteria, compare the severity to determine the relative risk.

This procedure has many difficulties, however, beyond the considerable resources required to carry it out. The units to be scanned could be internationally recognized states (the most common reporting unit), subregions of states, ethnic groups, or multistate regions. Scanning the entire globe requires choice of a common unit; but different areas may require different levels of focus. Analysis of central Africa is more effective with a focus on both the entire multistate region and on substate regions such as eastern Zaire. Evaluation of the risk for Russia requires focus on particular subregions such as the Caucasus as well as transnational networks linking that subregion to other societies. Data just on Russia as a whole or Rwanda as a whole would be insufficient or even misleading. Focus on ethnic or communal groups overcomes the disparities among states, but it overlooks cases not based on ethnicity (Tajikistan, Afghanistan at some stages, Somalia, Uzbekistan), the differences in types of identity, and interaction effects across borders. For instance, neither the Hutu-Tutsi conflict in Rwanda nor the problem of the citizenship of the Banyamulenge in eastern Zaire sufficed to predict the events of fall 1996; the interaction of these two trajectories (combined with the genocide in Rwanda, the pressure for elections in Zaire, and longer-term processes of state formation and breakdown) led to the war. Furthermore, as discussed earlier, there is no metric for comparative risk.

Social scientists have made efforts to develop more formal models for comparative risk assessments. The results of such statistical analysis enable the researcher to identify factors associated with conflict and to estimate the risk of conflict for any country or case. If the estimate is valid, it can also be applied to later periods not included in the original data set or to other units (countries or groups). Some units will fit the model well: they will be at peace or war, as predicted. Others, however, will not. Those with less conflict than predicted by the model might possess preventive factors worthy of study or simply be at greater risk for future conflict and hence candidates for more intensive monitoring.[17]

Barbara Harff and Ted Robert Gurr, who have done as much as anyone to develop such models, finally argue that such models "are not sufficient to bridge the gap between risk assessments and early warning" and that "explaining and forewarning of humanitarian crises also requires the systematic, close to real-time monitoring of potential crisis situations identified in risk assessments."[18] Although such an assessment, by the leaders in the field, is a useful corrective to excessive expectations of such methods, the critique may overlook some uses of such work.

A causal analysis that identifies factors that increase the risk of conflict helps identify priorities for structural prevention, such as inequality among identity groups, lack of education and opportunities for youth, reliance on primary commodities, especially those easily looted, and links with ethnic diasporas. Cases with high risk but little or no active conflict should also become the focus of intensive conflict monitoring, as early warning of accelerators or triggers can signal the need for operational prevention. As Harff and Gurr suggest in the foregoing citation, however, such estimates are finally of little help in making decisions about allocation of resources to different problems. The probability of conflict is a concept quite different from its political importance.

Conflict Monitoring

Efforts to develop conflict-monitoring systems for early warning of escalation processes in particular places have developed in two strands: "remote" monitoring, based on analysis of events data, and "engaged" monitoring, through the strengthening of networks. Some organizations try to combine the two, as do the Forum on Early Warning and Early Response (FEWER) and the FAST (Früh-Analyse von Spannungen und Tatsachenermittlung [Early Warning of Tensions and Fact Finding]) project of the Swiss Peace Foundation.

The predominant formal approach to monitoring conflict escalation relies on data series on measures of conflict and cooperation as well as accelerators and triggers of conflict.[19] Events data code "events" (the unit of analysis) into categories dictated by a conceptual framework. Every event is, of course, composed of smaller events and is also part of a larger event, so that the definition of an event is inherently arbitrary. Events data research uses different definitions: some techniques focus on the headlines of wire service reports, while some automated expert systems examine each clause in a wire service report.[20]

For purposes of early warning, coders classify events as indicating either conflict or cooperation among groups. Such systems use categories of accelerator events such as those developed by Harff and her collaborators, summarized in the previous discussion of escalation.[21] Other systems seek to identify trends in conflict or cooperation in the relationship among named actors (states, communal groups, movements) from news accounts.[22]

Events can be coded into these categories by hand, by hand with machine assistance, or with fully automated systems.[23] These events are then counted. In events data, the basic unit is the number of events of a given type occurring over a shorter time period, generally a month. Such monitoring remains a blunt instrument. As one group compiling indicators has observed, in the conflict profiles for Burundi in 1993, "most of the accelerators in the last three months fell on the final day before war broke out (reflecting the actions of army coup plotters and international reactions to the coup attempt)." In some cases, they note, "dynamic escalation to communal war will be abrupt and difficult to anticipate using any early warning model."[24]

Such models cannot substitute for field reporting and analysis. They depend on analysis of some text. But media cover only events deemed news-worthy. Reporters have access only to certain types of information. Furthermore, there is no way to compare intensity of acceleration across conflict situations, as the intensity of news coverage affects the number of events uncovered as much as the number that actually occur (which is not a well-defined concept in any case).

Most important, like other technical models, events data models of early warning tend to ignore the political and interactive nature of conflict. Like analyses that compare conflicts to mechanical problems (requiring the right "tools" to fix them) or diseases (requiring a public health system), such analyses "deny agency to the actors who are in conflict and who decide whether and how to use violence to pursue their goals."[25] Because early warning requires not only indicators of imminent danger but also informa-tion relevant to strategic and tactical decisions about how to respond, it requires additional, highly contextual information about the actors, their goals, and their capacities.

Stephen John Stedman, for instance, proposes a typology of "spoilers— leaders and parties who believe that peace emerging from negotiations threatens their power, worldview, and interests, and use violence to under-mine attempts to achieve it."[26] All spoilers are not alike, however. They differ in their goals and commitment: some totally oppose peace, others are greedy but opportunistic, and some have limited goals. Even to distinguish among actors in such broad terms requires information that is difficult to obtain, because actors have many incentives to disguise their preferences: total spoil-ers may appear to compromise to gain tactical advantage, greedy or limited spoilers may articulate outrageous demands in the hope of strengthening a bargaining position for a compromise they intend to accept.

Hence quantitative models will not and should not replace the judgment of policymakers. Such models bring clarity to a confusing situation by imposing analytical simplicity: choosing a level of analysis; presenting an operational definition of the phenomenon under study so that, for instance, we can actually count wars and determine whether they are increasing; and analyzing seemingly commonsensical conclusions that may or may not be true. The same positivistic and linear methodology that accounts for their success, however, also limits their appreciation of complexity, interactions, and feedback among different levels and units.[27]

At a meeting of the Great Lakes (then Burundi) Policy Forum shortly after the outbreak of the first war in Kivu (fall 1996), an expert noted that this war posed a puzzle question about warning. Many people had been monitoring the region, warning, for instance, that the arming of militias in the Rwandan camps in Zaire would lead to conflict. But no one, at least in Washington, seemed to have realized that the conflict might take the form of an uprising by Banyamulenge organized by Rwanda and Uganda or that such an uprising could develop into a major civil war in what was then Zaire.

The U.S. National Intelligence Council also missed such interactions in the Asian financial crisis. It accurately warned of a crisis of the Thai *baht* in August 1997, but decisionmakers did not perceive a crisis of the *baht* as a threat. Neither they nor the intelligence apparatus sensed the complex pattern of intricate interrelationships and feedback among currencies, banking systems, and financial markets around the world that turned the *baht* crisis into a global one.

In Central Asia the danger of conflict exceeds what any formal warning report would indicate. An analysis focused on "communal groups" would pick up the dangers of Uzbek-Kyrgyz conflict in southern Kyrgyzstan but miss the conflict based on subregional identity and Islamist networks in the Uzbekistan part of the Ferghana Valley or the north-south tensions in both Kyrgyzstan and Tajikistan. An analysis based on national-level indicators might show that all three countries were at risk, but it would miss the concentration in the Ferghana Valley of both structural factors and accelerators. Furthermore, among the factors promoting conflict in the region are cross-border networks. Civil war in Uzbekistan was promoted not by looting opportunities in Uzbekistan but by the economy of smuggling and drug trading, as well as the presence of the al-Qaida network, in neighboring Afghanistan and Tajikistan. As in all such complex systems, the system is not simply more than but is also different from the parts, and the risk of conflict is greater than analysis of the parts can suggest. Of course, such critiques might be taken into account by a different generation of models. But there is something about the complexity of human experience that suggests that a different kind of knowledge will also always be needed, that quality called by the ancient Greeks *metis*, or practical wisdom, the practitioner's knowledge.[28] Sometimes *metis* needs to be tested against models, but models also need to be tested against *metis*, especially that of accountable political leaders.

Such knowledge is gained mainly from the experience of actors engaged on the ground. Hence Janie Leatherman and her colleagues argue that "the need for culturally sensitive, politically astute and practical information calls for *engaged monitoring*."[29] Engaged monitoring is most likely to develop from a long-term presence on the ground that builds trust. Such trust, of course, precludes neutrality in such charged situations—hence the need for networking among organizations that may have access to different aspects of the conflict's deep structure.

The essential element in engaged transnational monitoring is the communication of information to actors outside the national boundaries; effective action will then require mutual exchange of information about potential interveners and other factors as well. There are two ways this can happen: between local actors and external actors, both of whom are physically present within the state's borders, or between local actors and external actors who are beyond the state's borders. Changes in means of communication, especially the development of the Internet, have transformed the process of warning by greatly reducing the cost and time required to communicate information across boundaries.

The first model dominates much discussion of engaged monitoring. According to this common paradigm, international NGOs already present on the ground develop working relationships with social actors at the grassroots level, where information about impending conflict is most likely to be found. The international NGOs in this model of early warning seem generally to be those engaged in development or humanitarian assistance. They tend to have a long-term presence in the field and contacts at all levels of society. These organizations, however, have to negotiate access to the populations they serve with the government or de facto authorities as well as with the populations themselves. Communicating information about abuses of power or other factors that might lead to external pressure or intervention can put both their presence and security at risk. In addition, such organizations generally produce and analyze information necessary for accomplishing their mission, which may not be identical to the information needed for conflict prevention. Indeed, just as policy interests can at times contaminate government intelligence, NGOs' need for access and definition of their mission may distort the information they collect.[30]

Some humanitarian and development NGOs, however, self-consciously collect such information as they attempt to integrate conflict prevention into their mission. This broadening of their mission has resulted from their heightened awareness of the political and social consequences of their assistance. In Burundi both ActionAid and Oxfam have undertaken such analyses, but this required making special efforts once they had decided to expand their missions.[31] Some of the best information on the political situation in parts of rural Afghanistan under the Soviet occupation was to be found in confidential files of the Swedish Committee for Afghanistan, which provided direct assistance in these areas.[32]

Other international actors present on the ground are diplomats and representatives of international agencies. Special representatives of the UN secretary general often have explicit preventive mandates, though such officials are usually dispatched only after violence has occurred. Boutros-Ghali sent Ould Abdallah to Burundi as his special representative only after the massacres that followed the attempted coup of October 1993. Nonetheless, after this round of bloodletting had subsided, Ould Abdallah's mission was essentially preventive. In his memoirs he describes how he established relationships needed for conflict monitoring. He met frequently and repeatedly with all major political and social groups, and not just with the leadership but also with those several levels down. In his view, success at building such relationships depended on his behaving in an honorable way and communicating a sense of commitment to his interlocutors. The information he was able to develop as a result was key to his relative success during his tenure of nearly two years.[33]

Although the first model of engaged monitoring, with an international presence on the ground playing the key role, is more familiar, the second model is gaining in importance and has, for instance, been incorporated into the structure of the Forum on Early Warning and Early Response. This model recognizes that the local society contains organized groups—including various types of NGOs—that can collect information because of their local relationships and analyze it in ways relevant to international preventive action. As in Margaret Keck and Kathryn Sikkink's model of transnational issues networks, the local organizations then share their information with partners.[34] The obvious advantages of this style of work lead to the increased emphasis on building the capacity of local civil society to carry it out.

Nongovernmental organizations resist incorporation into formally defined networks and the imposition of formal reporting or analysis requirements. Networks of NGOs are typically based on the informal ties and personal relationships that constitute "networking."[35] Furthermore, one should not romanticize local civil society. Like other actors in early warning and conflict prevention, civil society organizations are political. They may provide a refuge for opposition politicians, spring up in response to available funding, reflect ethnic or other identities, and so on, like any other human activity.[36] In making such evaluations, however, one should bear in mind that they also apply to oneself.

There is no reason for complacency about our understanding of global trends in conflict, risk factors, or escalation processes. The key element in the warning problem in preventive action, however, lies elsewhere. Because of the political nature of the problem and the shifting reality of sovereignty, prevention of violent conflict or humanitarian crises is unlikely ever to become the mission of a formal hierarchical system with clear entry points for warning. There will never be a single key decisionmaker who needs to be informed or whose "will" must be strengthened.

9

Systemic Prevention

> It is not in heaven, that thou shouldest say, Who shall go up for us to
> heaven, and bring it unto us, that we may hear it, and do it? Neither is it
> beyond the sea, that thou shouldest say, Who shall go over the sea for us,
> and bring it unto us, that we may hear it, and do it? But the thing is very
> nigh unto thee, in thy mouth, and in thy heart, that thou mayest do it.
>
> —*Deuteronomy 30:12–14*

Violent conflicts are embedded in an international system that often
provokes them. The world is not divided between societies at risk of
conflict and well-intentioned but sometimes indifferent "outsiders" who
might intervene. The global economy is creating an ever more yawning
divide between a globally integrated élite, disproportionately represented in
richer countries, and a fragmented population of those excluded from the
system.[1] Movements of the excluded may rebel in the name of mobilized
identities or antisystem ideologies, whether leftist, rightist, religious, or coming out of some as yet undiscovered dimension like Aum Shin Rikyo—or
they may simply employ violence against their neighbors to loot rather than
be looted. Unless we confront the way in which our own institutions and
practices foment violence, we beneficiaries of this global economy engaged
in the work of international prevention are no more than halfheartedly
patching up damage we have an interest in perpetuating. A global economy
needs a global social policy and a global politics.

Systemic prevention has several advantages; it avoids dilemmas of foreign intervention and affects many conflicts or potential conflict situations simultaneously. For instance, developed countries can implement banking regulations that prevent corrupt rulers from exporting their funds without intervening to depose those rulers, and the same laws will also restrain their successors—not to mention global terrorist organizations. Some systemic measures seek to gain better control over flows of economic resources that strengthen incentives and capacities for violence. Others seek to institutionalize sanctions and incentives tied to standards of behavior.

Markets in Resources for Conflict

The media impact of the atrocities in Sierra Leone—in particular, the amputations practiced by the Revolutionary United Front—as well as the collapse of peace accords in Angola focused attention on funding of wars in Africa by diamond sales. United Nations reports documented both the illicit diamond trade from Angola and the looting of gold, diamonds, coltan, timber, coffee, and wildlife from the Democratic Republic of the Congo.[2] Unlike the drug trade, these markets dealt in otherwise legal commodities for first-world markets. Merchants in the chicest neighborhoods of the world's leading cities offer diamonds for sale, while cutting-edge industries use the tantalum refined from coltan for key parts of cellular phones and computers. The link of common commerce to bloody atrocity could hardly be more shocking and clear.

For several years NGOs and specialists had called for regulation of the diamond trade.[3] After years of official indifference and arguments that diamonds were too generic for their origins to be traced, the shocking photos from Sierra Leone threatened a consumer backlash. The harsh public reaction, combined with a strong interest by the United Kingdom, a permanent member of the UN Security Council, forced creative thinking on the part of both major states and the corporations that controlled so much of the trade. The diamond business did not want to see its product's image of eternal love stained with blood.

Following UN sanctions against the sale of "conflict diamonds" from both Angola and Sierra Leone, major diamond trade associations and corporations formed the World Diamond Council to develop a plan for global certification of diamond origins. Industry leader De Beers also announced it would no longer trade in diamonds from conflict areas. Nongovernmental organizations generally praised the effort while criticizing the absence of a timetable for implementation. The high-technology industries that depend on less visible coltan supplies also began to consider ways to confront this challenge.[4] Belgian activists mounted an Internet campaign asking supporters to send e-mails or cell phone text messages saying, "No blood on my GSM!" in French or Flemish.

Other gems fund wars, as do emeralds in Afghanistan, but that war, like those in the Andean region, has been largely funded by drug trafficking. International drug policy, however, is formulated not as a policy toward conflict but as an extension of the domestic drug policies of the major consumer states, and particularly the United States. The so-called war on drugs treats narcotic production, trafficking, and consumption as crime and uses largely coercive measures to deal with all aspects of the trade. This approach itself, however, creates some of the pathologies it fights. Only the illegality of drugs makes them such lucrative resources for violence. A Council on Foreign Relations task force found that interdiction and source-country crop reduction have accomplished little in reducing the supply of drugs. Interdiction and coercive supply-reduction programs—such as are present in the current U.S. package of assistance to the Colombian armed forces— besides being ineffective, also escalate civil wars. The task force recommended, instead, a greater emphasis on reducing worldwide demand.[5] Regulations short of criminalization would reduce the risk premium, leading to price reductions that would facilitate crop substitution. The effect on war and conflict of both the current legal regime (prohibition) and the response (the war on drugs) should be factored into the debate on drug policy. Any policy that reduced the superprofits on narcotics would defund armed groups from Putumayo to Qandahar.

As noted earlier, the glut of small arms on post–cold-war markets reduced their price. The few arms control efforts dealing with conventional arms, rather than with nuclear weapons and weapons of mass destruction, deal mainly with high-tech heavy weapons. Because the actual mass destruction of human life in today's world, however, is mainly carried out through the massive application of small arms, NGOs have launched a campaign to limit their proliferation.[6] The UN became seized of the issue in 1994 through a démarche by the newly elected president Alpha Oumar Konare of Mali. In November 1994, Konare told Marrack Goulding, UN under secretary general for political affairs, that the trafficking of small arms across the Sahara greatly complicated his attempt to negotiate with insurgent Tuareg tribesmen. A UN study and arms collection program eventually culminated in a peace bonfire of weapons in the capital, Bamako, on March 27, 1996.[7]

For some NGOs, the focus on small arms constituted a more challenging follow-up to the international convention outlawing the use of antipersonnel landmines. That cause, initially championed by a network of NGOs, won the support of major governments, leading to an international agreement on a treaty at a conference in Ottawa in 1997. They founded new organizations and alliances to deal with small arms, but the issue of small arms has proved far more complex than landmines.[8] In the latter case, NGOs succeeded in stigmatizing a class of weapons, and major states (except for the largest states with extensive land borders and international security commitments) signed on.

Defining the agenda for small arms, however, has proved more difficult. No one advocates a ban on small arms. The movement focuses on preventing their "proliferation and misuse."[9] One can define "misuse" with respect to specific conflicts fueled by arms trafficking, and the movement has supported arms embargoes targeted at specific conflicts, but these are rarely preventive. International organizations impose them solely after serious escalation. More proactive approaches focus earlier in the supply chain. About 80 percent of all arms are still produced and exported by the United States and Europe, and preventing proliferation of small arms begins with manufacturers, dealers, and brokers rather than the more numerous and diffuse end users. The weapons used in many of today's wars are still being churned out by factories in the former Soviet bloc, in Belarus, Moldova, Ukraine, Bulgaria, Russia, and elsewhere, where locally produced arms sometimes provide the only competitive export, while many governments are still armed by traditional suppliers, including the United States, which has supplied most of the state parties to the war in the Democratic Republic of the Congo.[10]

Governments and international organizations, including not only the UN but also the European Union, NATO, the OSCE, the Organization of American States, and other regional organizations, have accepted portions of this agenda. As they have done so, however, fault lines have grown between the official and NGO bodies and between the United States and other major states. Official bodies focus their attention almost entirely on controlling illicit trafficking. At a 1998 conference in Oslo on controlling small arms, at which Canada proposed a treaty that would bar governments from selling light weapons to nonstate actors, the United States joined twenty other governments in supporting the general aim of controlling illegal and illicit sales of small arms. Washington and several other governments, however, argued that a ban on sales to nonstate actors would impinge on foreign policy and commercial interests by barring covert shipments of arms to guerrillas and legal sales to companies.

Although the NGOs support efforts against illicit trade, they argue that "licit" state-to-state arms transfers and sales also fuel wars and support abusive governments. The United States, of course, has some rarely invoked legislation on the books prohibiting arms transfers to governments that consistently engage in gross violations of human rights, and the EU has recently adopted a nonbinding code of conduct on arms transfers by member states. The NGO movement has called for full reporting of transfers and sales of small arms as well as more extensive licensing and monitoring mechanisms to subject such transfers to public debate. Under the administration of George W. Bush, however, the United States has also retreated from previous positions, resisting any restrictions on nonmilitary weapons as well as requirements that manufacturers mark weapons or report transactions to a registry. The EU and NGOs, at least, support such measures for transparency as a basic minimum. As in the case of drugs, the Bush administration is treating this global issue as an extension of domestic politics.

Systemic approaches to arms trafficking confront the humanitarian dilemma in conflict prevention. General measures to reduce access to arms affect movements of resistance to tyranny and foreign occupation as well as predation by genocidal warlords. The arms embargoes on Bosnia and Rwanda weakened those resisting genocide and aggression. The UN Security Council imposed a one-sided arms embargo in Afghanistan in 2000 partly because member states estimated that a comprehensive arms embargo would lead to a swift victory by the Taliban.

One resource needed for all the transactions described here, of course, is money. Although fighters can purchase some modern weaponry and other supplies locally for suitcases full of cash, long-distance transactions involving arms brokers, drug and gem wholesalers, mineral and oil companies, and other global organizations increasingly predominate in the international war economy. War finance thus passes through international banks and their electronic transfer systems.

Bank secrecy, taxation, and offshore banking laws that facilitate the laundering of proceeds from corruption or illicit transactions facilitate not only drug trade, arms trafficking, or terrorism, which provide direct resources for violence, but also the looting of countries by corrupt or predatory rulers like Mobutu Sese Seko or Sani Abacha. Abetted by their international partners in white-collar crime, such rulers destroy institutions and infrastructure, leaving whole societies to fester and decay. Although such societies need domestic political and economic reform, potentially aided by international efforts, the most important preventive effort the international community could offer would be an effective crackdown on the deposit, laundering, and use of corrupt proceeds by such predatory rulers. Inquiries into the wealth of the Abacha family, for instance, have found that these Nigerian kleptocrats deposited hundreds of millions, perhaps billions, of dollars into major banks in the United States, the United Kingdom, and Switzerland.

Several organizations have addressed these problems. The Organization for Economic Cooperation and Development is working on harmonizing laws prohibiting companies in member states from engaging in corrupt practices through its Convention on Combating Bribery; the organization also houses the Financial Action Task Force on Money Laundering, which has identified both policy loopholes and jurisdictions that facilitate the circulation of proceeds from criminal and corrupt activity. The NGO Transparency International works against corruption in a number of ways—sponsoring an agreement, for instance, among major international banks on principles to combat money laundering. Members of the U.S. Senate Banking Committee proposed legislation to prohibit banks from accepting proceeds from foreign official corruption, as they are now forbidden to accept the proceeds of other foreign criminal activity, but lobbying by banks defeated the measure.[11] The banks argued that the bill imposed too heavy a burden of monitoring on them, especially regarding account holders in their foreign correspondent banks. Such measures would also be useful in strengthening the international community's ability to impose and implement targeted financial sanctions, such as the CPA proposed on Nigeria.[12] Such regulations may finally be imposed as part of the war against terrorism.

Another phenomenon undergirding the development of war economies in some regions is transborder trade.[13] In several regions of the world, long-distance smuggling often facilitated by ethnic diasporas along routes that predate the states that stigmatize such commerce constitutes a major part of the economic system. The trans-Sahara trade routes across the Sahel, plied largely by Hausa-speaking traders, formed the infrastructure for the arms trafficking that led President Konaré of Mali to seek help from the United Nations. The infrastructure of aid to the Afghan fighters during the Soviet occupation reinforced the transborder trade through that country, as did the refugee flows that formed an Afghan and Pashtun diaspora in the Persian Gulf, Pakistan, and Central Asia. That transborder trade provided the Taliban with the bulk of their resources, perhaps more than the drug trade, and provides infrastructure for both the latter and arms trafficking.[14]

Although the contemporary transborder trade builds on long-standing links among commercial groups, it also responds to global phenomena such as long-term conflicts, migration, trade policy differentials, and covert actions by states. Smuggling may constitute a survival strategy for some populations, especially transborder groups such as Kurds, Baluch, Pashtuns, Hausa-speakers in West Africa, and Swahili and Kinyarwanda speakers in East and central Africa. Yet it undermines state structures, provides a mechanism for evading sanctions (which, in turn, often reinforce the transborder trade structures), and creates an ideal infrastructure for arms trafficking. A long-term approach to conflict prevention focusing on global economic factors will require a better understanding of transborder trade and a strategy for bringing those who survive from it within the ambit of the legitimate global economy.[15]

Institutionalized Standards of Behavior: Sanctions and Incentives

Attempts to limit economic resources for conflict seek to prevent violence by reducing the capacities of violent actors. Such instruments work, in a sense, ex ante—affecting the conditions for action. Others work ex post, aiming to affect how actors calculate the consequences of their action. These measures include both sanctions and incentives linked to specific standards of behavior.

The major attempt to institutionalize global sanctions against certain categories of violent behavior has been the effort to establish an International Criminal Court (ICC) with jurisdiction over war crimes, crimes against humanity, genocide, and aggression.[16] This proposal—another initiative largely promoted by "citizen diplomacy," like the ban on landmines or the campaign against proliferation and misuse of small arms—owes its recent advances to the examples of the ad hoc International Criminal Tribunals on the former Yugoslavia and on Rwanda.

The effect of these tribunals on peacemaking remains controversial. Advocates of the tribunals, in addition to arguing that justice requires punishment for such serious crimes, also contend that enforcement of the courts' mandates would promote peace and reconciliation. Judging those responsible for such crimes would both individualize guilt (undermining notions of ethnic or collective responsibility) and remove from the community spoilers with an interest in perpetuating conflict. In Bosnia-Herzegovina, for instance, human rights organizations that have pressed NATO forces to arrest indicted war criminals speedily argue that such arrests would facilitate measures for refugee return and reintegration. The NATO command's policy has vacillated, but on the whole it has favored a more cautious approach, fearing that arrests might push the Bosnian Serbs, in particular, away from cooperation.

This debate is simply one instance of the general debate as to whether creating an independent judicial organ to charge and try leaders might interfere with the political task of negotiating with them. This dispute informed one of the main controversies over the statute of the ICC: whether the prosecutor would be completely independent or subject to regulation by the Security Council. The final compromise allows the prosecutor to initiate cases independently, while empowering the Security Council to suspend investigation or prosecution for up to twelve months.

Prevention, of course, is not the sole purpose of the ICC, but the latter could prevent mass killings more effectively than ad hoc tribunals. The UN establishes ad hoc tribunals only after major crimes have occurred. The long delays involved in setting up new tribunals and making the first indictments, combined with the lack of effective authority or means to arrest suspects, greatly weaken preventive effects. Their retroactive and restrictive jurisdiction (such as the time limit of the International Criminal Tribunal on Rwanda, which includes only acts in Rwanda during 1994) leaves ad hoc tribunals open to charges of bias. Because leaders have already established their positions through conflict even before the creation of such ad hoc tribunals, they do risk perverse effects on peacemaking. The overthrow and arrest of Slobodan Milosevic shows that these perverse effects are not insuperable; but many advocates of criminal sanctions against atrocities neglect the presence in this case of significant incentives as well (joining "Europe," for example), incentives that are much weaker elsewhere.

Unlike the ad hoc tribunals, the ICC has a prospective jurisdiction. As leaders contemplate future careers based on atrocities, they will have to take such a tribunal into account, and those engaged in preventive diplomacy can use its jurisdiction as leverage. This creates a much different calculus from that faced by the authors of crimes against humanity in the former Yugoslavia and Rwanda when they decided to take such actions.

The tribunal's effectiveness will depend, as much as on the content of its statute, on the willingness of the United States and other major powers to cooperate with and support it. Although President Bill Clinton signed the treaty in the last days of his administration, he reiterated U.S. objections to the jurisdiction of the court over U.S. citizens, objections that led the Bush administration to retract the U.S. signature. Lack of U.S. participation will handicap the ICC.

More generally, creating a court without a corresponding police force could turn out to be an exercise in futility unless the Security Council is willing to undertake enforcement measures. The ICC has no police powers and depends for enforcement on the states party to it, which will not be able to enforce its mandates on those living in nonparty states without Security Council authorization.

These institutionalized sanctions, like the ones targeted on Nigeria and Yugoslavia, are more effective when complemented with incentives. One form of systemic incentive that international institutions offer is conditional membership.[17] Such incentives vary greatly by region, as part of a general pattern of regional disparity of all sorts in peace operations and humanitarian assistance.[18] Such incentives function only in "Europe," among states that hope to be admitted to the EU, NATO, or those that have some other form of association with the lands of peace, plenty, and six-week vacations. The proposed "stability pact" for the Balkans attempts to institutionalize these incentives even during the period before these countries are eligible for full membership in the European Union.[19]

Membership in the EU requires adherence to human rights standards as well as economic reforms (the "acquis communitaire") in return for substantial benefits in market access and free movement of people. States cannot enter NATO unless they settle disputes with other potential or actual NATO members—a condition that encouraged Hungary, for instance, to settle disputes with neighboring countries over Hungarian minorities.

It is not always easy to distinguish sanctions from incentives: the outer wall of sanctions against the Federal Republic of Yugoslavia deprived that country of incentives—namely, membership in international organizations and financial institutions. This case illustrates the way sanctions and incentives can work in tandem: the indictment of Milosevic made it clear that his removal was a necessary, if not sufficient, condition for "joining Europe." The same "power of attraction" of "Europe" underlies the success of other conflict prevention measures on that continent.[20] When the OSCE's high commissioner on national minorities, Max van der Stoel, visits the Baltic states to discuss the status of the ethnic Russians, or when he participates in roundtables on the Hungarian minority in various central European countries, hovering in the background is the implicit offer that, if the states comply with "European" standards, they will ultimately receive European benefits. A similar emissary might find it difficult to duplicate van der Stoel's efforts elsewhere without comparable systemic incentives.

The main set of incentives available for the world's poorest nations involves relief or forgiveness of debt. The international financial institutions are indeed using an offer of debt relief to the poorest states as an incentive for them to adopt a package of policy reforms, though the reforms are linked to conditions for a market economy, not to peace and stability. Critics of the package argue that the conditions are so stringent that few nations will be able to meet them. Donors have been tardy in providing funding; and, in any case, debt relief would at most provide a one-time improvement in a country's economic standing rather than a continued spur to growth and support for welfare, such as access to the EU offers.

The biggest question about systemic effects on conflict, of course, is the effect of the increasing globalization of economic activity and the triumph of an economic model based on the "Washington consensus." Despite the undeniable benefits of globalization to many, economic inequalities both within and among countries have grown in the past two decades. So has the impoverishment of the poorest and the economic instability of many countries, which increasingly depend on poorly regulated private capital flows. Quantitative inequality alone does not lead to violent political conflict; but in a world with faster and broader communications and more efficient global markets in the means of violence as well as other commodities, greater disparities create an environment hospitable to violent entrepreneurs who can offer alternative survival strategies to young men with few prospects. Countries destabilized by capital flight can suffer general economic declines that contribute to insecurity and intergroup tensions. The quest for financial stability and for greater global equity, as a counterpart to greater global integration, also figures on the agenda of conflict prevention.

Systemic prevention can change the background conditions that promote conflict. But some areas—states, regions, subregions—will always be more prone to violent conflict than others, more vulnerable to whatever global factors may promote or facilitate violence. Identification of and intervention in such areas constitutes what most have in mind when they speak of conflict prevention or preventive action.

10

Targeted Prevention

Anushirvan the Just encamped while hunting. When his servants went to make kababs, they had no salt. They sent to a village for it. Anushirvan told them, "Pay full price for it." They asked, "What harm can a little salt do?" He answered, "The foundation of oppression in the world was small. Each came and added to it, until it reached this level."

When the King eats one apple from the peasant's orchard, his servants uproot an entire tree.
For each five eggs the ruler takes away, his army skewers a thousand chickens.

—Sa`adi, *Gulistan*

Systemic prevention affects many conflicts simultaneously but indirectly. Most of what people think of as conflict prevention, however, consists of programs targeted at specific situations. Such programs are aimed at affecting both risk factors (structural prevention) and escalation (operational prevention). In practice the two always have to be integrated in common strategies.

Strategies

Much literature on conflict prevention discusses "tools"—programs to accomplish a given end in a given place, like fact-finding missions, support for reform of judicial systems, preventive military deployments, or economic sanctions. Such tools may accomplish a subsidiary goal in an overall strategy: fact-finding missions might engage protagonists in discussion of new problem-solving mechanisms; judicial reform might increase security,

161

reduce impunity, and strengthen the rule of law; preventive deployment might deter expansion of a conflict; economic sanctions might induce a government to cease escalation of violence or violations of human rights. Analysts have defined strategy mostly as a list of tools, linked to either causes of conflict or stage of conflict.[1] But tools "succeed" only if the strategy works.[2] Holding a national presidential election that leads to civil war and massacres, as in Burundi in 1993, might be the equivalent of bombing a mistakenly identified target (like the Chinese embassy in Belgrade) with precision-guided "smart" missiles. Evaluating the effectiveness of tools tells only whether a particular intermediate objective is likely to be achieved, not whether that intermediate objective is appropriate to the overall goal or whether the overall goal is the right one.

Strategy requires that intermediate goals be related to an overall objective through some sort of sequencing or interdependence. The CPA's proposed strategy for the Balkans aimed at preventing the outbreak of war in Kosovo or its spread to Macedonia by promoting a negotiated settlement that respected international principles concerning both borders and human rights. Preventing the spread of conflict from Kosovo to Macedonia, in turn, required a strengthening of external security (through the UN Preventive Deployment Force) and internal security (through dialogue and reforms), each of which implied a set of programs. Choice of these approaches was based on the judgment that the existing governments were legitimate in Macedonia and illegitimate in Kosovo. Promoting a solution in Kosovo required de-escalation and confidence building, leading to dialogue and negotiations over the province's status. Sanctions and incentives for the Federal Republic of Yugoslavia would induce de-escalation, while second-track meetings would prepare the grounds for negotiation. The major controversy over the proposed strategy was not whether the programs (tools) proposed for the intermediate goals were effective—though this was at issue, especially regarding sanctions on Belgrade—but whether the goal (a negotiated settlement that respected international principles) was desirable or feasible and whether these intermediate steps would reach the goal. Alternative strategies could have sought to overthrow Milosevic or prevent the arming of the Kosovo Liberation Army. Some who disagreed with our approach argued for greater emphasis on such goals, but their arguments had more to do with the nature of the problem and of the desired outcome than with the effectiveness of tools.

Although the debate on strategic approaches to conflict has focused more on intervention and settlement, the same considerations apply to prevention.

The most common subject of this debate—whether conflicts explode because of ancient hatreds or manipulation by leaders—disguises, as I have argued in discussing the causes of conflict, a debate on strategy. The thesis that most contemporary wars are ethnic conflicts derived from deep-rooted hatreds supports a strategy of isolating conflicts until they burn themselves out or separating opposing groups through partition. Supporters of the view that power-seeking leaders strategically manipulate people into conflict argue for firm opposition, up to and including military action or arrest for war crimes, to the leaders responsible.

This debate identifies a major issue: Should prevention address structures, such as culturally determined beliefs, or actors, such as politicians who manipulate people for political gain? Cultural beliefs are hardly the only structural factors that increase the risk of conflict, however. They are less important than social, economic, and institutional factors. These determine the situations in which actors make choices without fully explaining those choices. Privileging structural sources of conflict leads to a strategy focusing on transforming social structures and institutions to prevent conflict, while explanations emphasizing intentional action lead to strategies focused on the capacity and behavior of actors. Thus the problem of strategy in preventive action is related to the general problem of structure and agent in social thought.[3]

Different organizations, with their associated analytic frameworks, propound different strategies, based predominantly on either actors or structure. Human rights organizations tend to frame violent conflict as crime and advocate strategies based on individual accountability.[4] They tend to reject structural explanations as excuses. To the extent that human rights groups advocate conflict prevention, they most frequently advocate ending impunity through international criminal tribunals, domestic justice, or forceful interventions. Human rights organizations sometimes also recommend institutional reforms that would deter abuse in the future. Related organizations focus on "democracy building" and support for elements of civil society like human rights organizations and independent media. These form part of an institutional strategy focused on governance.

Realists emphasize security, both the political-military security of states and the physical security of groups in civil wars. They argue that only a stable, defensible basis for state power can provide both domestic and international security. Unless enforced with an overwhelming international military presence, attempts to reunify warring societies like the ethnic components of Bosnia or Kosovo-Serbia are doomed to failure. Some versions of realism applied to ethnic conflict draw on the "ancient hatreds" argument to support partition as a solution, claiming that communities that hate one another cannot live together. More sophisticated versions note that state collapse creates security dilemmas, in which the resulting fear and hatred make living together difficult, regardless of how ancient or modern, deeply rooted or manipulated, such feelings may be.[5] Redrawing borders or strengthening states will prevent conflict. In the absence of such changes, the incentives for violence on the part of leaders and their followers are simply too great.

Developmentalists emphasize human security, which derives from entitlement to basic needs and the right to participate in fair decisionmaking processes. Economic and social structures, not just political and military ones, can threaten people's integrity and well-being. People so threatened are more likely to resort to violence. Hence long-term prevention of violent conflict requires development that not only increases aggregate wealth but also ensures the basic security of all. Such development requires both the growth in assets of the most deprived people and institutions of governance to manage inevitable conflicts. The governance strategy that development agencies are increasingly promoting overlaps with that of democracy promotion.[6]

Organizations devoted to conflict resolution or transformation frame violent conflict as resulting from disputes or contradicting claims. The claims need not be considered symmetric or equally valid, except that all, even if in a distorted, unjust, or even criminal way, express some human need. Conflict resolution or reconciliation aims at helping actors transform their relationships. This transformation, in turn, can enable them to change structures that place them in conflict. Thus agents can transform structure through interaction with one another. Such a process seeks changes that create new opportunities for cooperation and prevent actors from trying to satisfy needs through violence. Hence it holds a potential for reconciliation, the key value of this approach. Conflict resolution approaches tend to frame the conflict as internal to a society and to ignore structures (such as international financial flows, global strategic interactions, or international drug policy) that the parties to the conflict cannot change; however, they transform their relationship. The model does not rule out punishment for crimes committed in the course of conflict, any more than the demand for an end to impunity rules out any attempt at reconciliation with perpetrators of past violence.[7] The paradigms frame the problem differently, however, and often lead their adherents to different prescriptions.

These strategic approaches address different aspects of conflict. They can be linked and interrelated. The realist emphasis on states and the developmentalists' emphasis on livelihood are both essential to the security and capacity that societies need to govern themselves better and protect human rights. Measures to counter criminal violence and, under different circumstances, to facilitate dialogue on how to transform state structures and pursue development may provide conditions that make it possible to build those institutions.

Strategies fit some cases better than others. Conflict resolution is most appropriate when relatively well defined parties are able to reach and implement agreements. Especially when all parties have some justified claims and violence has not overwhelmed the actors, this approach holds out hope for transformation. When, on the other hand, violence is escalating rapidly, particularly when one party is more guilty than others of aggression or atrocity, a more partisan and forceful intervention may be needed. International human rights standards provide legitimate benchmarks for political judgment.

Sanctions against the behavior of leaders are also more likely to be effective when institutions can sustain a change of leader and function as instruments for implementing policy—for example, in Yugoslavia rather than Zaire-Congo. In a failing or collapsing state, some arguments of the realists deserve attention, though their advocacy of partition is usually misplaced. Political change or problem solving is virtually impossible without basic institutions that can provide security and a mechanism with which to carry out policy. Because effective governance provides the only sustainable basis for conflict management, and effective governance within the current world order requires a state, prevention requires that state institutions be built. The poor fit between the state institutions required by today's international system and many societies incorporated into that system by colonialism or conquest, however, accounts for much of today's conflict.[8] Effective governance may rest on the foundation of a strong state that emerges from war or revolution, as did, for instance, the government of the United States, which experienced revolution, civil war, two world wars, and massive domestic turmoil over racism. Sometimes the violent creation of order is a necessary condition for a longer-term peace from which, alas, those who lose their lives along the way will never benefit.

Building human security lays the foundation for all other efforts, but such efforts require the security to make long-term plans. Hence it can work best either before violence breaks out (as the CPA's working group advocated for the Ferghana Valley) or when conclusion of a conflict increases confidence in the future. The dominant paradigm of development has often failed to take into account the need to sustain peace and social and political inclusion.

No one can apply strategies directly to cases. The ultimate goal of any targeted prevention strategy should be to address structural problems sufficiently to reduce the need for operational prevention. Without operational measures to halt escalation, however, addressing structural issues is often impossible. Structural reforms require engagement with partners in an open environment. Violent conflict destroys that atmosphere, putting a premium on immediate considerations—as when a Burundian negotiator told Nyerere's team in Arusha that he could not agree to reform measures for fear of losing his life.

Hence an idealized targeted conflict-prevention strategy would combine operational measures to reduce open violence with structural reforms. The operational measures against escalation should minimize contradiction of longer-term goals, and over the life of the program the emphasis should be shifted from operational to structural measures.

Political obstacles will be encountered in implementing such a strategy. Some parties, often those with the most power, oppose them. Both structural programs and many cooperative conflict management programs require access to the society or parties to the conflict, access that governments can block or use as a bargaining chip. Governments may permit access only for parts of programs they approve in ways that distort the goals. The government of Uzbekistan has been eager to cooperate with the UN Office of Drug Control and Crime Prevention against drug trafficking, organized crime, and terrorism, which fit its definition of its problems, but has blocked efforts by the development and political agencies of the UN to work on economic, social, and political sources of conflict.

Nongovernmental organizations may be able to gain access by providing relatively nonthreatening services of development or humanitarian aid; but without official action to complement the NGOs' engagement with political change, the latters' work remains incomplete. Falling back on sanctions or other externally applied punitive measures is often ineffective, especially when pursued alone. Attempts at coercion or stigmatization by outside forces may lead a government to forbid outside efforts to work on the ground.

Hence one of the most important distinctions we found in the CPA's work was that between governments that welcomed international conflict-prevention initiatives, which they considered as aid in solving their society's problems, and those that rejected them as unacceptable interference aimed at strengthening opposition (which they often are). This distinction surfaced in every region in which the CPA's project included more than one country. Some governments had political reasons to welcome or reject outside involvement:

—The government of Burundi welcomed international involvement, starting with the first Buyoya presidency. After the 1993 attempted coup and massacres, the FRODEBU presidency called for a more active UN role to bolster its position vis-à-vis the Tutsi-dominated military. Buyoya's military government continued to welcome international involvement to legitimate itself and to counter the sanctions imposed by neighboring countries. It also preferred to involve a range of international actors to balance Nyerere's perceived pro-opposition orientation. The Democratic Republic of the Congo's president, Laurent Kabila, opposed external involvement that would strengthen civil society and opposition political parties. As long as he was allied with Rwanda, he also opposed the commission of inquiry into the disappearance of Rwandan Hutu refugees. When he broke with Rwanda in 1998, he changed his position on this issue, though now the war and rebel policies, rather than the government's refusal, blocked the commission's work.

—Macedonia, isolated by Greece's blocking of international recognition and potentially threatened by Serbian aggression and Albanian nationalism, welcomed the recognition signaled by an international presence. Kosovar Albanians wanted international intervention to free them from Serbia-Yugoslavia and support their contention that they were sovereign international actors. Milosevic, on the other hand, used his refusal to admit international observers to insist on Yugoslav sovereignty and as leverage in bargaining over the outer wall of sanctions against the Federal Republic of Yugoslavia, though he did agree to allow the United States, a major power he was courting, to establish a library and information center in Pristina.

—The Kyrgyz Republic tried to use international organizations' conflict prevention agenda as leverage over its more powerful neighbor, Uzbekistan, whose domestic and foreign policies appeared to pose threats to this tiny state. Uzbekistan opposed this attempt. President Karimov also did not want to risk empowering local actors in the Ferghana Valley, as he feared any regional program would do, by bringing local actors into direct contact with international agencies and donors.

The 1995 *Supplement to an Agenda for Peace* notes that one major obstacle to prevention is the "reluctance of one or another of the parties to accept

UN help." Kofi Annan, in his May 2001 report to the Security Council on conflict prevention, repeated the same concern. His report notes that the UN can do little "if the Government concerned refuses to admit it has a problem that could lead to violent conflict and rejects offers for assistance."[9] No formula will solve these political dilemmas. Certainly, a key shortcoming of the recommendations of both the CPA's Ferghana Valley Working Group and the UNDP Ferghana Valley Development Project was the absence of measures to convince the government of Uzbekistan to participate in such efforts. Now that the United States and Russia have largely defined the problem in Central Asia as a terrorist threat emanating from Afghanistan, they too may support Uzbekistan's resistance to programs that frame the problem differently, though the State Department says it will continue to focus on human rights. International actors face an alternative not between political will and a lack thereof but between different political wills based on different interests and problem definitions that lead to different strategies.

Structural Prevention: Development and Governance

Structural prevention aims at transforming characteristics of groups, states, and regions that increase their risk of violent conflict. Those directly affected must ultimately own and lead such transformation, but international actors can do much to shape, support, and sustain their efforts. Roughly speaking, we can divide structural prevention between programs affecting development and those affecting governance.

Development

Research suggests that poverty—or, even more intensely, a rapid increase in poverty—interacts with two main factors to produce risk of conflict: with lootable or taxable wealth that both provides resources for conflict and centralizes the state and with group identities that provide both claims to resources and social capital for political organization. Poverty especially affects the likelihood of civil war through its effect on the education and employment of young men, who provide a cheap recruitment pool for armed groups. Education of women, which many studies have shown to improve social welfare, strengthens society's capacity to build peace.

These conclusions provide guidelines for integrating conflict prevention into an economic development strategy. Aggregate growth can aggravate disparities among regions or groups as capital flows to the most efficient. The breakup or reform of inefficient economic institutions can reduce security and produce the floating population of unemployed young men most susceptible to recruitment to violence. Measures imposed by Western powers on an indebted Yugoslavia required the central government to curb employment-creating but economically inefficient expenses in the federating units, which generated incentives for the wealthier republics to disengage from the federation.[10] Accelerated land privatization in the Kyrgyz Republic in accord with an International Monetary Fund (IMF) program will release superfluous labor from kolkhozes. Some will migrate to seek work, others will join the Islamic Movement of Uzbekistan.[11] These reform proposals, though they address real problems, will not succeed if they also aggravate war in the region.

Some proposed mechanisms incorporate such concerns into the work of international financial institutions and donors. The World Bank, working with the Carter Center, developed pilot programs of "participatory stabilization" in Uganda and Guyana, engaging citizens in discussions with the World Bank and public authorities. Such public consultations or roundtables between international organizations and both civil society and the political authorities are used in a variety of conflict management activities, as well as in forms of engaged research on conflict, such as that of the War-Torn Societies Project.[12] Others have suggested integrating conflict prevention into development policies through conflict-impact assessments of projects.[13]

Such assessment instruments should not aim only at avoiding harm. Some donors and development agencies are thinking about how to use assistance more proactively, both by integrating governance into development, as discussed later in this chapter, and by modifying economic development strategies to decrease the risk of conflict in more targeted ways.[14] These include support for policies and projects that reduce imbalances among identity groups, diversify the economy away from dependence on natural resource extraction, insist on transparency and accountability of public resources as a condition for assistance, and increase education and reduce unemployment, including addressing gender disparities in both.

Others have proposed incorporating conflict prevention into programs of international financial institutions through peace conditionality. James Boyce developed this concept for postconflict reconstruction in response to an influential argument by UN officials that the IMF fiscal austerity program for El Salvador conflicted with the political goals of the El Salvador peace process, which required certain expenditures—notably, on forming a national police force integrating former guerrillas. Boyce concluded that the Salvadoran government was using the IMF program as an excuse to avoid implementing policies it opposed and that more explicitly political conditionality, not less economic conditionality, would enable IFI policies to support implementation of the peace agreement.[15] In a later paper, presented at one of the CPA's conferences, he and Manuel Pastor argued for extending such "peace conditionality" to preconflict situations as well. The outbreak of civil war or mass violence destroys chances for economic improvement, and governance issues therefore must be part of conditionality along with strictly economic or fiscal ones.[16]

Programs to accomplish conflict prevention objectives may conflict with economic efficiency. Reducing intergroup disparities may require investment where returns are lower, one of the reasons that market-driven growth can increase disparities. Economic diversification can conflict with pursuit of comparative advantage and might be used to support a protectionist strategy like import-substitution industrialization, with all the risks of corruption and waste that entails. However, just as economists sought market-driven models that improved equity (such as redistribution through growth by investing in the human capital of the poor, largely through education), so it should not surpass human imagination to devise strategies and projects that capture most virtues of a market while reducing the risk of conflict.

Governance

Paul Collier and Anke Hoeffler of the World Bank have estimated that after five years of implementing an economic reform package the average country would reduce its risk of conflict by 30 percent. Applying this simulation to Zaire-Congo during the period from 1995 to 1999, the country with the highest estimated risk of conflict during that period, they argue that "had the government of Zaire implemented radical policy reform (approximately of the magnitude undertaken by Uganda between 1986 and 1992), and if donors had tripled their aid contribution, then civil war would have become unlikely."[17] Such a scenario, of course, is counterfactual in more ways than one. Neither Zaire under Mobutu nor the DRC under Kabila could have carried out such a reform program, which would have conflicted with the personal interests of the rulers and required administrative capacities the state did not have. For this and other reasons, therefore, agencies have attempted to take a broader view of development, including within it not only improved economic performance but also investments in institutions—that is, governance.

The United Nations Development Program and the Development Assistance Committee (DAC) of the OECD have drafted guidelines for integrating support for governance into development aid. As the DAC puts it, "Helping strengthen the capacity of a society to manage conflict without violence must be seen as a foundation for sustainable development."[18] An integrated strategy for long-term, structural prevention would combine policies for growth, targeted programs to reduce sources of conflict, and support for governance to "strengthen the capacity of a society to manage conflict without violence."[19]

Governance embraces state functions, the political arena, and the institutions of civil society that participate in making, implementing, and monitoring social choices. Although economic transformation might reduce some of the sources of conflict, political institutions can increase a society's ability both to carry out economic transformation and to manage the conflicts that inevitably continue or may even be provoked by the development process.

Democratic institutions, and most especially elections, have become an important focus of policy. Nonetheless, focusing governance programs solely on democratic institutions can be counterproductive. Elections in the absence of an effective, law-abiding state structure risk provoking conflict by providing a national arena for competition for power. Some analysts have therefore urged that programs for state building must precede those for democratization.[20] State building logically precedes democratization, but state building and democratization do not follow neat linear processes. Theorists can imagine an authoritarian state that gradually liberalizes as institutions become stronger.[21] But governments not subject to accountability through an electoral process monitored by an independent civil society too often degenerate into malign or predatory dictatorships. Furthermore, people increasingly demand the right to choose or judge leaders, making it difficult for rulers to remain benign while refusing such demands. Electoral processes, though they may provoke conflict, also help build institutions of representation and accountability that can ultimately restrain conflict. The goal should be not to halt elections but rather to ensure that elections are not treated as ends in themselves and are accompanied by other reforms.

Burundi provides an example of the dangers and potentials of elections. The 1993 elections placed the majority in control of all state bodies except the military, without protection for the dominant minority or means to enforce the election results against spoilers. The solution need not be international military intervention. Before the election, a small delegation from

FRODEBU had met with President Buyoya. The delegation told Buyoya that FRODEBU would allow him to run unopposed without party affiliation. Burundi would then have emerged with a reformist Tutsi military president owing political debts to all major parties and groups, together with a national assembly in which the majority received its rightful representation. Buyoya, however, decided to run as an UPRONA candidate and lost in an election with no prior agreement on power sharing, leading to the subsequent breakdown into coups and civil war. The offer from FRODEBU leaders illustrates the possibility of finding ways to ease the strains of transition in divided societies through pacts between groups to avoid confrontation.

External forces should not precipitate violence by pushing for off-the-rack reforms but should support initiatives like this one. They should be particularly cautious about pressing for rapid presidential elections. Regional and local elections may build a base for a national political arena. Electoral aid should be only one component of a broad program of assistance in building up the capacity of both the state and civil society. An important part of such programs would be combating official corruption. When the head of state himself rules through corruption or promotion of conflict, however, promoting a reasonably fair election may be the only way to start the necessary transformation.

Political acts like pressing a ruler to allow fairer elections and stronger independent institutions fall more within the ambit of preventive diplomacy than preventive development. Development organizations trying to integrate conflict prevention into their work without becoming directly involved in such political controversies propose to focus on strengthening and reforming parts of the state that most directly affect prospects for conflict. These include national human rights institutions, both official and nongovernmental; the legal system more broadly construed; security forces, especially civilian police; courts and other parts of the judicial system, including penal institutions; and various grievance mechanisms, such as ombudsmen. Of course, these programs can work only if the highest political leadership supports them, so that preventive diplomacy affecting the state's top leadership and capacity-building programs for institutions should complement each other.

A crucial nexus where these intersect is civil society. Even when the top leadership of the state is corrupt or repressive, to the extent that aid to official bodies would be wasteful or harmful, private groups may continue to function. Under corrupt or authoritarian governments civic groups may both take on some statelike functions, like service provision, and continue monitoring state actions, providing what little public space persists. Such was the case, in different ways, in Nigeria and Zaire under Abacha and Mobutu. The CPA's report on the Ferghana Valley recommended that in every policy area in which aid organizations were engaged in capacity building, they should seek to support not only the official institutions but also private ones that study and monitor the policy area. Such monitoring and complementarity between state and society strengthens both.

Democracy assistance has a place in this effort, but all "democracies" are not alike.[22] Systems that provide little compensation for losers or that concentrate too much power in one authority have an inherent penchant for conflict. The concentrated control of oil revenue in the person of the president has contributed to Nigeria's difficulties in establishing stable democracy. That is why both fiscal and political federalism are vital for Nigeria's future. Modes of power sharing can vary greatly; coalition governments are the least stable form. Power sharing can involve the design of the executive (presidential, parliamentary, and mixed systems), local government, fiscal systems, and administration.[23]

In some cases, institutional reform must take ethnonational identity into account. Realists often suggest that only partition of the state is a stable solution to ethnic conflict, especially once bloodshed has exacerbated fear, anger, and hatred. Others argue that ethnic conflicts should be overcome through integrationist measures, including power sharing, strengthening of nonethnic civic identities, and other measures.[24] The process of partition itself almost invariably involves bloodshed that embitters future relations. U.S. military planners working on a possible intervention in Burundi in 1996 did not seem to realize that by establishing "safe areas" for Hutus or Tutsis, they would also establish "unsafe areas." Such a provisional partition would have led to mass killing. Even short of partition, however, the identity or structure of the state is often at issue, as groups demand autonomy, devolution, revenue sharing, or other changes in state structure.

The normative structures of the international system generally oppose the creation of new states, despite the recent emergence of the largest number of new states since decolonization in the 1950s and 1960s. Borders will change from time to time, usually with some violence, but there is no way to reconcile a right to secession with a world of states; nor would the ministates that would result necessarily be stable themselves. Hence most attempts to find solutions to territorialized ethnic conflicts focus on schemes for decentralization such as devolution to local governments, federalism, or autonomy. Some intergroup conflicts can be resolved largely by strengthening civic institutions and providing greater fairness in distribution of assets, as the CPA's working group recommended for Macedonia; others require recognition of ethnonational claims, as in Kosovo. In several cases, such as the peoples of the Niger Delta, the distribution and management of state resources, not ethnic claims per se, are the core issues. Such cases cannot be resolved peacefully as long as the central state itself is so authoritarian or corrupt that it cannot be counted on to seek or implement an agreement.

Regional Structures

Neither governance nor development are exclusively national. Regional factors interact to make whole sets of countries prone to mutually reinforcing conflict processes. Landlocked countries (including all of Central Asia and the Great Lakes region) encounter particular development problems that only regional cooperation could overcome. Transborder trade and other markets in conflict resources, though they are articulated with global networks, often function mainly at a regional level.

Regional war economies are usually based on preexisting smuggling networks, which develop from interaction among economic policy differentials, lax border controls, transnational ethnic or other networks, and corruption. A bustling free port like Dubai, smack in the middle of a region of states with highly protectionist policies, corrupt bureaucracies, and numerous conflicts, creates opportunities and incentives for smuggling. Regional cooperation on these issues holds potential for reducing structural factors conducive to violence and its spread. Harmonization of customs duties, cooperation on border controls and law enforcement, and other measures might impede the development of regional war economies.

Most organizations dealing with international policy, however, whether politically or economically, have no structures focused on regional programs, because states are their usual counterparts. Nor do all regions possess regional institutions capable of engaging with international partners. The UN can more easily pursue a regional policy in West Africa than in the Great Lakes region or in Central Asia, because West Africa is organized as a region by the Economic Community of West African States (ECOWAS), a functioning subregional organization underpinned by a local hegemon, Nigeria, which can act as a partner. But such partnership was impossible or more difficult when Nigeria itself was the source of regional problems under General

Abacha. Both the organizational structure and politics of regions make some more amenable than others to comprehensive approaches.

Operational Prevention: Conflict Management, Coercive Diplomacy, and Intervention

Because assistance, capacity building, and other measures that require a presence on the ground and cooperative authorities are involved in so much of structural prevention, they are likely to be implemented only when a government enjoys a modicum of international political credibility, and they can succeed only when a government itself comes to support them. Some rulers, of course, stay in power by provoking conflict or undermining state and political institutions. For all these reasons, efforts at structural prevention—namely, measures aimed at changing the behavior of actors and preventing escalation owing to unforeseen crises—can rarely be isolated from operational prevention.

Operational prevention—that is, action to slow, halt, or reverse vertical or horizontal escalation of conflict—forms part of a continuum from structural prevention to crisis response. Analysts have distinguished two broad types of operational prevention: coercion or inducement and cooperative management.[25] On the one hand, external actors may try to affect the behavior of parties to the conflict by threats or promises; on the other, they can work with the parties closely in a more problem-solving mode, through negotiations, dialogue, training, and observer or fact-finding missions.

No formula can dictate the strategy for operational prevention in any case, and such decisions tend to be even more politicized than those about structural prevention. Whether to engage a party in dialogue and negotiations, impose sanctions against it, or threaten it with a military response for certain actions depends not only on a calculus of what will be effective but also on what one wants to accomplish as a result of a political stance on the conflict and on the legitimacy of each party's claims. Although the underlying risks of conflict are largely social, economic, and institutional, escalation is above all political, resulting from the strategies of actors. Sometimes economic and social factors push actors to extremes: sudden financial crises may threaten a population's security and lessen a government's control, or food shortages may trigger population movements. In such cases, rapid, targeted humanitarian aid (as well as the incorporation of conflict prevention criteria and peace conditionality in rescue packages) may help ease the immediate strains. The crisis remains essentially political, however.[26]

Cooperative Conflict Management

Cooperative management of conflict includes a range of techniques from traditional preventive diplomacy, sometimes shading into coercive diplomacy, to a variety of conflict resolution techniques practiced largely by NGOs, including some religious organizations.

On the more official part of the continuum lie methods and institutions of preventive diplomacy. The UN secretary general can employ fact-finding missions to engage governments in discussion and bring issues to the attention of the Security Council; but, though this method was highlighted in the *Agenda for Peace* in 1992 and recommended again in the Brahimi report of 2000 and the secretary general's 2001 report on prevention, member states still resist it.[27] Both Uzbekistan and Indonesia, for instance, have refused UN proposals for fact-finding missions.

The UN, regional organizations, and some states have appointed various special envoys and representatives to conflict areas.[28] The most effective seem to be those who reside in the area, but states that allow such special representatives to set up shop are still a small minority. Most envoys have ad hoc mandates for a particular country or, in a useful innovation, a region, like the Great Lakes. More such regional envoys would be useful in consolidating and coordinating efforts in West Africa or Central Asia, including Afghanistan.

A few organizations have established offices with permanent mandates for preventive diplomacy. The high commissioner on national minorities of the OSCE, for instance, has the right of initiative. His initiatives have had a higher rate of acceptance than proposals for UN fact-finding missions. The Organization of African Unity also established a Mechanism for Prevention, Management, and Resolution of Conflict, including a mandate to work on internal conflict.[29] The effectiveness of these envoys depends greatly on the nature of the regions in which they are working; any envoy working in Europe has more tools at hand, especially incentives, than one working in Africa or Asia.

The character of the individuals chosen also matters. Envoys such as Ahmedou Ould Abdallah (Burundi), Lakhdar Brahimi (South Africa, Haiti, Afghanistan), or Jean Arnault (Guatemala, Burundi) generate confidence in their interlocutors and an atmosphere of cooperation among the international actors. The better envoys also stray far from traditional diplomatic techniques. They engage interlocutors in a variety of ways, making use of NGOs and supportive states to mobilize resources and carry out programs.[30]

Some have adopted methods used by NGOs, such as roundtables or second-track discussions. Often they reach out to the international research community to obtain information and perspectives they do not find within the UN or other institutional frameworks in which they are operating.

Techniques that engage parties to an actual or potential conflict in dialogue or discussion, as advocated in the conflict resolution approach, inherently confer a kind of legitimacy on those who participate. Some explicitly start from the presumption that all parties have legitimate, if not necessarily equal, claims. Even when it is claimed that inclusion in the negotiations constitutes only value-free recognition that a group has power, participation in a negotiation process carries with it the implicit offer of a political role as part of the outcome. Negotiations can thus involve a kind of moral hazard; if realism requires inclusion of any group with real power, and if real power is demonstrated through the exercise or threat of violence, then violence becomes the starting point on a path to legitimacy. Different actors use this problem in different ways: governments refuse to negotiate with those they label terrorists or extremists (Uzbekistan and the IMU, Milosevic and the KLA); diplomats attempt to craft agreements among moderates excluding extremists (Ould Abdallah in Burundi) or hold all-party talks to bring "extremists" into a legitimate political process (Nyerere and Mandela in Burundi); realists and proponents of reconciliation argue for inclusiveness on different grounds (recognition of power realities, the need for forgiveness after violence to reconstitute society); human rights advocates argue against impunity for and negotiations with abusers who should be arrested and tried, not empowered.

If there is any general rule that can be applied invariably, I have not discovered it. As in most political situations, normative or legal standards can at best set some bounds. The following, sometimes contradictory guidelines might be helpful in deciding whom to engage:

—Seek to include all parties in consultations or negotiations.

—Consult with legitimate local actors on the process they prefer.

—Try not to legitimate gross abusers of human rights; avoid both self-righteousness and disregard for the needs of victims, recognizing that people in terrible situations are liable to do terrible things but that victims need dignity, recognition, and a measure of justice.

—Take into account the degree of symmetry: an abusive insurgency against a relatively legitimate government should face a higher hurdle to recognition than an abusive insurgency against an abusive government or other opponent.

—An abusive group that nonetheless enjoys a political constituency based on genuine grievances deserves more respect than one based largely on greed or ambition; especially in ethnic conflicts, beware of allowing accusations of atrocity or "terrorism" to exclude any group's legitimate claims.

—Acknowledge current reality while trying to change it; if no one is willing or able to defeat or weaken a powerful abusive group, there may be no alternative but to engage it, but do so on principled terms. Negotiators should also refuse to provide a political excuse for powers unwilling to act against perpetrators of atrocities—if necessary, by withdrawing.

These criteria are vague and inherently political, especially in the use of terms like *legitimate* and *abusive*. They are a guide to, not a substitute for, political judgment and political processes among international actors.

Some argue that neutrality on the part of any mediator, facilitator, or convener is necessary.[31] Whether neutrality is appropriate depends on one's political and ethical evaluation of the conflict as well as the balance of forces. A slightly different, and more principled, approach argues not for neutrality but for impartiality. Neutrality in conflict management risks going too far in ignoring normative criteria. As the Brahimi report on UN peacekeeping operations argues, impartiality means above all applying the principles of the UN Charter, which are binding not only on the UN itself but also on member states and other international organizations composed of such states.[32]

Even if there is no general formula for what works, there do seem to be certain forms of negotiations aimed at preventing crisis that do not work—in particular, those like the Rambouillet meeting between representatives of Serbia and Kosovar Albanians or the Israeli-Palestinian negotiations at Camp David in September 2000, which preceded the renewed Palestinian *intifada*. Forcing antagonists to seclude themselves for a fixed (usually short) period to reach an agreement for which their people are not prepared, under pressure from conveners who are clearly closer to one side than the other, seems likely to intensify rather than avoid crisis. Even if negotiators reach an agreement, it is difficult to implement accords reached under such circumstances. When negotiators represent ethnic or political groups in conflict, including either weak states or nonstate actors, it takes even more time and work to build a base for the process and outcome in the larger society. The Tajikistan dialogue group convened by the Kettering Foundation and the Russian Institute of Oriental Studies eventually spawned a group of NGOs and outreach projects founded by members in order to overcome this problem, as did the Harvard problem-solving workshops on the Israeli-

Palestinian conflict, but the limited success of these two initiatives shows how difficult this "transfer" problem is.[33]

On the continuum of prevention measures, some of these "talking cures" lie closer to structural interventions, especially those that focus on capacity building or dialogues on transforming the sources of conflict. The Arusha negotiations on Burundi under the successive leadership of Julius Nyerere and Nelson Mandela, for instance, dealt with all major institutional issues of Burundi, as well as with future plans for the economy and even differing views of the past. The latter may appear to be irrelevant to a purely political negotiation, but civil wars among parties linked to different identities are never purely political in a superficial sense. Although conflicts are not attributable to differences in "culture" in the sense of immutable differences in group beliefs and values, the process by which enemies become co-citizens or good neighbors also involves human relationships, in what is sometimes called reconciliation. Although people in conflict tend to demonize their enemies as less than human, the process of reconciliation enables the parties to see how former enemies, too, acted as human beings, imprisoned by their histories and circumstances. Civil society, including religious and other groups, is more often the agent of reconciliation than are political or official bodies.

Although negotiations, dialogue, and discussion among parties to an actual or potential conflict predominate in common conceptions of conflict resolution, they form only part of a strategy and often not the most important one. Operational prevention should include an array of other measures to change the environment in which negotiations take place, whether by supporting and strengthening forces for peace or weakening those aggravating the conflict.

One part of an operational strategy consists of engagement or capacity building to inhibit or counter escalation processes. These strategies can include supporting peace constituencies, media projects, monitoring, and civilian, police, or military deployments. International capacities for such engagement and deployment need to be developed much further.

Negotiations among belligerents exclude most of the society. When international actors focus exclusively on those who are fighting, they may increase the importance and credibility of combatants to the detriment of forces in the society that would be able to sustain a more stable and peaceful form of governance. This debate became intense in Somalia, where many Somalis bitterly criticized the U.S. force for interacting exclusively with warlords rather than with clan leaders and other parts of civil society.

Some organizations have consequently defined the support of constituencies for peace as a central goal. Work with women, who rarely take part in armed conflict, often constitutes the focal point of this effort.[34] Other organizations attempt to work with religious leaders, elders, business leaders, or other groups with an interest in ending fighting in order to build up pressure for a search for nonviolent solutions. They may seek to revive or strengthen traditional methods of conflict management. Search for Common Ground organized a Women's Center in Burundi, which has served as a safe zone for intergroup cooperation. The CPA advocated Christian-Muslim cooperation and dialogue in Nigeria as a way both to prevent the political manipulation of this division and to promote an agenda for social and political change.

Mass media play a central role in promoting fear and violence in many conflicts. The Rwandan "hate radio," Radio Mille Collines, whose director is on trial for genocide in Arusha, explicitly incited and guided the genocide to the extent of issuing operational instructions; Serbian television under Slobodan Milosevic drummed into the population the concept that Serbs were under threat everywhere from vicious enemies held at bay only by war and violence. Some have even advocated attacks on "hate media," a recommendation that NATO seemed to adopt when it bombed Serbian television on April 24, 1999, in an action that Human Rights Watch suggested violated international law.[35]

A growing number of projects attempt to counter such media through more peaceful means. In both Macedonia and Burundi, Search for Common Ground has established journalism projects that emphasize both interethnic cooperation in reporting (to avoid one-sided depictions) and objective professional standards. The Swiss Fondation Hirondelle has established a radio and news service covering both the International Criminal Tribunal on Rwanda and the Burundi peace negotiations. The United States and the EU made major efforts to keep alive independent media in Serbia, which played important roles in both the abortive demonstrations of 1996–97 and the successful postelection uprising of 2000.

International organizations have developed a variety of official monitoring deployments to provide timely and accurate information as well as incentives for officials and opponents to refrain from violence. These include conflict monitors, humanitarian monitors, human rights monitors, civilian police monitors, and military observer missions as well as preventive military deployments (such as those in Macedonia and Guinea). The OSCE has particularly developed such missions. Its Conflict Prevention Center is in charge of resident missions of long duration in member countries, which monitor and offer good offices in solving internal problems, sometimes in conjunction with a UN or other peacekeeping mission and sometimes on their own. Such monitors can generally be deployed only with the consent of the controlling authorities, though in Kosovo Milosevic permitted the autumn 1998 deployment of OSCE monitors under threat of NATO bombing.

Civilian deployments of this type are much cheaper than military deployments, but in certain ways they are more difficult to implement. Although nearly all states have standing armies, until recently none of them had standing or on-call bodies of trained civilian monitors. Each mission has to be recruited, trained, and funded from scratch. Hence the EU, the OSCE, the United States, Canada, and several European countries, at least, are developing on-call corps of civilian police or other monitors. The Brahimi report emphasizes the need to separate police and other civilian components of the legal system from military peacekeeping in peace operations and advocates greatly enhancing the UN's capacity to recruit and manage such forces. Given their relatively modest cost, these and other organizations should consider training many people for such tasks. It will still be easier to send them to postconflict areas if such missions are foreseen in a formal agreement, but if such standing capacities existed, they might be used in other circumstances as well. The UN and major states, for instance, could have offered to deploy them in the Maluku islands of Indonesia to deter or monitor the communal conflict between Muslims and Christians before it reached the stage of near warfare.

Coercive and Inducive Measures

Where the greatest risk of conflict is posed by a predatory, corrupt regime, as in Abacha's Nigeria or Mobutu's Zaire, the primary task remains removing or neutralizing the ruler through a combination of sanctions and incentives combined with support for other forces. Sanctions, especially unilateral sanctions by the United States, have become the subject of a major debate in recent years.[36] Most of the debate and research, however, has revolved around sanctions as a tool of interstate relations rather than as a tool for preventing civil or transnational wars, humanitarian emergencies, massive human rights violations, state failure, or ethnic conflict. Furthermore, the term is often associated with a trade embargo, which is only one form of sanctions. Sanctions can include measures designed to sap the capacity for violence, such as arms embargoes, the freezing of assets, or embargoes on specific commodities, such as diamonds, from conflict areas. Such targeted sanctions against resources for violence would be greatly strengthened by a global regulatory regime aimed at the same types of resources.

Sanctions can also target individuals by denying them visas or placing them on watch lists. A higher level of sanctions, of course, would be criminal sanctions. Although ad hoc war crimes tribunals are necessarily postconflict rather than preventive, the International Criminal Court could provide a background threat of sanction that would be useful in conjunction with other measures.

Broad-gauged economic embargoes, such as the trade embargo against Burundi, the embargo against the Federal Republic of Yugoslavia, and the oil embargo against Nigeria that many NGOs advocated, have to be applied with great care, especially against extremely poor countries. The sanctions against the FRY probably worked, to the extent that they did, because they were combined with incentives. The greatest risk of such embargoes, besides the suffering they cause, is that in seeking to achieve the goals of operational prevention, they actually undermine those of structural prevention by impoverishing people, encouraging smuggling and corruption, and subverting legitimate state functions.

For these very reasons, it is vital to supplement systemic measures against global money laundering with greater capacity to levy targeted financial sanctions. Such "smart sanctions" would require greater intelligence capacity within the international financial system and extensive cooperation among governments and financial institutions. Some additional legislation might also be necessary to stipulate the circumstances under which such assets might be embargoed. As mentioned previously, sanctions are much more effective when twinned with incentives. Although incentives have been much less studied, they are widely used, though, again, largely in interstate diplomacy.[37]

Force itself can play a role in prevention. Most of the discussion about use of force assumes it should be used as a last resort. The so-called Powell doctrine virtually guaranteed that the United States would use military force, if at all, only in pursuit of total victory when it had exhausted other options. Some in the field of prevention, however, argue that relegating force to the last resort almost guarantees its failure. Instead, argues Jane Holl Lute, for instance, the threat or use of force should be integrated into preventive efforts from the start.[38] Such a position requires confidence in the good will and judgment of major military powers, most of all the United States. It also entails the substantial risk of escalation and thereby risks producing the very result it intends to forestall.

Thus far, however, though military deployments are sometimes part of crisis response, they have played little or no role in preventive action except for the UN Preventive Deployment Force, the ECOWAS deployment on Guinea's border with Sierra Leone, and the preventive component of post-agreement peace-building operations. One of the principal reasons to deploy a broad range of other preventive measures is to obviate the need for military force. Nonetheless, the deployment in Macedonia was so well received that the international community might consider whether there are other areas (such as the vulnerable regions of southern Kyrgyzstan) where such a deployment might prove useful. In January 2001, ECOWAS decided to deploy a preventive force in Guinea on that country's border with Sierra Leone in an attempt to halt the spread of conflict and deal with an escalating refugee crisis. In Guinea, however, unlike in Macedonia, a full range of international preventive efforts does not yet accompany the preventive deployment.

Finally, there are times when preventive measures fail, or are not tried, and the resulting atrocities cross a threshold at which basic human solidarity requires forceful action. Making international decisions for such intervention requires both fact finding and a standard. The UN Charter would seem to require a Security Council resolution to authorize such action, but NATO took it nonetheless in Kosovo, and the Security Council, though vetoes prevented it from authorizing the action, overwhelmingly refused to condemn it. In practice, the processes for deciding on such intervention are political.[39]

It is not only norms, however, but also capacities that are lacking, unless, as in Kosovo, the crisis affects the security interests of major states—most of all the United States, the only state with global military reach. In theory, strengthening the UN's ability to deploy military force in a timely manner for crisis response might both have a dissuasive effect and provide the required capability when needed. That proposal, however, would require command, control, and reserve capabilities that the UN will not have in any foreseeable future.[40] The Brahimi report instead contains recommendations for coordinating standby arrangements with willing states for crisis response and quick deployment to peacekeeping, but implementation of some of these recommendations has been held up by opposition from G-77 states that fear the interventionist use of the UN by the United States and its allies. Resistance to effective measures to ensure such intervention comes from two sources: states that do not want to be the objects of intervention (including India, China, Russia, Egypt, and many other third-world states) and powerful states, first of all the United States, that, even if they claim the right of humanitarian intervention, do not want to bear the corresponding duty to intervene. Although discussions on this subject continue at the UN and elsewhere, a consensual regime on humanitarian intervention remains quite distant.

11

Organizing for Prevention

> The secret lies in the regulations about jurisdiction. In fact, it is not true
> and in a great living organization cannot be true that there's only one
> authorized secretary for each case. It's just that one of them has chief
> authority, while many others have a lesser degree of authority. Who—
> even if he were the greatest worker—could keep together on his desk the
> ramifications of the smallest incident?
>
> —FRANZ KAFKA, *The Castle*

In the preceding chapters of this book, I have sketched elements of a global
strategy for prevention; but there is no global strategist to implement it.
No authority has legal or political responsibility for preventing violent conflicts. Any entity enjoying such responsibility would, in effect, exercise the
authority of a global sovereign, but conflict prevention consists of a process
of global governance, not world government. Although international norms
are gradually shifting toward giving the responsibilities of sovereignty more
weight compared with the rights of sovereignty, international efforts to
enforce those responsibilities remain subject to ad hoc political decisionmaking of transnational governance through networks, unlike the routinized
law-enforcement processes of effective government.[1] Prevention of violent
conflict requires not just international cooperation—that is, cooperation
among states—but also transnational cooperation—cooperation across borders among a variety of different types of actors.

Any global preventive framework to which such a process could refer
would depend largely on whether the UN and the United States—one global

in legitimacy but relatively small and weak, the other particular in legitimacy but global in power—can define terms of collaboration with each other and with other partners. Secretary General Kofi Annan has increasingly defined prevention of violent conflict as the core of the UN's mandate.[2] In doing so, he has sought to provide moral leadership in the effort to establish a "culture of prevention" not only in the organization but also in the world. Such a normative commitment would constitute the apex of any global architecture for prevention. The secretary general and the UN, of course, could credibly assume such a role only after frankly recognizing the deep flaws of previous UN operations in Bosnia and Rwanda, for some of which Kofi Annan bore personal responsibility as head of the UN Department of Peacekeeping Operations.[3]

Others have reinforced these efforts. Under the chairmanship of Germany (in 1999), Japan (in 2000), and Italy (in 2001), the G-8 group of leading states has made conflict prevention a major theme of its meetings. Communiqués have focused on systemic issues, such as small-arms trading and conflict diamonds, as well as on the need to strengthen the capacity of international institutions to deal with conflict.[4]

Although the U.S. government has not made a comparable effort to raise the priority of conflict prevention in foreign policy, the Clinton administration did undertake some initiatives. It appointed a national intelligence officer for humanitarian emergencies and established a small "early warning" office in the State Department's Bureau of Intelligence and Research. It had the intelligence community produce an "atrocity watch list" of situations that might give rise to massive human rights violations. The administration consolidated lessons it had learned about how to upgrade interagency collaboration in crisis response through Presidential Decision Directive 56 (PDD 56) in 1997. The United States Agency for International Development, especially through the Office of the Transition Initiative, increasingly incorporated governance and structural prevention into its mandate. Internationally, the United States provided both sustained support to some targeted efforts that coincided with U.S. interests and some intermittent and diffuse support to more general efforts.

Although the UN, the G-8, and the United States might give general direction, an international architecture for prevention would be anchored in regional organizations and regional networks of civil society. The EU (the only regional organization with a prevention agenda beyond the region of the member states), the OSCE, the Organization of African Unity and its successor, the African Union, the Organization of American States, even the

Association of Southeast Asian Nations, as well as subregional organizations such as the Inter-Governmental Authority on Development in the Horn of Africa and the Economic Community of West African States have developed early warning or conflict prevention units. To varying degrees, these units are seeking partners in regional NGOs and civil society.[5] A major task of the United States, other donors, and the UN would be to support efforts to enhance such regional capabilities.

If structured transnational cooperation evolves within these frameworks, it can help to create, and will in turn be strengthened by, more stable and convergent expectations for behavior in this issue area. These convergent expectations, values, and practices, whether or not they are associated with a formal institution, would constitute what scholars of international relations call a "policy regime."[6]

Such a regime for prevention of deadly conflict remains a project rather than a reality. The implications of the events of September 11, 2001, for the global approach to violent conflicts have hardly been identified, let alone processed. Nonetheless, development of a framework for prevention need not await—and has not awaited—the full empowerment of the UN, the consistent engagement of the United States, or successful capacity building of regional organizations. In a much more decentralized, networked way, a variety of organizations and movements have begun programs and established links aiming at the prevention of violent conflict. Even in the absence of a regime, these networks may gradually affect the way parts of the international system work. For the foreseeable future, this model of transnational cooperation, not a structured, multilevel regime, constitutes the organizational future of preventive action.[7]

Prevention: Operations and Processes

Because comprehensive strategies require a mix of structural and operational measures, implementing such a strategy would require a correspondingly broad set of actors with varying capacities. The Carnegie Commission and others have proposed models of leadership and coordination for prevention based on peacekeeping and peace-building operations, with a lead actor, explicit strategy, division of labor, and exit strategy.[8] Unlike other types of "peace operations," however, prevention generally lacks a clear mandate or organizational structure.[9] Peacekeeping and peace-building operations are led by states or international organizations. They involve the UN, regional organizations, national forces, and NGOs. They are conducted under an

explicit international mandate—typically, a UN Security Council resolution—that defines the goals and fixes responsibility for authority and
coordination.[10]

Preventive efforts rarely have such a mandate. Other than immediate crisis response, the few cases of formally mandated preventive operations aim
at preventing regional spillover or recurrence—rather than outbreak or escalation—of mass violence. Such, for example, are the two much-studied
examples of Macedonia and Burundi. These operations resembled postconflict operations. A formal mandate, moreover, normally requires the
consent of a host government, creating a strategic dilemma discussed earlier.
Academic analyses usually focus on (often hypothetical) official operations
after a political decision to act has been made. It is more accurate, however,
to conceive of the entire effort to mobilize action as the preventive effort,
including campaigns, advocacy, and warnings. We should not artificially
separate this process, in which activists and others pressure governments
and international organizations to act, from a subsequent phase in which the
official actors then exert influence on the society at risk. The advocacy or
warning effort also exerts pressure. The preventive effort on Nigeria, for
instance, included uncoordinated campaigns by NGOs, limited sanctions
from the Commonwealth and the United States, and UN fact-finding and
human rights missions. Preventive efforts more often take place through
such a networked process than through an "operation."

Networking and Advocacy for Prevention

As scholars and practitioners work on the common theme of conflict prevention, they have begun to develop a common analytical framework. In
other issue areas, especially those involving science and technology (notably,
the environment), such interaction has created a transnational group of
specialists and policymakers whose common understanding facilitates communication and cooperation across national boundaries, a phenomenon
some have called an "epistemic community."[11] Strengthening these epistemic
(knowledge-based) communities can assist conflict management efforts.[12]
Epistemic communities can also form an operational constituency for policy regimes.

Such networks include parts of international organizations, parts of governments, and nongovernmental organizations, including those in the areas
of conflict themselves. Networks have emerged linking these organizations—
both formal networks (such as the European Platform for Conflict Prevention

and Transformation and the Forum on Early Warning and Early Response [FEWER]) and informal networks that develop through collaborative work.[13]

Broader sectors of civil society, including religious, labor, and civic groups, political parties, and, in some countries, party foundations, are also developing an interest in conflict prevention and resolution. Some specialized media are creating links among those dealing with conflict around the world and helping to provide both better early warning and the infrastructure for networks. Finally, all of these groups are becoming more aware of the potential role of international business, just as business is trying to adjust to a much more visible global role for itself, including its operations in conflict areas. As in the CPA's project on Nigeria, business and NGOs have often seen each other as adversaries. Yet the profits of worldwide corporations depend more than ever on the public image of brands, which can be tarnished by sordid foreign involvement; and business operations are far easier in countries where corruption is curbed and legality and peace prevail. Especially in view of the increasing prominence of economic causes of civil wars, the predominance of private capital flows for development, and business's on-the-ground presence in many areas of conflict, possible cooperation is certainly worth exploring. The UN is doing so through its Global Compact, and a number of NGOs have also launched projects in this area.[14]

No single organization coordinates or directs these activities. Networks form and function largely through the Internet, punctuated by meetings at various locations; those who cannot attend physically are informed by e-mail or reports on web pages. When I started working in preventive action in 1994, I had concerns that reliance on Internet communication would marginalize activists in poor countries. In only a couple of years, however, as "capacity-building" efforts focused on, among other things, distribution and connection of computers for activists around the world, the Internet has become the major medium through which global networks form.

In the summer of 1995, for instance, at a meeting in Vienna about information sharing between the OSCE and NGOs, senior staff of the OSCE Conflict Prevention Center told the NGOs that member states had prevented the OSCE secretariat from obtaining Internet connections, for fear that the staff would be too open to outside information or perspectives. The OSCE obtained its first web page during the Swiss chairmanship in 1996, and the web page was still hosted on the Swiss government site rather than by the OSCE itself. By now, of course, the OSCE has its own web page, and all staff members have private Internet addresses, enabling NGO activists to communicate with them directly.[15] A similar evolution took place at the UN, and member states may not realize the degree of direct, horizontal communication that staff now have with NGOs and others.

The rhetoric of networking often depicts it as a frictionless method for developing synergy. Sometimes networking can resemble the process sketched by Keck and Sikkink for transnational advocacy that I describe in the discussion of warning.[16] However, such networked partnerships can provoke conflict among participants. Organizations sometimes treat exchanges as an opportunity not to broaden their perspectives but to advocate their positions against opposition. Nor does participation in networks by NGOs and civil society in the societies in conflict provide a reliable reference point for accountability. The best networking structures recognize and deal with these issues explicitly.

Interference or intervention in another society's affairs risks unintended consequences whose ill effects may harm many, though rarely those who caused them. Even within developed societies with strong administrative and political systems, social engineering fails, and reforms fall short of their goals. That is no reason not to attempt reforms, but it is a reason always to subject their implementation to monitoring and accountability through democratic institutions. Transnational preventive action rarely incorporates such mechanisms. Consequently, the greatest strategic and ethical principle in preventive action is that outsiders must at every step consult with, learn from, and act with those inside the society or societies who are locked in the conflict and have no exit strategy from it. Effective transnational action is based on strategies constructed through partnerships and networks with those directly involved.

Of course, external organizations and actors cannot check their principles at the border in the interest of solidarity, if only because they will never find a unanimous society with which to ally. Every society consists of a field of conflicts and disagreements, and, inevitably, any course of action places one closer to some than to others. It is hard to overestimate, however, the tendency of outsiders to substitute their certainty of good intentions for a genuine understanding of the complexities of a given situation. Whenever I have been able to spend time in the field with people closely involved in conflicts, I have always been struck by the understanding, resourcefulness, and creativity of so many of those on the ground who lack the resources to implement their ideas. Nor can one romanticize local NGOs or social and political leaders, and distinguishing those with real capacities to transform their societies from those who live from conflict, have exaggerated or unrealistic ambitions, or seek to manipulate outsiders in their own interests can be a tricky and dangerous political task. Nevertheless, I have had enough surprises to conclude that whenever possible one should advance with caution, together with allies who know the terrain from a lifetime of experience.

The experience of the Great Lakes Policy Forum illustrates some of the conundrums of such collaboration. Its participants have included Burundians and others from the region. Some international officials in Burundi, however, opposed the participation of Burundians. They told us that, after the monthly meeting, Burundians telephoned home (this was before the spread of e-mail to Burundi) and spread rumors that the United States was taking sides in the conflict. As Africans, they accused us of liberal guilt and asked us to close the meetings to Burundians. This we could not do, but we did establish a smaller, more action-oriented Security Working Group that focused much more on operational coordination between NGOs in the field and government, without the same degree of transparency.

This experience exposed a key problem in the discourse of networking and empowerment: local NGOs and local civil society in areas of conflict are not apolitical repositories of humanitarianism but are themselves political actors.[17] Governments of the countries that are the object of prevention demand that international actors subject themselves to accountability by, first of all, recognizing their status as the representatives of their peoples. Because so many of these governments consist of unaccountable cliques, NGOs sometimes instead attempt to meet the challenge of accountability by working with other local partners. International Alert, for instance, now defines one of its main operational goals as the strengthening of local constituencies and capacities for peace. In Burundi it has helped organize a multigroup organization, Les Apôtres de la Paix (Apostles of Peace), that advocates and practices dialogue and collaborative problem solving. The Women's Center established in Bujumbura by Search for Common Ground organizes women as a constituency for peace.

Nongovernmental organizations in the conflict zones, however, sometimes experience these relationships as patronizing and one-sided, as, inevitably, those with the resources ultimately decide which local perspectives or capacities to strengthen. Local organizations often define their priorities quite differently than the coordinators of global networks. In one case, for instance, local NGOs resisted an attempt to train them to provide better "early warning" to a global network, on grounds that they mainly sought to improve their ability to act directly in their own region. Nor are the local actors passive recipients of outsiders' networking: they actively seek international allies and sometimes succeed to the point that the international organizations working on a conflict become as polarized as the parties themselves.

Although the imbalance of power and resources can create feelings of manipulation, so does the politics of conflict management. Someone must take responsibility for the choices made. Failure to establish clear political accountability can lead to confusion about what is the message and who is the messenger. The front page of some FEWER reports carries a box stating that the report "has been translated and edited to reflect local nuances and keep the local voice intact" and that the views are "those of the author," not of FEWER or its partners.[18] Nonetheless, FEWER states that reports are "quality assured" through the use of indicators as well as "expert group feedback." This feedback is itself political, however, not merely technical.

For instance, FEWER has enlisted scholars and activists from the Great Lakes region and East Africa to write papers supplying background analysis for policy on the Great Lakes region, in order to bring local expertise to bear on international conflict prevention efforts. The secretariat sent draft papers to board members (including me) for review. I found an anonymous paper on Burundi to be marred by a pro-Tutsi bias. Another author, of a guide to political groups in the region, gave what I thought was too benevolent an interpretation of the goals of the Hutu groups fighting the current government of Rwanda, overlooking their continued support for genocide. I offered the comments, of course, in my capacity as an objective "expert," but my own "balanced" view, as I saw it, in favor of peace, security, compromise, and so on was itself a political position.

The International Crisis Group takes a different approach, relying directly on advocacy, for which it takes political responsibility. The group employs field-based researchers, sometimes from the areas of conflict. Nonetheless, though its analyses benefit from local knowledge, its reports do not claim to transmit "local" voices. Reports go through a vetting process at headquarters in Brussels, and the final products represent the political judgment of the organization, as interpreted by the president (currently, Gareth Evans, the former minister of foreign affairs of Australia). This model attempts to combine the access to information provided by networking with the more centralized organizational model needed to take political responsibility.

These examples describe networking mainly for advocacy and warning, rather than networking on the ground for direct action. In practice, the latter is difficult without recognized access and a formally authorized operation, which, as mentioned earlier, is rare in preventive action. Networking and coordination, often under a UN umbrella, are vital to peace implementation operations, and many of these have a preventive component. Ould Abdallah, as special representative of the UN secretary general in Burundi, saw coordination of NGO networks working in the country as important both to supplement the meager resources at the disposal of the UN and to increase coherence of international policy. He encouraged the formation of forums in London and Washington and remained in contact with NGOs as well, through weekly meetings on the ground.

Even when no formal international presence explicitly deals with conflict issues, however, some humanitarian or development organizations, international and local, usually carry out programs for reconciliation, defense of human rights, or another component of nonviolent governance. Even in Nigeria under Abacha or in Zaire under Mobutu, some such groups, often anchored in local religious organizations, continued to function. Often they are isolated from one another and from the international community. Groups from the eastern DRC with whom I met in Nairobi in 1998 complained bitterly that what little international support or recognition their efforts at reconciliation between the Banyamulenge and other ethnic groups had received had been swept away in the 1998 war. The CPA's Nigeria report transmitted the desire of many groups we spoke with for assistance in networking and coalition building through, for instance, communications technology. Finding better ways to support such efforts and link them to international ones may be the most important frontier in preventive action. One interesting attempt to use information technology for this purpose is the Harvard-UN website on conflict prevention, which, among other activities, hosts closed (password-protected) global web conferences on prevention.[19] The first one, which for eight days in January and February 2001 discussed the challenges posed by the Maoist insurgency in Nepal, was notable not only for the wide participation but for the fact that the Nepali participants clearly saw international actors as mostly harmful, and at best irrelevant, to solving the problem, which few if any of them defined as "conflict prevention."[20]

These networks are promoting greater collaboration at the working level. Because they include not only private organizations but also practitioners and policymakers in international organizations and governments, they do not constitute solely a form of privatization of international affairs. An attempt to rely exclusively or excessively on NGOs would not succeed, as the experience of Sant' Egidio in Kosovo illustrates. For some efforts, not only donor funding but official political action is required. Sometimes even high-level engagement is needed. Networks and epistemic communities, consequently, do not constitute an adequate alternative to an effective global regime. They do not wield enough power, and they do not enjoy sufficient accountability. However, they can provide a second-best solution and a political base of support for efforts to strengthen official institutions.

Organizational Restructuring for Prevention: Warning, Response, and Accountability

Organizational changes cannot substitute for leadership, but without them policy changes remain mere rhetoric. Prevention must rely on daily, coordinated efforts that involve top leadership only at relatively rare moments. A model is beginning to emerge. The U.S. model of interagency coordination embodied in PDD 56 and the UN's Framework for Coordination Mechanism embody different aspects of these lessons. Both provide mechanisms for coordination but with insufficient mechanisms for accountability.

In addition to restructuring existing organizations, more effective prevention would also require new capacities. Most debate has revolved around crisis response and hence around proposals for new kinds of military forces, whether a UN rapid-reaction force, the EU's military force, or portions of the U.S. military that might be dedicated to peace operations rather than the traditional mission "to fight and win the nation's wars." The main need for prevention, however, is elsewhere: in creating, training, and sustaining corps of civilian monitors, police, and humanitarian workers, preferably drawn from all regions of the world and connected to regional bodies, to undertake preventive work under international auspices. Increasing preventive capacity by forming such bodies would change the decisionmaking process, as it would offer policymakers instruments they now lack and help them avoid the dilemmas of committing military forces that are either needed for other tasks or not appropriate to the task at hand.

Nonetheless, the decisionmaking and analytic processes will still need to be restructured. The fundamental reality of all organizations is that resources are limited, and the most precious and limited resource is the time of the top leadership. Immediate crises usually fully occupy the time of the highest echelons, which in turn demand support for those concerns from those lower down. Concerns with a shorter time frame tend to crowd out those with a longer time frame. Key dilemmas of focusing organizations on prevention include

—how to link warning to response;

—whether to establish a separate unit for prevention or "mainstream" it by mandating all line units to incorporate it into their work; and

—how to combine interagency or interorganizational cooperation and coordination with accountability in such a way that someone with adequate resources is clearly responsible.

In discussions of the organizational challenge of prevention, someone usually claims that it is difficult to reward people for prevention, because it is impossible to know what did not happen as a result of their efforts. Hence there are no political or professional incentives for officials to devote time or energy to prevention. Let me dismiss this issue before moving on to others. Prevention does not consist of unobservable counterfactuals, any more than does any other area of policy. No one could prove that nuclear deterrence had prevented any specific nuclear attack, but that did not prevent nuclear deterrence from being implemented. The goal of preventing a nuclear attack was considered an important enough goal to justify undertaking an extremely expensive and risky program in hopes of accomplishing it. The results, furthermore, could be observed in crisis management in the Cuban missile crisis, the Middle East, and elsewhere. Prevention of deadly conflict is similarly concrete. It consists of observable actions with observable results, even if one can never document exactly what would have happened in their absence. The problem of counterfactual hypotheses is endemic in social science and policy, both of which deal with nonreplicable events. It is not peculiar to or uniquely prominent in the problem of conflict prevention.[21]

Two opposing approaches to focusing organizations on prevention each have their own advantages and disadvantages. Given that daily tasks and crisis management tend to crowd out longer-term concerns, one solution is to create a separate office responsible solely for prevention. The World Bank did something analogous in a related field by establishing a Post-Conflict Unit. A dedicated unit, however, tends to become marginalized within an organization. Often, it is given a mandate without the resources to carry it out. Even if the unit does manage to carry out some preventive activities, other parts of the same organization may undertake policies that contradict it, often with more resources. The alternative is "mainstreaming." However, simply assigning people to integrate prevention with their regular work, exhorting them, and training them does not address the problem they face when they get back to their desks, unless prevention receives some dedicated institutional structure that creates accountability for carrying it out.

A hybrid system establishes an interagency forum that brings together sources of information and action officers from a variety of departments and links them to external networks. Such an institution will function effectively for prevention only if

—it is integrally linked to warning as a response mechanism;

—it meets regularly, not only when top leadership convenes it in response to a crisis; and

—someone is held accountable for its effectiveness.

The framework established by the U.S. government's Presidential Decision Directive 56, in May 1997, meets some of these criteria. It sets out procedures for dealing with "complex contingency operations," including peace implementation and foreign humanitarian assistance operations.[22] It addresses the same type of crises as conflict prevention does ("territorial disputes, armed ethnic conflicts, and civil wars that pose threats to regional and international peace") and notes that its procedures can help "develop strategies for early resolution of crises." Such "early resolution," however, is mentioned as one of several consequences of the PDD, not its primary goal.

The directive calls upon the Deputies Committee (the interagency committee consisting of the seconds-in-command of all agencies comprising the National Security Council) to form an Executive Committee (ExCom), bringing together all relevant agencies to oversee joint planning for an operation. One of the major difficulties in implementation is the divergence between military and civilian agencies' concepts of planning. The armed services find that the State Department and other civilian agencies have no process equivalent to the military's elaborate and well-funded process of planning, divided among strategic, operational, and tactical levels. This imbalance leaves the civilian agencies at a disadvantage, something that both the military and others would like to address. Presidential Decision Directive 56 continues the pursuit of "jointness" in operations that began with placing the military services under unified command with common systems of control and communication and joint planning. Despite the obstacles that any such interagency process faces, within the U.S. government the executive authority of the president is strong enough to impose an increasing level of coordination on these operations.

The gravest weakness of the process is its failure to distinguish prevention from crisis response and a lack of specific accountability. Only a decision of the Deputies Committee triggers the mechanism set up in PDD 56. Intelligence products like the atrocity watch list are not formally linked to the interagency policy process as a response mechanism. At one time, around

1997, the State Department convened a monthly meeting known as the Secretary's Initiative on Preventive Diplomacy, at which regional bureaus could raise concerns regularly for interagency follow-up, but the practice fell into desuetude. In December 1999, National Security Adviser Sandy Berger proposed that the Contingency Planning Interagency Working Group set up under PDD 56 meet regularly to examine the atrocities watch list and other indicators, but the process was not institutionalized.[23] The process might be improved by requiring regular meetings of an ExCom assigned the task of prevention to consider action on these products and other concerns.

The ExCom could also establish regular contact with NGOs. The government already consults NGOs and private analysts through the United States Institute of Peace and other mechanisms. The government could also establish more regular contact with networks like the Conflict Prevention and Resolution Forum, a monthly forum established by the same NGOs that set up the Great Lakes Policy Forum, to air more general preventive concerns. Such regular meetings already take place between InterAction (the private humanitarian organization umbrella group) and the humanitarian agencies. The U.S. government has set out on paper a framework for integrated response; it needs to make the framework more proactive by better linking it to warning and making deliberations on conflict prevention more regular. Finally, a specific official with adequate authority, not just a committee, needs to be made responsible for preventive action.

Though the UN Framework for Coordination Mechanism (FCM) partly resembles the U.S. government's interagency process, its failings are mirror images. The FCM focuses on prevention and integrates warning with response, but as a whole the mechanisms for interagency coordination and accountability are too weak to ensure implementation. The UN secretary general has far less authority over the UN than the president does over the U.S. government. Furthermore, the UN has far fewer resources and often finds itself unable to implement strategies that it devises.

The FCM was created in 1995, originally to promote better planning of peacekeeping missions; now, however, "the overall goal of the Framework Process is to produce a swift and integrated UN system-wide response in the form of a comprehensive preventive action strategy to potential crises."[24] The FCM includes a two-tiered structure like that set out in PDD 56. Whereas the latter has the Deputies Committee, the FCM has established the Framework Team, including senior managers from eleven participating organizations.[25] The Framework Team, unlike any entity concerned with prevention in the U.S. government, "normally meets monthly or even more often if needed to review and prioritize countries/situations of concern." According to UN internal memos on the FCM, "The criteria for nominating a country or situation is that . . . in the opinion of the desk officer, the situation presents a potential to develop into a complex emergency, conflict, or other circumstance where there may be a *prima facie* case for UN preventive action."[26] The team submits a proposed situation for examination by all other members, resulting in additional analysis and reporting from the field.

The Framework Team can then decide to convene a Country/Situation Review Meeting, including all Framework Team member organizations at the working level and also involving resident coordinators and others from the field. This meeting can "determine and recommend further courses of action which may include a range of coordination or preventive measures."[27] The review meeting's report then goes to the Framework Team for further action at the executive level, as needed.

The structure of the FCM aims at increasing ownership and jointness in both analysis and action. Opposition from member states has so far prevented the UN from establishing an intelligence or analysis unit. The Brahimi report recommends the establishment of such a unit, called EISAS, which would report to the Executive Committee on Peace and Security (ECPS).[28] The information to be analyzed by EISAS would come partly from UN development and humanitarian agencies present on the ground, and many host states oppose integrating those agencies into an intelligence or political unit that might lead to efforts directed against them. The framework process, however, to some extent turns this defect into a virtue. Agencies feed raw information into the policy process, then they analyze the reporting and make decisions together. Hence, though the UN badly needs greater analytic capacity, the framework process potentially integrates warning and response for prevention better than does PDD 56.

The FCM's major weakness is that of the UN. Especially because so many UN agencies have their own budgets, and because most field operations are funded by donors through voluntary contributions, the secretary general lacks authority to coordinate the agencies. The weakness of membership support for prevention in general and the FCM in particular also compromises its effectiveness. Sometimes a preventive strategy might require the UN to mobilize support among some member states for action directed at another. The FCM, however, was set up entirely by the secretariat without explicit authorization from the General Assembly, and the secretariat has not made public any of its operational documents. Many member states oppose bringing development and humanitarian agencies into an integrated structure for conflict warning and response, which might, they fear, lead to political conditionality on assistance.

The UN is also seeking to expand its contact with global civil society for conflict prevention. Through the UN conferences on population, environment, human rights, women's rights, and other issues, the UN has associated NGOs with the setting of standards and policy objectives, a process that forms part of the agenda of systemic prevention. Through a variety of other initiatives it is now trying to open up its more operational activities a bit more to global civil society. I have already mentioned the attempt to engage business and human rights organizations together through the Global Compact. Specifically to provide itself with access to better information on prevention, the UN has collaborated with efforts such as the conflict prevention website based at Harvard and the Conflict Prevention and Peace Forum. The former sets up informational resources on conflict on a dedicated website, including both a library and conferencing facilities. The interactive portion of the website, in particular, could facilitate inclusion of field and headquarters, as well as NGOs and independent analysts. The Conflict Prevention and Peace Forum provides the UN with access to independent experts and NGOs with direct knowledge of conflict situations. The British Department for International Development, which has emerged as a major supporter of efforts to strengthen UN capacity, funded the start-up of both projects.

Presidential Decision Directive 56 instructs U.S. government educational institutions to establish appropriate training programs, and the UN, through its Staff College in Turin, has inaugurated a training course in early warning and conflict prevention (also funded by the Department for International Development). The course's workshops, held in the field, are meant to strengthen the framework process by creating a stronger epistemic prevention community across agencies and departments, between field and headquarters, and also with NGOs, some of whose representatives have also participated.

Such efforts are not limited to the United States and UN. The EU has named conflict prevention as a key goal of its Common Foreign and Security Policy. It set up and then closed a Conflict Prevention Network to link it to academic expertise. The EU has identified dealing with "root causes" of conflict as its principal role.[29] Many other regional organizations and governments have established some institutional framework or program for prevention. At a series of regional consultations on the Brahimi report, participants from Africa, Latin America, and Asia expressed a clear preference for regional organizations, states, and civil society as agents for prevention, rather than the UN or other global actors.[30] If the results are not too visible, the effort is also not yet mature. Virtually all of these efforts were initiated after 1990, and most after 1995.

Politics and Leadership

Necessary as they are, neither organizational reforms nor a better-stocked "tool box" will prevent violent conflicts. The principal challenge of warning and prevention of civil wars and collapsed states lies either in showing how they impinge on those able to do something about them or increasing the capacity of those on whom they clearly impinge. Some international organizations, notably the UN, have embraced the prevention of mass violence and atrocity as a mission, but this goal remains marginal to how the United States, at least, defines its official interest in international affairs. As one study argues, "As a matter of practical action if not conviction, many policymakers in Europe and North America view the confinement of war to internal conflict, and the containment of humanitarian disasters to peripheral regions of the Third World, as the solution, not the problem."[31] The clear evidence that the abandonment of Afghanistan following the Soviet withdrawal helped nourish al-Qaida should place this outlook in question. Afghanistan is not a special case: al-Qaida and other such malign organizations draw their support from the long-standing conflicts over Palestine and Iraq, and they also exploit opportunities in other failed states and civil war situations, including Somalia, Yemen, and markets in conflict diamonds.

Nongovernmental organizations and others committed to the prevention or humanitarian agenda tend to cluster around the UN, the EU, and a few other international organizations, as if these were autonomous actors. Supporters and critics of the UN, respectively, call for or criticize "UN action," obscuring the extent to which this body remains largely a coordinator of national actions. The UN depends closely on decisions of its members—and despite the tensions in the relationship, especially on the United States, the world's largest economy, military power, and source of information. One might wish for a smoother partnership of these two institutions, but there are limits to how much it will improve. The United States will never treat the UN as Canada and Scandinavian countries do. Participation in international organizations augments the influence of small but wealthy countries, whereas for the United States the benefits of multilateralism inevitably compete with an option of unilateral action (or inaction) that other states do not have.[32] This superpower remains, at least in the eyes of its own citizens, a nation-state with particular interests, even if the unprecedented magnitude and scope of its power combined with the ideals of its founding make many around the world insist that it should—or hope that it will—behave as a global institution.

Polls show that Americans are generally willing to support global efforts, though without any deep or intense commitment, provided the burden is shared fairly with others,[33] but the Bush administration seems intent on renouncing any globalist perspective on the national interest, preferring to focus on narrowly defined security threats and economic interests.[34] During the 2000 presidential campaign, neither George W. Bush nor Al Gore showed any initiative in rethinking the United States' role. In the second presidential debate, both candidates supported the decision to remain aloof from the Rwandan genocide; and despite a question from the moderator about sending civilian peace monitors rather than the military to conflict areas, neither candidate could or would expand the discussion beyond the sterile debate about when or whether to send in the U.S. military. This debate seems archaic now that U.S. troops are engaged in Afghanistan and the United States is supporting UN and other allied efforts at "nation-building" there, but public debate has not yet drawn the more general conclusions.

The reluctance of the United States to put more of its power resources at the service of preventing violence in seemingly remote places hinders the development of a preventive regime from one side. From another, states that fear they might be the objects of prevention, or that worry that "prevention" could become a flag of convenience for intervention by the powerful, also resist such efforts. Only the immense pressure brought to bear by the United States after the attack on its own territory enabled it to create the fragile interventionist antiterrorism coalition. The deceptive triumphalism over Kosovo, portraying a limited-liability air offensive to preserve security in Europe and the credibility of NATO as a general precedent for military "humanitarian" intervention, intensified real fears and provided ammunition to regimes that also wished to insulate themselves. They recognize, if many of its proponents do not, that prevention is political. If a global regime for prevention means putting international institutions at the service of the political interests of the most powerful nations to intervene in others, many states will oppose it.

Partnership of the UN with regional actors, at least in cases not directly involving the security of the United States, might provide a more acceptable alternative, in that it might reduce fears of superpower domination, but it would at best complement, not replace, global efforts, just as private efforts can at best only complement official ones. Not all regions have the resources or political cohesion to carry out preventive action. States and societies may be too weak, impoverished, or undermined by disease—notably, HIV/AIDS. Political factors may impede the formation of stronger regional organizations or coalitions, as when a major state is too preponderant or at odds with its neighbors (India in South Asia) or is itself an object of concern (Indonesia, Nigeria, the DRC). The regions with the greatest ability to support preventive action are, almost by definition, those that least need it.

The hopes of the immediate post–cold-war era have given way to the anxieties of the age of globalization and terrorism. When the USSR and the United States ended their decades-long dispute, some imagined that great powers, now no longer at odds, would establish a more effective structure of global governance. The Security Council summit meeting that received Boutros Boutros-Ghali's *Agenda for Peace* symbolized that hope. However, competition among states continued, the loss of strategic value of whole areas of the world created opportunities for entrepreneurs of violence, and nations, though they became less isolated, seemed to become more selective in the ways they engaged.

The age of globalization or of the network society has itself given rise to new fears.[35] Parts of our own society are becoming increasingly linked to other parts of global society, and it can no longer be disputed that the effects of mass killing elsewhere can hardly be safely contained. Besides its role in nurturing terrorism, violence has also proved to be a major vector for the spread of HIV/AIDS. Mass movements of people and looting activities devastate valuable environmental and wildlife resources, from the gorilla reserves of Rwanda to the tropical hardwood forests of Indonesia. The toll on education and development and the loss of security accelerates the flight of desperate people risking their lives to crash through the borders of the United States and Europe. These effects may be harder to perceive, but they may be as vast as the damage perpetrated by terrorist attacks.

Even if foreign policy and security experts, by and large, still dismiss mass violence in poor countries as a mere humanitarian concern, a movement is growing around the world that is affecting not only the societies at risk but also the governments of all our major allies and consequently all the multilateral institutions through which the United States carries out so much of its global affairs. The devastated country of Afghanistan that provided a haven for Osama bin Laden is not a unique case but the symbol of a global problem.

The threat of mass violence and killing constitutes one of several inter-linked global threats that will be confronted only through cooperative efforts. In the next decade, HIV/AIDS and other epidemics, partly spread by violent conflict, are likely to kill more people than political violence in Africa and, soon enough, in parts of Asia as well. Climate change and deforestation appear to be spreading mosquito-borne and other diseases into new regions. Global warming may already be a factor in the unprecedented droughts that threaten famine in parts of Asia and Africa and is likely to stress some of the world's most vulnerable parts even further. These processes reinforce one another in ways that are predictable in general if not in their specifics.

Together with the stresses and inequities triggered by the latest stage of economic globalization—the combination of concentrated wealth creation with greater insecurity and marginalization for many—these processes add up to a challenge intimately connected to that posed by terrorists. The new gen-eration of terrorist organizations exploits these global linkages and networks just as do other forms of NGOs. Political violence is largely a response to the stresses of globalization, whether by canny leaders, opportunistic armed groups, idealistic rebels, or panicked masses. That violence forms part of our modern condition, not an irrational leftover from a "traditional" past. The stresses that provoke it pose tricky problems of collective action and interna-tional cooperation, especially burden sharing, and they require new capacities that could be almost as difficult to create as national missile defense.

Reducing the incidence of political violence requires, as I have argued, a range of actions targeted at both actors and institutional structures at differ-ent levels of organization of the international system. External intervention and social engineering have their limits, both empirically and ethically, and it is hence even more important to focus on what I have called "systemic pre-vention"—changes in global institutions and processes that affect the proclivity and capacity for violence of many societies. These include mon-itoring and regulating sales of commodities that fund conflict; improving transparency of and control over the trade in small arms and light weapons; revisiting the international legal regime for prohibited drugs so as to reduce the illegal superprofits on these commodities; better regulating interna-tional banking and financial practices to improve controls over illegal transactions and the looting of states by corrupt rulers; and complementing the globalization of capital flows and trade with an increasingly global safety net and political voice for individuals, groups, and societies vulnerable to the resultant displacement and insecurity. International financial institutions establish a global regime for development— what is commonly known as "globalization"—and that regime needs to respond to the stresses it causes. International institutions can also incorporate humane standards of behavior into their functioning both through institutionalized sanctions, as in the International Criminal Court, and incentives, as in conditions for membership in organizations that provide aid and other benefits to members.

Regions and states that suffer more than others from the stresses that lead to violence require targeted attention, most of all to support efforts by some political forces there to develop their own capacities for accountable governance and regional cooperation. Though such societies and regions need "development," they in particular need capacities to deal with natural resource endowments that are so often associated with corruption and violent conflict, with disparities among identity groups exacerbated by certain styles of economic growth, and with the transparent management of public resources. Politically, outsiders should not destabilize fragile states with pressure to adopt any specific model of democracy but should, rather, support indigenous experiments and efforts, especially concentrating on helping citizens strengthen the state's more benign capacities—public order, accountability, and service provision, in particular. Regional cooperation in both development and governance becomes increasingly vital as transnational networks play larger roles in economic development, economic decay, governance, and armed conflict.

As violent conflict starts to escalate, it becomes ever more difficult to address those challenges of development or governance. It is remarkable how underdeveloped are international capacities to inhibit such escalation, compared with the highly developed military capacities to meet force with force. Only a few groups and envoys regularly engage in the various forms of mediation and capacity building that help societies manage conflict peacefully. Missions to monitor human rights violations or conflict situations, whether through political or civilian policing activities, have to be assembled from scratch for every case, and few people are available or trained for such roles. Increasing the ability of states, the UN, and regional organizations to mobilize and deploy such missions registers high on the agenda for preventing armed conflict.

International actors are similarly in need of greater ability to impose targeted sanctions, especially financial ones, against individuals or groups escalating bloodshed, including terrorists. Broad-gauged sanctions are of limited use and have too many unintended consequences for innocent victims, but they are far easier to impose. Incentives, which seem more costly, are also underused, though they have proved their value, especially when broad incentives are combined with targeted sanctions, as in Serbia-Yugoslavia. The use of force in "humanitarian intervention" is a moral imperative when genocide is under way, as in Rwanda, but it is hardly a preventive measure. It is as likely to accelerate escalation as to end it, especially when it is applied waveringly and inconsistently.

Hard as these measures might sound when they are listed so summarily, they are even harder in practice. Violent conflicts are not irrational eruptions to be contained by calmer and wiser powers but strategic choices in an international system still predicated on violence as the ultimate measure of power and even legitimacy. The very goal this book sets itself—the prevention of violent conflict—implicitly creates incentives for those with grievances to turn to the use of force because they perceive that only then will actors concerned with security pay attention to their claims. Even then, unless violence menaces the interests of those with the most power, its victims may largely be ignored or offered mild palliatives. And when powerful interests are indeed engaged, they are as likely to compete as to cooperate. Preventing violent conflict is not a purely humanitarian goal; it is part of an agenda for stable management of global affairs, as political an agenda as any other and one that is as unlikely to coalesce a consensus as any other high-stakes contest.

Such a goal forms part of a liberal agenda of global governance. That agenda, like other schemes for the improvement of the human condition, is full of pitfalls and is unlikely to be realized as envisioned. The need for accountability is one major concern I have signaled, but there are others. Many in the military realize that the conflicts dealt with here are those their institution will confront in the future, and they welcome attempts to forestall them. Despite the rejection of "nation building" or humanitarianism as foreign policy goals by some on the right, I have found throughout my work that concern with these issues need not be confined to one side of the political spectrum. Even before September 11, John McCain, in the Republican presidential primary debate in New Hampshire on October 28, 1999, declared his desire "to inspire a generation of Americans to commit themselves to a cause greater than their self-interest. There are great causes in the world, where there are hungry children, where [there are] seniors without shelter, and where people are killing each other because of ethnic and tribal hatreds."[36] One may quarrel with the diagnosis but not with the priorities. Even if we cannot end violence or deprivation, we can resist them. The deaths of millions of people are not just troublesome images on an electronic screen; for millions of our fellow human beings, they are the end of life, of the only life they know with certainty. These people are part of our world, not just in imagination but also more and more through countless encounters and interactions. The despair they feel and the blood they spill can indeed overflow our doorstep. They challenge our policy, they challenge our humanity, and they challenge the uses to which we put our wealth and power.

Notes

Chapter 1

1. Leslie H. Gelb, "Quelling the Teacup Wars," *Foreign Affairs*, vol. 73, no. 6 (1994), pp. 2–6.

2. Michael E. Brown and Richard N. Rosecrance, eds., *The Costs of Conflict: Prevention and Cure in the Global Arena* (Lanham, Md.: Rowman and Littlefield for the Carnegie Commission on Preventing Deadly Conflict, 1999), especially the table on p. 225. This multiauthor study uses a careful methodology, comparing several types of counterfactuals in a total of nine potential or actual conflicts. For earlier estimates of the effects on the directly affected societies, see Michael Cranna, ed., *The True Cost of Conflict: Seven Recent Wars and Their Effects on Society* (New York: New Press and Saferworld, 1994).

3. Katherine Q. Seelye, "Clinton Blames Milosevic, Not Fate, for Bloodshed," *New York Times*, May 14, 1999, p. A12.

4. Thomas L. Friedman, *The Lexus and the Olive Tree: Understanding Globalization* (Farrar, Straus and Giroux, 1999), especially pp. 93–119.

5. Margaret E. Keck and Kathryn Sikkink, *Activists beyond Borders: Advocacy Networks in International Politics* (Cornell University Press, 1998); William S. Reno, *Warlord Politics and African States* (Boulder: Lynne Rienner, 1998); Friedman, *The Lexus and the Olive Tree*; Martha Finnemore, *National Interests in International Society* (Cornell University Press, 1996); Thomas Risse-Kappen, ed., *Bringing Transnational Relations Back In: Non-State Actors, Domestic Structures, and International Institutions* (Cambridge University Press, 1995).

6. Hugh Miall, *The Peacemakers: Peaceful Settlement of Disputes since 1945* (St. Martin's, 1992).

7. Carnegie Commission on Preventing Deadly Conflict, *Preventing Deadly Conflict: Final Report, with Executive Summary* (New York: Carnegie Corporation of New York, December 1997), p. xviii.

8. Anthony Giddens, *The Nation-State and Violence*, vol. 2 of *A Contemporary Critique of Historical Materialism* (University of California Press, 1987).

9. Thomas Friedman, "The New Human Rights," *New York Times*, July 30, 1999, p. A19.

10. *Nomination of Madeleine Korbel Albright, of the District of Columbia, to Be Secretary of State,* Hearings before the Senate Foreign Relations Committee, 105 Cong. 1 sess., January 8, 1997, p. S598.

Chapter 2

1. The estimate of numbers of deaths comes from the Carnegie Commission on Preventing Deadly Conflict, *Preventing Deadly Conflict: Final Report* (New York: Carnegie Corporation of New York, 1997). Besides the difficulty of obtaining accurate data, the meaning of the concept is difficult to define. The strictest definition would include only those killed by weapons; others, however, include excess mortality owing to the destruction of infrastructure. A survey conducted by the International Rescue Committee, published after the Carnegie Commission report, estimates that from 1996 to 2001, 2.5 million people died in the eastern provinces of the Democratic Republic of the Congo directly or indirectly as a result of the fighting in that region (International Rescue Committee, "IRC Study Points to Horrific Death Toll in Eastern Congo: 2.5 Million 'Excess' Deaths in Thirty-three Months of Unrest," May 8, 2001). Inclusion of such estimates would push the total much higher. See also International Institute for Strategic Studies, "The 2000 Chart of Armed Conflict," in *The Military Balance, 2000–2001* (Oxford University Press, 2000).

2. Ludwig Wittgenstein, *Philosophical Investigations,* translated by G. E. M. Anscombe (Oxford: Blackwell, 1967).

3. For similar lists, see Michael S. Lund, *Preventing Violent Conflicts: A Strategy for Preventive Diplomacy* (Washington: United States Institute of Peace, 1996), pp. 49–50; and Raimo Väyrynen, "Complex Humanitarian Emergencies: Concepts and Issues," in *Analysis,* vol. 1 of E. Wayne Nafziger, Frances Stewart, and Raimo Väyrynen, eds., *War, Hunger, and Displacement* (Oxford University Press, 2000), pp. 43–89.

4. Ted Robert Gurr, "Minorities, Nationalists, and Ethnopolitical Conflict," in Chester A. Crocker and Fen Osler Hampson, eds., with Pamela Aall, *Managing Global Chaos: Sources of and Responses to International Conflict* (Washington: United States Institute of Peace, 1996), pp. 53–78; Ted Robert Gurr, "Ethnic Warfare on the Wane," *Foreign Affairs,* vol. 79, no. 3 (2000), pp. 52–64; Ted Robert Gurr, *Minorities at Risk: A Global View of Ethnopolitical Conflicts* (Washington: United States Institute of Peace, 1993).

5. Donald Horowitz, *Ethnic Groups in Conflict* (University of California Press, 1985).

6. Interviews (with confidential informants), Bujumbura, October 1998.

7. Peter Wallensteen and Margareta Sollenberg, "Armed Conflict, 1989–1998," *Journal of Peace Research,* vol. 36, no. 5 (1999), pp. 593–606.

8. Kalevi J. Holsti, *The State, War, and the State of War* (Cambridge University Press, 1996); Martin van Creveld, *The Transformation of War* (Free Press, 1991); Peter Wallensteen, ed., *Preventing Violent Conflicts: Past Record and Future Challenges* (Uppsala, Sweden: Uppsala University, Department of Peace and Conflict

Research, 1998); Michael Mandelbaum, *The Dawn of Peace in Europe* (New York: Twentieth Century Fund, 1996); Bruce Russett, *Grasping the Democratic Peace: Principles for a Post–Cold War World* (Princeton University Press, 1993); Barry Buzan, *People, States, and Fear: The National Security Problem in International Relations* (Brighton, England: Wheatsheaf, 1983); Mary Kaldor, *New and Old Wars: Organized Violence in a Global Era* (Cambridge: Polity, 1999).

9. Yahya Sadowski, *The Myth of Global Chaos* (Brookings, 1998).

10. Kaldor, *New and Old Wars*.

11. Myron Weiner, "Bad Neighbors, Bad Neighborhoods: An Inquiry into the Causes of Refugee Flows," *International Security*, vol. 21, no. 1 (1996), pp. 5–42; Raimo Väyrynen, "Regional Conflict Formations: An Intractable Problem of International Relations," *Journal of Peace Research*, vol. 21, no. 4 (1984), pp. 337–59; Buzan, *People, States, and Fear*, pp. 186-229; David A. Lake, "Regional Security Complexes: A Systems Approach," in David A. Lake and Patrick M. Morgan, eds., *Regional Orders: Building Security in a New World* (Pennsylvania State University Press, 1997), pp. 45–67; Peter Wallensteen and Margareta Sollenberg, "Armed Conflict and Regional Conflict Complexes," *Journal of Peace Research*, vol. 35, no. 5 (1998), pp. 621–34. Väyrynen develops the idea of "regional emergencies" in "Complex Humanitarian Emergencies."

12. Taylor B. Seybolt, "Major Armed Conflicts," Stockholm International Peace Research Institute Yearbook 2001, *Armaments, Disarmament, and International Security* (Oxford University Press, 2001), chap. 1; Wallensteen and Sollenberg, "Armed Conflict and Regional Conflict Complexes."

13. François Jean and Jean-Christophe Rufin, eds., *Économie des guerres civiles* (Paris: Hachette, 1996).

14. Barnett R. Rubin, "The Political Economy of War and Peace in Afghanistan," *World Development*, vol. 28, no. 10 (2000), pp. 1789–803.

15. Gerald B. Helman and Steven R. Ratner, "Saving Failed States," *Foreign Policy*, no. 89 (Winter 1992–93), pp. 3–20; Robert H. Jackson and Carl G. Rosberg, "Why Africa's Weak States Persist," *World Politics*, vol. 35 (October 1982), pp. 1–24; Robert H. Jackson, *Quasi-States: Sovereignty, International Relations, and the Third World* (Cambridge University Press, 1990); Joel S. Migdal, *Strong Societies, Weak States: State Society Relations and State Capabilities in the Third World* (Princeton University Press, 1988); William S. Reno, *Warlord Politics in African States* (Boulder: Lynne Rienner, 1998).

16. Barnett R. Rubin, "Russian Hegemony and State Breakdown in the Periphery: Causes and Consequences of the Civil War in Tajikistan," in Barnett R. Rubin and Jack Snyder, eds., *Post-Soviet Political Order: Conflict and State Building* (London: Routledge, 1998), especially pp. 143–52.

17. Michael Ignatieff, *Blood and Belonging: Journeys into the New Nationalism* (Toronto: Penguin, 1994), cited in Janie Leatherman, William DeMars, Patrick D. Gaffney, and Raimo Väyrynen, *Breaking Cycles of Violence: Conflict Prevention in Intrastate Crises* (West Hartford, Conn.: Kumarian, 1999), p. 64; Barry R. Posen,

"The Security Dilemma and Ethnic Conflict," *Survival,* vol. 35, no. 1 (Spring 1993), pp. 27–47.

18. Barbara Harff, *Genocide and Human Rights: International Legal and Political Issues,* Monograph Series in World Affairs, vol. 20, bk. 3 (University of Denver, Graduate School of International Studies, 1994); Helen Fein, *Genocide: A Sociological Perspective* (Newbury Park, Calif.: Sage, 1993).

19. Alain Destexhe, *Rwanda and Genocide in the Twentieth Century,* translated by Alison Marschner (New York University Press, 1995); David Rieff, "Hell and Humanitarianism," *New Republic,* December 7, 1998, pp. 36–42.

20. Physicians for Human Rights, "Statement on Genocide in Kosovo," National Public Radio editorial, April 8, 1999.

21. Aryeh Neier, *War Crimes: Brutality, Genocide, Terror, and the Struggle for Justice* (New York: Times Books, 1998).

22. Major websites dealing with humanitarian emergencies are Reliefweb (www.reliefweb.int), maintained by the UN's Office for the Coordination of Humanitarian Affairs; the United Nations High Commissioner for Refugees site (www.unhcr.ch); and the International Committee of the Red Cross site (www.icrc.org).

23. Väyrynen, "Complex Humanitarian Emergencies," pp. 57–76.

24. Michael Ignatieff, *The Warrior's Honor: Ethnic War and the Modern Conscience* (London: Chatto and Windus, 1998).

25. An early work in this field, so early that it is often forgotten, was François Jean, *L'Ethiopie: Le bon usage de la famine* (Paris: Médecins sans Frontières, 1985). See also Rakiya Omaar and Alex de Waal, "Humanitarianism Unbound? Current Dilemmas Facing Multi-mandate Relief Operations in Political Emergencies," Africa Rights Discussion Paper 5 (London: Africa Rights, November 1994); Alain Destexhe, *L'humanitaire impossible, ou, Deux siècles d'ambigüité* (Paris: A. Colin, 1993); Rony Brauman, *Humanitaire: Le dilemme* (Paris: Textuel, 1996); François Jean, "Aide humanitaire et economie de guerre," in François Jean and Jean-Christophe Rufin, eds., *Économie des guerres civiles* (Paris: Hachette, 1996), pp. 543–89.

26. Kenneth Neal Waltz, *Man, the State, and War* (Columbia University Press, 1962).

27. Czechoslovakia and Ethiopia also divided during the same period, for reasons also linked to the end of the cold war, but without such pervasive geopolitical effects.

28. Lund, *Preventing Violent Conflicts.*

29. See, for instance, Mark Duffield's précis of the career of Jonas Savimbi, in "Globalization, Transborder Trade, and War Economies," in Mats Berdal and David M. Malone, eds., *Greed and Grievance: Economic Agendas in Civil Wars* (Boulder: Lynne Rienner, 2000), pp. 69–89.

30. Gurr, "Ethnic Warfare on the Wane"; Barnett R. Rubin, "Conclusion: Managing Normal Instability," in Barnett R. Rubin and Jack Snyder, eds., *Post-Soviet Political Order: Conflict and State Building* (London: Routledge, 1998), pp. 162–79.

31. Daniel Yergin, *The Commanding Heights: The Battle between Government and the Marketplace That Is Remaking the Modern World* (Simon and Schuster, 1998).

32. Thomas L. Friedman, *The Lexus and Olive Tree: Understanding Globalization* (Farrar, Straus and Giroux, 1999).

33. David Ricardo, *On the Principles of Political Economy and Taxation* (London: John Murray, 1817), chap. 7.

34. United Nations, *Report of the Panel of Experts on the Illegal Exploitation of Natural Resources and Other Forms of Wealth of the Democratic Republic of the Congo,* S/2001/357, April 12, 2001.

35. United Nations Development Program, *Human Development Report 2000* (Oxford University Press, 2000), pp. 3–4, 6.

36. United Nations Development Program, *Human Development Report 1997* (Oxford University Press, 1997), pp. 3, 7, 9.

37. Paul Collier and Anke Hoeffler, "Justice-Seeking and Loot-Seeking in Civil War," World Bank, February 17, 1999 (www.worldbank.org/research/conflict/papers/justice.htm [May 3, 2002]); Paul Collier and Anke Hoeffler, "Greed and Grievance in Civil War," World Bank, October 21, 2001 (www.worldbank.org/research/conflict/papers/greedandgrievance.htm [May 3, 2002]); Daniel C. Esty, Jack A. Goldstone, Ted Robert Gurr, Pamela T. Surko, and Alan N. Unger, "State Failure Task Force Report," working paper, Science Applications International Corporation, McLean, Va., 1995.

38. Anne-Marie Gardner, "Diagnosing Conflict: What Do We Know?" in Fen Osler Hampson and David M. Malone, eds., *From Reaction to Prevention: Opportunities for the UN System in the New Millennium* (Boulder: Lynne Rienner, 2002), pp. 15–40; John L. Davies and Ted Robert Gurr, eds., *Preventive Measures: Building Risk Assessment and Crisis Early Warning Systems* (Lanham, Md.: Rowman and Littlefield, 1998); Esty et al., "State Failure Task Force Report"; Daniel C. Esty, Jack A. Goldstone, Ted Robert Gurr, Pamela T. Surko, and Alan N. Unger, *State Failure Task Force Report: Phase II Findings* (McLean, Va.: Science Applications International Corporation, 1998); several contributions in Ted R. Gurr and Barbara Harff, eds., *Early Warning of Communal Conflicts and Genocide: Linking Empirical Research to International Responses,* Monograph Series on Governance and Conflict Resolution 5 (United Nations University Press, 1996), especially Barbara Harff, "Early Warning of Potential Genocide: The Cases of Rwanda, Burundi, Bosnia, and Abkhazia," pp. 47–78; Ted Robert Gurr and Will H. Moore, "Ethnopolitical Rebellion: A Cross-Sectional Analysis of the 1980s with Risk Assessments for the 1990s," *American Journal of Political Science,* vol. 41, no. 4 (1997), pp. 1079–103; A. J. Jongman and A. P. Schmid, *Monitoring Human Rights: Manual for Assessing Country Performance* (Leiden [Netherlands] University, Faculty of Social Sciences, Interdisciplinary Research Program on Root Causes of Human Rights Violations, 1994); *Early Warning of Communal Conflict and Conflict Management,* Proceedings from a Workshop Held at the Center for International Development and Conflict Management, University of Maryland, November 5–6, 1993, *Journal of Ethno-Development,* vol. 4 (July 1994);

Pauline H. Baker and John A. Ausink, "State Collapse and Ethnic Violence: Toward a Predictive Model," *Parameters,* vol. 26 (Spring 1996), pp. 19–36; Jürgen Dedring, "Social-Political Indicators for Early Warning Purposes," in Kumar Rupesinghe and Michiko Kuroda, eds., *Early Warning and Conflict Resolution* (St. Martin's, 1992); Susanne Schmeidl, "Exploring the Causes of Forced Migration: A Pooled Analysis, 1971–1990," *Social Science Quarterly,* vol. 78, no. 2 (1997), pp. 284–308.

39. These are the terms used by Leatherman and her colleagues in *Breaking Cycles of Violence,* but they have equivalents in most of the schema. Lund, in *Preventing Violent Conflicts,* presents such an analysis, which he develops further with John Prendergast in *Preventing and Mitigating Violent Conflict: A Practitioner's Handbook* (Washington: Creative Associates, 1997).

40. Charles Tilley, *From Mobilization to Revolution* (Reading, Mass.: Addison-Wesley, 1978); Ted Robert Gurr, *Why Men Rebel* (Princeton University Press, 1970); Collier and Hoeffler, "Justice-Seeking and Loot-Seeking."

41. Frances Stewart, "The Root Causes of Humanitarian Emergencies," in *Analysis,* vol. 1 of E. Wayne Nafziger, Frances Stewart, and Raimo Väyrynen, eds., *War, Hunger, and Displacement* (Oxford University Press, 2000), pp. 1–41.

42. Collier and Hoeffler, "Greed and Grievance in Civil War," and other papers at the World Bank website (www.worldbank.org/research/conflict/papers). See also Berdal and Malone, *Greed and Grievance.*

43. Stephen John Stedman, "Spoiler Problems in Peace Processes," *International Security,* vol. 22, no. 2 (1977), pp. 5–53, p. 5; Collier and Hoeffler, "Justice-Seeking and Loot-Seeking."

44. Samuel P. Huntington, *The Clash of Civilizations and the Remaking of World Order* (Simon and Schuster, 1996).

45. Anthony Lake, "Confronting Backlash States," *Foreign Affairs,* vol. 73, no. 2 (1994), pp. 45–55.

46. Collier and Hoeffler, "Greed and Grievance in Civil War."

47. See, for instance, the analysis of how institutional design could help prevent conflict in Macedonia in Steven L. Burg, "Nationalism and Civic Identity: Ethnic Models for Macedonia and Kosovo," in Barnett R. Rubin, ed., *Cases and Strategies for Preventive Action,* vol. 2 of *Preventive Action Reports* (New York: The Century Foundation Press, 1998), pp. 23–45.

48. See, for instance, the discussion in Leatherman et al., *Breaking Cycles of Violence,* pp. 73–94.

49. Ibid., pp. 86–92.

50. This account and the lists are taken from John L. Davies and Barbara Harff, with Anne L. Speca, "Dynamic Data for Conflict Early Warning," in John L. Davies and Ted Robert Gurr, eds., *Preventive Measures: Building Risk Assessment and Crisis Early Warning Systems* (Lanham, Md.: Rowman and Littlefield, 1998), pp. 83–84.

51. One example that did not provoke the reaction it should have was the repression unleashed by the regime of President Juvénal Habyarimana of Rwanda after the invasion by the Rwandan Patriotic Front in 1990. The small-scale localized killings

organized by the regime prefigured the later genocide. See Commission internationale d'enquête sur les violations des droits de l'homme au Rwanda depuis le 1er octobre 1990, *Rapport de la commission internationale d'enquête sur les violations des droits de l'homme au Rwanda depuis le 1er Octobre 1990: Rapport final* (Paris: Fédération internationale des droits de l'homme [FIDH], 1993).

52. Human Rights Watch, *Playing the Communal Card: Communal Violence and Human Rights* (New York, 1995).

53. For the most detailed account yet available for any contemporary conflict, see Alison Des Forges, *Leave None to Tell the Story: Genocide in Rwanda* (New York: Human Rights Watch, 1999).

54. Davies and Harff, with Speca, "Dynamic Data," pp. 83–84.

55. Ahmedou Ould Abdallah, *Burundi on the Brink, 1993–1995: A UN Special Envoy Reflects on Preventive Diplomacy* (Washington: United States Institute of Peace, 2000); Michael S. Lund, Barnett R. Rubin, and Fabienne Hara, "Learning from Burundi's Failed Democratic Transition, 1993–1996: Did International Initiatives Match the Problem?" in Barnett R. Rubin, ed., *Cases and Strategies for Preventive Action,* vol. 2 of *Preventive Action Reports* (New York: The Century Foundation Press, 1998), pp. 47–92.

56. Nick Megoran, "Calming the Ferghana Valley Experts," *Central Asia Monitor,* vol. 8, no. 5 (2000), pp. 20–25.

Chapter 3

1. Numbers of victims are, of course, highly contested in this region. Alison Des Forges (*Leave None to Tell the Story: Genocide in Rwanda* [New York: Human Rights Watch, 1999]) accepts a figure of about 500,000 killed in Rwanda. Gérard Prunier (*The Rwanda Crisis: History of a Genocide* [Columbia University Press, 1995], p. 304) estimates that between 800,000 and 850,000 were killed. Howard Adelman ("Difficulties in Early Warning: Networking and Conflict Management," in Klaas van Walraven, ed., *Early Warning and Conflict Prevention: Limitations and Possibilities* [The Hague: Kluwer Law International, 1998], p. 53, n. 6) thinks that even figures in excess of a million may be justified.

2. For an application of a set of indicators to Burundi, see Michael S. Lund, Barnett R. Rubin, and Fabienne Hara, "Learning from Burundi's Failed Democratic Transition, 1993–1996: Did International Initiatives Match the Problem?" in Barnett R. Rubin, ed., *Cases and Strategies for Preventive Action,* vol. 2 of *Preventive Action Reports* (New York: The Century Foundation Press, 1998).

A World Bank project estimates that in the 1990s Zaire had a higher risk of civil war than any other country (Paul Collier and Anke Hoeffler, "Aid, Policy, and Peace," World Bank working paper, August 17, 2000 [www.worldbank.org/research/conflict/papers/aidpolicy.htm (May 4, 2002)]).

3. United Nations Development Program, *Human Development Report 2000* (Oxford University Press, 2000), p. 160.

4. Mahmood Mamdani, *When Victims Become Killers: Colonialism, Nativism, and the Genocide in Rwanda* (Princeton University Press, 2001).

5. Ibid.

6. James Scott, *Seeing Like a State: How Certain Schemes to Improve the Human Condition Have Failed* (Yale University Press, 1998).

7. René Lemarchand, *Burundi: Ethnic Conflict and Genocide* (Cambridge University Press, 1996); Jason S. Abrams, "Burundi: Anatomy of an Ethnic Conflict," *Survival,* vol. 37, no. 1 (1995), pp. 144–64; David Callahan, *Unwinnable Wars: American Power and Ethnic Conflict* (Hill and Wang, 1997).

8. Mamdani, *When Victims Become Killers.*

9. Peter Uvin, *Aiding Violence: The Development Enterprise in Rwanda* (West Hartford, Conn.: Kumarian, 1998).

10. The agreements were finalized on August 3, 1993, but were backdated to April 7, 1992. Most of the government consisted of moderate Hutus opposed to Habyarimana. See Astri Suhrke and Bruce Jones, "Preventive Diplomacy in Rwanda: Failure to Act or Failure of Actions?" in Bruce W. Jentleson, ed., *Opportunities Missed, Opportunities Seized: Preventive Diplomacy in the Post–Cold War World* (Lanham, Md.: Rowman and Littlefield, 2000), pp. 238–64. Jean-Pierre Mugabe ("Declaration on the Shooting Down of the Aircraft Carrying Rwandan President Juvénal Habyarimana and Burundi President Cyprien Ntaryamira on April 6, 1994" [April 21, 2000]) claims that the RPF also planned to sabotage the accords and ordered the downing of the presidential plane. Thanks to Carole Collins for making this available. See www.afroamerica.net/habyara_ass_mugabetest1.html.

11. UPRONA stands for Parti de l'Unité pour le Progrès National (National Unity and Progress Party), and FRODEBU for Front pour la Démocratie au Burundi (Front for Democracy in Burundi). It is not quite accurate to state that UPRONA is predominantly Tutsi: its principal leader (though perhaps a figurehead) and many of its members of parliament were Hutus, who constituted the vast majority of the population. Virtually all Tutsi support either UPRONA or smaller Tutsi extremist parties, whereas the support for FRODEBU is nearly all Hutu (though some prominent Ganwa are active in the party). The most important Tutsi "party" is the army, not UPRONA.

12. On the Rwandan genocide, see Prunier, *The Rwanda Crisis;* Philip Gourevitch, *We Wish to Inform You that Tomorrow We Will Be Killed with Our Families: Stories from Rwanda* (Farrar, Straus and Giroux, 1998); Des Forges, *Leave None to Tell the Story;* Mamdani, *When Victims Become Killers;* Howard Adelman and Astri Suhrke, with Bruce Jones, *Early Warning and Conflict Management,* vol. 2 of *The International Response to Conflict and Genocide: Lessons from the Rwanda Experience* (Copenhagen: Joint Evaluation of Emergency Assistance to Rwanda, 1996).

13. For a detailed analysis of the failure of warning, see Adelman and Suhrke, with Jones, *Early Warning and Conflict Management;* and Suhrke and Jones, "Preventive Diplomacy in Rwanda." See also United Nations, *Report of the Independent Inquiry*

into the Actions of the United Nations during the 1994 Genocide in Rwanda, S/1999/1257, December 16, 1999.

14. United Nations, *Report of the Independent Inquiry into the Actions of the United Nations during the 1994 Genocide in Rwanda;* Belgian Senate, *Parliamentary Commission of Inquiry Regarding the Events in Rwanda,* 1997–98 session, December 6, 1997; French National Assembly, *Rapport d'information déposé en application de l'article 145 du règlement par la mission d'information de la commission de la défense nationale et des forces armées et de la commission des affaires étrangères, sur les opérations militaires menées par la France, d'autres pays et l'ONU au Rwanda entre 1990 et 1994,* December 15, 1998; Organization of African Unity, "International Panel of Eminent Personalities to Investigate the 1994 Genocide in Rwanda and the Surrounding Events," July 7, 2000.

15. "Clinton Meets Rwanda Genocide Survivors," CNN World News, March 25, 1998 (www.cnn.com/World/9803/25/rwanda.clinton [May 4, 2002]).

16. Michael Ignatieff, *The Warrior's Honor: Ethnic War and The Modern Conscience* (London: Chatto and Windus, 1998), pp. 84–89.

17. For a more detailed analysis, see Lund, Rubin, and Hara, "Learning from Burundi's Failed Democratic Transition, 1993–1996."

18. See table 1 (pp. 153–57) in Fabienne Hara, "Burundi: A Case of Parallel Diplomacy," in Chester A. Crocker and Fen Osler Hampson, eds., with Pamela Aall, *Herding Cats: Multiparty Mediation in a Complex World* (Washington: United States Institute of Peace, 1999), pp. 139–58.

19. Janie Leatherman, William DeMars, Patrick D. Gaffney, and Raimo Väyrynen, *Breaking Cycles of Violence: Conflict Prevention in Intrastate Crises* (West Hartford, Conn.: Kumarian, 1999), pp. 11, 24, 125, 202–03, 217 n. 1; Callahan, *Unwinnable Wars,* p. 125.

20. The main Tanzania-based group was PALIPEHUTU, the Parti de la Libération du Peuple Hutu (Party for the Liberation of the Hutu People), which professed an explicitly "ethnic" agenda. The newer group, founded by Léonard Nyangoma, minister of the interior in the first FRODEBU government, was the CNDD (Le Conseil National de Défense de la Démocratie [National Council for Defense of Democracy]). The CNDD's military forces, the FDD (Forces de la Défense de la Démocratie [Force for the Defense of Democracy]), split from the CNDD in 1998 under the leadership of Jean-Bosco Ndayikengurukiye.

21. The report finally came out in 1996 (United Nations, *Letter Dated 96/07/25 from the Secretary-General Addressed to the President of the Security Council,* S/1996/682). It was submitted at the end of July, just as a military coup replaced President Sylvestre Ntibantunganya with Pierre Buyoya. The UN delayed release of the report for fear of contributing to destabilization of Burundi as the coup was occurring, a decision criticized by human rights organizations.

22. Human Rights Watch, *Rwanda: Rearming with Impunity* (New York, 1995).

23. InterAction, "U.S. Coalition Warns of Escalating Violence in Central Africa; Hundreds of Thousands More People Could Die in Burundi, Rwanda," news release, July 13, 1995, Washington.

24. United Nations, *Letter of the Secretary-General to the Security Council on the Situation in Burundi*, S/1995/1068, December 29, 1995.

25. The mission consisted of Fabienne Hara and Michael Lund. The findings of this mission are reported in Lund, Rubin, and Hara, "Learning from Burundi's Failed Democratic Transition, 1993–1996."

26. On the sanctions, see International Crisis Group, "Burundi under Siege," report, Brussels, April 28, 1998.

27. Hara, "Burundi: A Case of Parallel Diplomacy"; International Crisis Group, "Burundi under Siege"; International Crisis Group, "Burundi's Peace Process: The Road from Arusha," report, Brussels, July 20, 1998.

28. The sponsors of the Burundi Policy Forum had already (as of January 1997) renamed it the Great Lakes Policy Forum, in recognition of the growing interdependence of conflict and peacemaking in the region.

29. Mamdani, *When Victims Become Killers.*

30. Human Rights Watch, "Democratic Republic of Congo: What Kabila Is Hiding: Civilian Killings and Impunity in Congo," report, New York, October 1997; Marie Beatrice Umutesi, *Fuir ou mourir au Zaïre: Le vécu d'une refugiée Rwandaise* (Paris: L'Harmattan, 2000).

31. French intelligence sources claim that they helped repatriate four American bodies who fell in the Congo with the Rwandans, but U.S. involvement seems to have taken place at the policy level rather than on the ground.

32. Council on Foreign Relations, "Consultation on the Great Lakes Region of Central Africa with Ambassador Mohamed Sahnoun, March 6–7, 1997," report, New York, March 31, 1997.

33. One of these companies, the Canadian firm American Mineral, went to the length of purchasing a post office box in Bill Clinton's hometown of Hope, Arkansas, a ploy that gave the impression they were acting on behalf of President Clinton (Robert Block, "Taking Sides: As Zaire's War Rages, Foreign Businesses Scramble for Inroads," *Wall Street Journal,* April 14, 1997).

34. Philip Gourevitch, "Letter from the Congo: Continental Shift," *New Yorker,* August 4, 1997, pp. 42–55, p. 42.

35. United Nations, *Report of the Panel of Experts on the Illegal Exploitation of Natural Resources and Other Forms of Wealth of the Democratic Republic of Congo,* S/2001/357, April 12, 2001.

36. International Rescue Committee, "IRC Study Points to Horrific Death Toll in Eastern Congo: 2.5 Million 'Excess' Deaths in 33 Months of Unrest," May 8, 2001.

37. United Nations, *Report of the Independent Inquiry into the Actions of the United Nations during the 1994 Genocide in Rwanda;* United Nations, *Report of the Secretary-General Pursuant to General Assembly Resolution 53/35: The Fall of Srebrenica,* A/54/549, November 1999.

38. Barbara Crossette, "Town, Awaiting Peace, Reels from Congo War," *New York Times,* May 6, 2000, p. A6.

39. International Crisis Group, "From Kabila to Kabila: Prospects for Peace in the Congo," Brussels, March 16, 2001.

40. For a more detailed analysis of the situation in Rwanda in early 2000, see Human Rights Watch, *Rwanda: The Search for Security and Human Rights Abuses* (New York, April 2000).

Chapter 4

1. Michael Ignatieff, *The Warrior's Honor: Ethnic War and the Modern Conscience* (London: Chatto and Windus, 1998), p. 141.

2. "Blair Sets Out Intervention Doctrine in Chicago," *Washington Post,* April 23, 1999, p. A33.

3. In Serbian (or, as it used to be called, Serbo-Croatian), "Kosovo" ends with an *o* and is accented on the first syllable. Serbian nationalists generally refer to the province as Kosovo and Metohija, the latter term an explicit reference to the lands belonging to the Serbian Orthodox Church there. In Albanian, "Kosova" ends with an *a* and is accented on the second syllable. The Albanian adjective and substantive "Kosovar" is generally used to refer to inhabitants of that province. Its use here does not imply any prejudice against the rights of other ethnic groups in that province. Macedonians call their country the Republic of Macedonia and refer to themselves (as both an ethnic group and citizens of that country) as Macedonians. There is a province in northern Greece called Macedonia, which contains both Greek-speaking residents of that province and Greek citizens who speak the southern Slavic language that Macedonians call Macedonian but that Bulgarians consider a Bulgarian dialect. Greece does not recognize a separate Macedonian ethnicity for those who speak that language. Greece has objected to the name of the Republic of Macedonia as irredentist with respect to Greece's homonymic province. I omit a discussion of the ethnic provenance and mother tongue of Philip of Macedon and his son, Alexander the Great, save to note that Alexander seemed more concerned that his subjects should worship him as a god than that they adopt his language. Greek texts refer to Macedonians as Slavo-Macedonians. Greece originally opposed any use of the term "Macedonia" by the newly independent country, but since 1994 Greece has not opposed the country's entry into international organizations under the transitional name Former Yugoslav Republic of Macedonia, abbreviated as FYROM. Neutrality of terminology in such a situation is perhaps a vain aspiration, and I cannot prevent anyone from inferring political views from the following choices: I use the internationally accepted "Kosovo" except when referring to Albanian institutions that use the word "Kosova" in their title. I refer to the state whose capital is Skopje simply as Macedonia and to both members of the Macedonian ethnic group and citizens of Macedonia as Macedonians. In the case of all ethnonyms that also denote citizens of ethnically named states, I try to indicate clearly whether I am referring to citi-

zenship or ethnicity. This principle also applies to the discussion of Central Asia further on. I also avoid expressions such as "the Albanians" or "the Serbs" as a shorthand for the political leadership of a state or group.

4. Michael T. Kaufman, "Meet Kosovo, the World's Biggest Little Tinderbox," *New York Times,* July 5, 1998, sec. 4, p. 4.

5. Ivo Banac, "Sorting Out the Balkans," *Foreign Affairs,* vol. 79, no. 3, (2000), pp. 152–57.

6. Victor A. Friedman, "Observing the Observers: Language, Ethnicity, and Power in the 1994 Macedonian Census and Beyond," in Barnett R. Rubin, ed., *Toward Comprehensive Peace in Southeast Europe: Conflict Prevention in the South Balkans,* vol. 1 of *Preventive Action Reports* (New York: Twentieth Century Fund Press, 1996), pp. 81–106. Friedman's census analysis shows that Bulgarians counted almost all Slavic speakers as Bulgarians, Greeks counted those who went to "Greek" (Orthodox Christian) schools as Greeks, and Turks counted all Muslims as Turks (including Albanians). Today, some Muslim Macedonian speakers who wish to emphasize their religious identity send their children to schools in which classes are conducted in Turkish, a language they do not understand.

7. Kosovar Albanians boycotted the 1991 Yugoslav census and hence were not counted. Yugoslav statisticians estimated their number at 82.2 percent of the population of Kosovo at the time (Steven Burg, "Stabilizing the South Balkans," in Barnett R. Rubin, ed., *Toward Comprehensive Peace in Southeast Europe: Conflict Prevention in the South Balkans,* vol. 1 of *Preventive Action Reports* [New York: Twentieth Century Fund Press, 1996], pp. 30–31). It has become commonplace to speak of the population of Kosovo as more than 90 percent Albanian before the 1999 war, but a number of factors (including the large number of Albanian guest workers and asylum seekers abroad) seem to make that figure an exaggeration. Since the 1999 war and the expulsion and flight from the province of Serbs, Gypsies, and others, the higher figure may have become accurate.

8. On the linguistic basis for asserting a distinct Macedonian identity, see Friedman, "Observing the Observers," pp. 84–88.

9. Susan Woodward, *Balkan Tragedy: Chaos and Dissolution after the Cold War* (Brookings, 1995).

10. Marc Weller, *The Crisis in Kosovo, 1989–1999,* vol. 1 of *International Documents and Analysis* (Cambridge, England: Documents and Analysis Publishing, 1999), pp. 57, 58.

11. Woodward, *Balkan Tragedy;* Burg, "Stabilizing the South Balkans." Milosevic also staged takeovers of the Serbian Communist Party, Montenegro, and Vojvodina through the use of manipulated crowds and nationalist violence.

12. Burg, "Stabilizing the South Balkans," pp. 31–32.

13. Barnett R. Rubin, "Violence Pays in Kosovo," *Christian Science Monitor,* March 17, 1998, p. 20.

14. Burg, "Stabilizing the South Balkans," p. 33.

15. Ibid., pp. 32–33.

16. Ibid., pp. 34–35.

17. The Greek constitution contains a similar provision about overseas ethnic Greeks (ibid., pp. 35–36), and, indeed, Greece interceded actively on behalf of ethnic Greeks in southern Albania. See the earlier discussion on the consistent application of principles.

18. A recount of the Macedonian population, sponsored by the Council of Europe, affirmed the official figures; see Friedman, "Observing the Observers."

19. Exceptions were made for subjects directly related to Albanian language, culture, and pedagogy.

20. Janie Leatherman, William DeMars, Patrick D. Gaffney, and Raimo Väyrynen, *Breaking Cycles of Violence: Conflict Prevention in Intrastate Crises* (West Hartford, Conn.: Kumarian, 1999).

21. The two countries continued to disagree about the name of the country, a subject for further negotiations (Richard Holbrooke, *To End a War* [Random House, 1998], pp. 121–27).

22. At that time the organization was called the Conference on Security and Cooperation in Europe (CSCE), but for the sake of clarity and simplicity I have adopted the anachronism of using the new name throughout. The CSCE changed its name at the end of 1994.

23. Michael S. Lund, "Preventive Diplomacy for Macedonia, 1992–1999: From Containment to Nation Building," in Bruce Jentleson, ed., *Opportunities Missed, Opportunities Seized: Preventive Diplomacy in the Post–Cold War World* (Lanham, Md.: Rowman and Littlefield, 2000), pp. 173–208. On the Council of Europe census mission, see Friedman, "Observing the Observers."

24. John Marks and Eran Fraenkel, "Working to Prevent Conflict in the New Nation of Macedonia," *Negotiation Journal*, vol. 13, no. 3 (1997), pp. 243–52; Lund, "Preventive Diplomacy for Macedonia."

25. Stefan Troebst, "Conflict in Kosovo: Failure of Prevention? An Analytical Documentation, 1992–1998," Working Paper 1, European Centre for Minority Issues, Flensburg, Germany, 1998.

26. Ibid.

27. Project on Ethnic Relations, "Interethnic Relations in Serbia/Yugoslavia: Alternatives for the Future," Princeton, N.J., 1993; Project on Ethnic Relations, "Democratic Processes and Ethnic Relations in Yugoslavia," Princeton, N.J., 1995; Pax Christi International, *Kosovo: The Conflict between Serbs and Albanians and the Role of the International Community* (Brussels, 1995).

28. Barnett R. Rubin, "Executive Summary," in Barnett R. Rubin, *Toward Comprehensive Peace in Southeast Europe: Conflict Prevention in the South Balkans*, vol. 1 of *Preventive Action Reports* (New York: Twentieth Century Fund Press, 1996), p. 5 (footnote omitted).

29. Steven L. Burg, "Nationalism and Civic Identity: Ethnic Models for Macedonia and Kosovo," in Barnett R. Rubin, ed., *Cases and Strategies for Preventive Action*,

vol. 2 of *Preventive Action Reports* (New York: The Century Foundation Press, 1998), pp. 23–45.

30. The Carnegie Commission on Preventing Deadly Conflict argued for the importance of a "lead actor" in preventive efforts (Carnegie Commission on Preventing Deadly Conflict, *Preventing Deadly Conflict: Final Report* [New York: Carnegie Corporation of New York, 1997]), pp. 40–41.

31. Steven L. Burg and Barnett R. Rubin, "Recommendations," in Barnett R. Rubin, ed., *Toward Comprehensive Peace in Southeast Europe: Conflict Prevention in the South Balkans,* vol. 1 of *Preventive Action Reports* (New York: Twentieth Century Fund Press, 1996), pp. 11–24.

32. Lund, "Preventive Diplomacy for Macedonia," provides a careful analysis of these factors and the various counterfactual scenarios.

33. Susan Woodward, "CFSP: A Step Backward? Lessons from the Balkans," Working Paper 17/99, Helmut Kohl Institute for European Studies, Hebrew University, Jerusalem, 1999; Friedman, "Observing the Observers."

34. Lund, "Preventive Diplomacy in Macedonia."

35. Sant' Egidio's consultations originally included Croatia as well, as one of the ideas explored was an agreement under which Croatia would grant a large degree of autonomy to its ethnic Serbian population in Krajina and East Slavonia, while Serbia would do the same for Albanians in Kosovo. Croatia, however, evinced no interest in any concession to the Serbs and instead proposed arming the Kosovar Albanians for a rebellion. Sant' Egidio broke off the talks, as this proposal was not consistent with its ethic of resolving conflicts peacefully. In any case, the Kosovar Albanians also rejected the idea of autonomy as a solution.

36. Troebst, "Conflict in Kosovo," pp. 81–83, provides a summary as well as English translations of both documents.

37. Ibid., p. 82.

38. Laura Silber continued her distinguished record of reporting with "Ethnic Albanians to End Schools Boycott," *Financial Times,* September 3, 1996. In early 2000, one of the leading U.S. newspapers rejected an op-ed contribution by a prominent international leader calling for action to prevent a crackdown by Milosevic in Montenegro on the grounds that, in the absence of more violence, Montenegro was not newsworthy.

39. Troebst, "Conflict in Kosovo," pp. 58–67. For an analysis focusing on the failure of the EU's Common Foreign and Security Policy in Kosovo, see Woodward, "CFSP: A Step Backward?"

40. Troebst, "Conflict in Kosovo," pp. 51–56.

41. On August 3, 1995, the Taliban (presumably aided by Pakistan) forced down a plane over Qandahar, Afghanistan, on its way to deliver arms and ammunition to their foes in the north of the country. The plane, chartered from the official airline of the Russian Autonomous Republic of Tatarstan, was transporting supplies, mostly Chinese-manufactured ammunition, from Tirana, Albania, to the Afghan capital, Kabul, controlled at the time by Ahmad Shah Massoud.

42. Tim Judah, *Kosovo: War and Revenge* (Yale University Press, 2000).

43. Christopher Hedges, "Kosovo's Next Masters," *Foreign Affairs,* vol. 78, no. 3 (1999), pp. 24–42.

44. Burg and Rubin, "Recommendations," p. 24.

45. Human Rights Watch, *Humanitarian Law Violations in Kosovo* (New York, 1998), pp. 27–32, cited in Judah, *Kosovo: War and Revenge,* p. 140.

46. Only a few days before the start of the operation, the U.S. special envoy, Robert Gelbard, had criticized the violence of the Serb police but then added, "We condemn very strongly terrorist actions in Kosovo. The UÇK [Kosova Liberation Army] is, without any questions, a terrorist group." It seems likely that Milosevic took this statement as encouragement to eliminate the KLA. Judah, *Kosovo: War and Revenge,* p. 138.

47. For a detailed, if preliminary, account of the Rambouillet "negotiations," see Judah, *Kosovo: War and Revenge.* Judah quotes Holbrooke as telling Milosevic of the bombing, "It will be swift, it will be severe, it will be sustained" (p. 227).

48. Alissa J. Rubin, Tyler Marshall, and John-Thor Dahlburg, "Crisis in Yugoslavia: Allies, Russia Back Plan to End Kosovo Conflict," *Los Angeles Times,* May 7, 1999, p. A1.

Chapter 5

1. Peter M. Lewis, Pearl T. Robinson, and Barnett R. Rubin, *Stabilizing Nigeria: Sanctions, Incentives, and Support for Civil Society,* vol. 3 of *Preventive Action Reports* (New York: The Century Foundation Press, 1998).

2. Terry Lynn Karl, *The Paradox of Plenty: Oil Booms and Petro-States* (University of California Press, 1997), shows that many of these pathologies derive systematically from the political economy of an oil state.

3. This figure seems to include $2.3 billion looted from the treasury and about $1 billion each in contracts to fake companies and bribes from foreign contractors. See Emeka Nwankpa, "Obasanjo Puts Abacha's Loot at $4.3 billion," *Nigeria Today,* February 8, 2000; Tom Masland and Jeffrey Bartholet, "The Lost Billions," *Newsweek,* March 13, 2000; and various reports from Transparency International, such as "Nigeria: Accounts Frozen in Switzerland," January 2000.

4. Lewis, Robinson, and Rubin, *Stabilizing Nigeria,* p. 27.

5. The price of Nigerian Bonny Light crude doubled, from about $15 a barrel in 1979 to $30 a barrel in 1980 (U.S. Department of Energy, *Annual Energy Review* [July 2001], p. 324, table 11.6, tonto.eia.doe.gov/FTPROOT/multifuel/038400.pdf [May 12, 2002]).

6. Oil prices peaked in 1981, at $40 a barrel for Nigerian Bonny Light crude, and fell to $30 a barrel in 1983 (ibid.).

7. Karl, *The Paradox of Plenty.*

8. On the annulment, see Omo Omoruyi, *The Tale of June 12: The Betrayal of the Democratic Rights of Nigerians (1993)* (London: Press Alliance Network Limited, 1999).

9. *The Master-Plan: The Agenda That Conquered IBB [Ibrahim Babangida], by Yoruba Solidarity Forum* (1994). A prominent northern academic and political figure gave multiple copies of this obvious (almost comical) forgery to the CPA mission in Kano.

10. After the nullification of the election, a press release from Dasouki called for recognition of its results and a handover of power to Abiola. Nobel laureate Wole Soyinka reproduces the statement as an appendix to his book *The Open Sore of a Continent: A Personal Narrative of the Nigerian Crisis* (Oxford University Press, 1996), pp. 155–58. One prominent Yoruba Muslim, a supporter of Abiola who also knew Dasouki from his work in Islamic affairs, told the CPA delegation in Lagos that Dasouki had denied to him having issued the message circulating in his name. Whatever the truth behind this press release, Abacha clearly perceived Dasouki as a potential rival in his own home region, the North, and an alternative focus of legitimacy.

11. There were also charges of the movement's involvement in some other violent incidents; see European Platform for Conflict Prevention and Transformation with the African Centre for the Constructive Resolution of Disputes, *Searching for Peace in Africa: An Overview of Conflict Prevention and Management Activities* (Utrecht, Netherlands, 1999).

12. Ibid.; Onigu Otite and Isaac Olawale Albert, eds., *Community Conflicts in Nigeria: Management, Resolution, and Transformation* (Ibadan, Nigeria: Spectrum Books and Academic Associates PeaceWorks, 1999).

13. Cece Modupé Fadopé, "In Focus: Nigeria," *Foreign Policy in Focus*, vol. 2 (January 1997).

14. For a good sketch of the Nigerian oil industry, see Human Rights Watch, *The Price of Oil: Corporate Responsibility and Human Rights Violations in Nigeria's Oil-Producing Communities* (New York, February 1999).

15. While drafting this chapter I received the following e-mail entitled "VERY PRIVATE AND CONFIDENTIAL:

> PETROLEUM [SPECIAL] TRUST FUND, LAGOS LIAISON OFFICE
> KARIMU KOTUN STREET, VICTORIA ISLAND LAGOS
> Dear Prof. Richard [my middle name],
> Your contact and particulars were given to me by an official of our diplomatic mission in your country who vouched for you as an honest and trustworthy fellow who could champion a business of this magnitude. I am Dr. Graham Douglas, a Nigerian, who is currently the chairman of the contract award panel in the Petroleum Trust Fund. I happen to come from the Niger Delta Area which produces crude oil which accounts for about 95% of the country's foreign exchange earnings. The Northern oligarchy who have

ruled this country since our independence have used the oil wealth from my area to enrich themselves leaving nothing to national treasury, let alone the suffering masses of the Niger Delta. In order to silence us the more, our spokesman and mouthpiece Mr. Kenule Saro Wiwa with eight others kinsmen of mine were murdered on Nov. 9th, 1995 for pleading our course [sic].

In the spirit of reconciliation for the injustice done to my people, the present regime of Gen. Olusegun Obasanjo, appointed me the chairman contract award panel of the Petroleum Trust Fund, which is a body set up by the Late Head of State Gen. Sanni Abacha to manage the excess revenue accruing from the sale of petroleum and its allied products, as a result of domestic increase in pump price of petroleum products. Consequently, the estimated annual revenue for 1998 was 47 billion U.S. Dollars. Members of my panel and I over shot this target by 378 million USD by Nov 11 1998. We have declared the sum of 47.360 Billion USD to the Federal Military Government of Nigeria withholding the balance of 18 Million USD reference 115 Unit 3d, paragraph "F" of the Auditor General of the Federal Republic of Nigeria's report 1998 on Federal Republic of Nigeria Estimated Revenue. Because of the existing domestic laws forbidding Civil Servants from opening, operating and maintaining foreign accounts, we do not have the expertise to transfer this balance of funds into a foreign account. Moreover this balance of 18 Million USD has been secured in form of credit/payment to a foreign contractor. If you maintain a corporate/personal offshore account, could you please furnish me with your bank details including your personal telephone/fax numbers where I can always reach you. We have also arrived at a conclusion that you will be compensated to the tune of 25% of the total sum of money transferred into your account while 5% will be reserved for incidental expenses that both parties will incur in the course of executing and actualizing this transaction. The balance of 70% will be kept to our selves. If you are capable of helping us actualize our life's dream, send an E-MAIL to me today giving your personal details. This transaction is highly confidential because of the top ranking government officials involved in the transaction. The transaction is also risk free.

Let me hear from you today.
KIND REGARDS,
GRAHAM DOUGLAS (PH. D)

I sent this solicitation on to the Federal Bureau of Investigation.

16. Fadopé, "In Focus: Nigeria"; United Nations, *Report of the Special Rapporteur on the Situation of Human Rights in Nigeria,* E/CN.4/1997/62, February 1997, Add. 1, March 1997; United Nations, *Report of the Special Rapporteur on the Situation of Human Rights in Nigeria,* E/CN.4/1998/62, February 1998; United Nations, *Report of the Special Rapporteur of the Commission on Human Rights on the Situation in Nigeria,* A/S3/366, September 1998, Add. 1, November 1998; United Nations, *Report of the Special Rapporteur on the Situation of Human Rights in Nigeria,*

E/CN.4/1999/36, January 1999; United Nations, *Joint Report of the Situation of Human Rights in Nigeria of the Special Rapporteurs on Extrajudicial, Summary, or Arbitrary Executions, and on the Independence of Judges and Lawyers*, A/S1/538, October 1996, Add. 1, December 1996, *The Situation of Human Rights in Nigeria.*

17. Human Rights Watch, *The Price of Oil.*

18. Margaret E. Keck and Kathryn Sikkink, *Activists beyond Borders: Advocacy Networks in International Politics* (Cornell University Press, 1998), pp. 12–13.

19. Taft later became assistant secretary of state for population, refugees, and migration and then director of the Bureau of Conflict Prevention and Recovery of the UN Development Program. The story is used with her permission.

20. The Council on Foreign Relations does not take positions on policy issues. The CPA worked through a mechanism called a "task force," in which a group of individuals assembled by the council takes a position (possibly with dissenters) on their personal responsibility. The council does not endorse the task force's position but disseminates such reports as part of its public education function.

21. Archbishop Gabriel Gonsum Ganaka, Vision 2010 conference, Abuja, Nigeria, January 15, 1997.

22. Richard N. Haass, ed., *Economic Sanctions and American Diplomacy* (New York: Council on Foreign Relations, 1998); David Cortright and George A. Lopez, eds., *Economic Sanctions: Panacea or Peacebuilding in a Post–Cold War World?* (Boulder: Westview, 1995); Gary Clyde Hufbauer and Jeffrey J. Schott, assisted by Kimberly Ann Elliot, *Economic Sanctions in Support of Foreign Policy Goals* (Washington: Institute for International Economics, 1983); Gary Clyde Hufbauer, Jeffrey J. Schott, and Kimberly Ann Elliot, *Economic Sanctions Reconsidered* (Washington: Institute for International Economics, 1990).

23. The revised paper presented there was published as David Cortright and George A. Lopez, "Carrots, Sticks, and Cooperation: Economic Tools of Statecraft," in Barnett R. Rubin, ed., *Cases and Strategies for Preventive Action*, vol. 2 of *Preventive Action Reports* (New York: The Century Foundation Press, 1998), pp. 113–34.

24. U.S. Department of the Interior, *Minerals Yearbook* (Bureau of Mines, 1997). Oil revenues accounted for 80 percent of Nigerian government revenue in 1997, but no comparable figures are available for Iraq.

25. Lewis, Robinson, and Rubin, *Stabilizing Nigeria*, p. 17.

26. Jeff Gerth, "Hearings Offer View into Private Banking," *New York Times*, November 8, 1999, p. A6; Jeff Gerth, "U.S. May Bar Illicit Funds in Deposits by Foreigners," *New York Times*, November 11, 1999, p. A10.

27. Lewis, Robinson, and Rubin, *Stabilizing Nigeria*, p. 18.

28. As in Macedonia, privatization was an ethnic and political issue in Nigeria as much as an economic one. The northerners who dominated the state corporations feared that privatization would increase the power of the Yoruba economic élites and so imposed an unwieldy quota system by state on the shareholders in privatized state companies. We note in the report that privatization should not "unduly bur-

den the Nigerian public [for example, through sudden increases in prices] or intensify ethnic conflict" (ibid.).

29. Ibid., p. 93.

30. Ibid., p. 23.

31. Salih Booker, Darren Kew, and Barnett R. Rubin, "Nigeria's Transition: From End to Beginning: Report of the Conference on Nigeria, January 30, 1998, and Update on Nigeria, March 1999" (New York: Council on Foreign Relations, 1999). At the last minute, a crisis in Iraq prevented Pickering from attending, and Ambassador Howard Franklin Jeter delivered Pickering's speech in his stead. The meeting was cosponsored by the Council on Foreign Relations' African Studies Program.

32. The president also established a public website (www.nopa.net) through which I subscribed to public announcements—including the text of the June 14, 2000, memorandum of understanding between the president and the Nigerian Labour Congress on ending these strikes.

33. Remi Oyo and Toye Olori, "POLITICS—Nigeria: Sharia Controversy Far from Over," InterPress Service, Lagos, March 2, 2000.

34. I thank Mobolaji Aluko of Howard University for relaying, without endorsing, Governor Sani's account of these events.

Chapter 6

1. Sam Nunn, Nancy Lubin, and Barnett R. Rubin, *Calming the Ferghana Valley: Development and Dialogue in the Heart of Central Asia*, vol. 4 of *Preventive Action Reports* (New York: The Century Foundation Press, 1999), p. 35, table 3.1.

2. Ibid., p. 37, table 3.2.

3. Olivier Roy, *La nouvelle Asie Centrale, ou La fabrication des nations* (Paris: Seuil, 1997); Alisher Ilkhamov, "Center-Periphery Relations in Uzbekistan," paper presented at Olin Seminar Series conference, Reconceptualizing Central Asia: States and Societies in Formation, Harvard University, February 22, 2001.

4. If the official rate for the Uzbek *som* is S.50 to the dollar, whereas the market rate is S.150 (about the order of magnitude during our visit, rounded off for illustrative purposes), someone allowed to purchase dollars at the official rate could buy $10 with S.500, then change the $10 into S.1500, and then change the S.1500 into $30, and so on.

5. Roy, *La nouvelle Asie Centrale;* Alisher Ilkhamov, "Political Islam in Uzbekistan: Imported Ideology or Grass-Root Movement?" (Center for Social Research, "Expert-fikri," Tashkent, Uzbekistan, 2001).

6. As in much of the Soviet Union, nomenclature is complicated—in this case by both the Soviet heritage and multilingualism. The city and district of Khujand (Tajik) or Khojent (Uzbek) were part of Uzbekistan until 1929. They were both later renamed Leninabad. In post-Soviet Tajikistan, the city reverted to the name Khujand, and the district was officially known as Leninabad until being renamed Soghd, after an ancient kingdom.

7. Nunn, Lubin, and Rubin, *Calming the Ferghana Valley.*

8. This draft is reprinted ibid., appendix A, pp. 139–48.

9. Cited ibid., p. 144.

10. Strobe Talbott, "A Farewell to Flashman: American Policy in the Caucasus and Central Asia," speech delivered at the Central Asian Institute, Johns Hopkins University School of Advanced International Studies, Washington, D.C., July 21, 1997, as cited in Nunn, Lubin, and Rubin, *Calming the Ferghana Valley,* p. 11.

11. Nunn, Lubin, and Rubin, *Calming the Ferghana Valley,* p. 12.

12. See, for example, the Agence pour la Cooperation Technique et le Developpement (Agency for Technical Cooperation and Development) at www.acted.org/index2E.html?Chap='ACTED'.

13. The website is at www.ferghana.elcat.kg. The program was officially an interagency UN effort, with the UNDP as the lead agency and funder in the two countries (Tajikistan and Kyrgyzstan) where the program operated, not a UNDP project per se.

14. United Nations, *Text of Debate from General Assembly, Fifty-fourth Session, 7th Plenary Meeting, September 21, 1999,* A/54/PV.7.

15. Nunn, Lubin, and Rubin, *Calming the Ferghana Valley,* p. 61, table 4.1.

16. See Human Rights Watch, "Crackdown in the Farghona Valley: Arbitrary Arrests and Religious Discrimination" (New York, May 1998); Human Rights Watch, "Tajikistan, Leninabad: Crackdown in the North" (New York, April 1998); and Human Rights Watch, "Uzbekistan: Persistent Human Rights Violations and Prospects for Improvement" (New York, May 1996).

17. International Crisis Group, "Central Asia: Crisis Conditions in Three States," Brussels, August 7, 2000.

18. See Barnett R. Rubin, "Russian Hegemony and State Breakdown in the Periphery: Causes and Consequences of the Civil War in Tajikistan," in Barnett R. Rubin and Jack Snyder, eds., *Post-Soviet Political Order: Conflict and State Building* (Routledge, 1998), pp. 162-79, drawing also on works by Stéphane Dudoignon, Olivier Roy, and Shahrbanou Tadjbakhsh.

19. See the Hizb-ut-Tahrir website (www.hizb-ut-tahrir.org [May 6, 2002]) and International Crisis Group, "Islamic Mobilisation and Regional Security," report, Brussels, March 1, 2001.

20. Harold H. Saunders, *A Public Peace Process: Sustained Dialogue to Transform Racial and Ethnic Conflicts* (St. Martin's, 1999).

21. Barnett R. Rubin, "The Political Economy of War and Peace in Afghanistan," *World Development,* vol. 28, no. 10 (2000), pp. 1789–1803.

22. Barnett R. Rubin, Ashraf Ghani, William Maley, Ahmed Rashid, and Olivier Roy, *Afghanistan: Reconstruction and Peacebuilding in a Regional Framework,* Peacebuilding Report 1/2001 (Bern: Swiss Peace Foundation, Centre for Peacebuilding, 2001), www.swisspeace.ch/html/navigation/fr_program_koff.html.

Chapter 7

1. Karl Marx and Frederick Engels, *The Communist Manifesto* (London: Pluto, 1996); Karl Marx, *The Poverty of Philosophy* (New York: International Publishers, 1963); Francis Fukuyama, *The End of History and the Last Man* (Yale University Press, 1998); James Scott, *Seeing Like a State: How Certain Schemes to Improve the Human Condition Have Failed* (Yale University Press, 1998).

2. Carnegie Commission on Preventing Deadly Conflict, *Preventing Deadly Conflict: Final Report* (New York: Carnegie Corporation of New York, 1997).

3. Mark Bowden, *Black Hawk Down: A Story of Modern War* (New York: Monthly Press, 1999); François Jean, *L'Ethiopie: Le bon usage de la famine* (Paris: Médecins sans Frontières, 1985); Rakiya Omaar and Alex de Waal, "Humanitarianism Unbound? Current Dilemmas Facing Multi-mandate Relief Operations in Political Emergencies," Discussion Paper 5, Africa Rights, London, November 1994; Robert B. Oakley and John L. Hirsch, *Somalia and Operation Restore Hope: Reflections on Peacemaking and Peacekeeping* (Washington: United States Institute of Peace, 1995); François Jean and Jean-Christophe Rufin, eds., *Économie des guerres civiles* (Paris: Hachette, 1996); Rony Braumann, *Humanitaire: Le dilemme* (Paris: Textuel, 1996); Alain Destexhe, *L'humanitaire impossible, ou, Deux siècles d'ambigüité* (Paris: A. Colin, 1993); Jonathan Moore, ed., *Hard Choices: Moral Dilemmas in Humanitarian Intervention* (Lanham, Md.: Rowman and Littlefield, 1998).

4. Jeffrey Z. Rubin, Dean G. Pruitt, and Sung Hee Kim, *Social Conflict: Escalation, Stalemate, and Settlement* (McGraw-Hill, 1994).

5. Stephen John Stedman, "Conflict Prevention as Strategic Interaction: The Spoiler Problem and the Case of Rwanda," in Peter Wallensteen, ed., *Preventing Violent Conflicts: Past Record and Future Challenges* (Uppsala, Sweden: Uppsala University, Department of Peace and Conflict Research, 1998), pp. 67–86.

6. Mancur Olson, *The Logic of Collective Action: Public Goods and the Theory of Groups* (Harvard University Press, 1965); contributions to Inge Kaul, Isabelle Grunberg, and Marc A. Stern, eds., *Global Public Goods: International Cooperation in the Twenty-first Century* (Oxford University Press, 1999), especially David A. Hamburg and Jane E. Holl, "Preventing Deadly Conflict: From Global Housekeeping to Neighborhood Watch," pp. 366–81.

7. Project on Ethnic Relations, *The New York Roundtable: Toward Peaceful Accommodation in Kosovo* (Princeton, N.J., 1997).

8. Valery Tishkov, Institute of Ethnology, Russian Academy of Sciences, personal communication, Brussels, March 1998.

9. The former term is from Carnegie Commission on Preventing Deadly Conflict, *Perspectives on Prevention: Preventive Diplomacy, Preventive Defense, and Conflict Resolution: A Report of Two Conferences at Stanford University and the Ditchley Foundation* (New York: Carnegie Corporation of New York, October 1999), p. 5; the latter from Graham Allison and Hisashi Owada, *The Role of Democracies in Pre-*

venting Deadly Conflict (Washington: Carnegie Commission on Preventing Deadly Conflict, 1999), p. 9.

10. International Alert, "Code of Conduct for Conflict Transformation Work" (www.international-alert.org/text/code_e.htm [May 6, 2002]); Gunnar M. Sorbo, Joanne Macrae, and Linnart Wohlgemuth, *NGOs in Conflict: An Evaluation of International Alert* (Bergen, Norway: Christian Michelson Institute, 1997).

11. European Platform for Conflict Prevention and Transformation, *People Building Peace: Thirty-five Inspiring Stories from Around the World* (Utrecht, Netherlands, 1999).

12. This schema, of course, builds on many previous efforts to develop such typologies—notably, the Carnegie Commission for the Prevention of Deadly Conflict, *Preventing Deadly Conflict: Final Report;* and Michael S. Lund, *Preventing Violent Conflicts: A Strategy for Preventive Diplomacy* (Washington: United States Institute of Peace, 1996). Kalypso Nicolaïdis, "International Preventive Action: Developing a Strategic Framework," in Robert I. Rotberg, ed., *Vigilance and Vengeance: NGOs Preventing Ethnic Conflict in Divided Societies* (Brookings, 1996), pp. 23–73, formulates the concept of "systemic prevention," though Nicolaïdis's definition is slightly different from the one presented here.

13. Boutros Boutros-Ghali, *An Agenda for Peace: Preventive Diplomacy, Peacemaking, and Peace-Keeping,* A/47/277-S/24111, June 17, 1992 (United Nations, 1992), p. 20.

14. René Lemarchand, *Burundi: Ethnocide as Discourse and Practice* (Cambridge University Press, 1994); Liisa H. Malkki, *Purity and Exile: Violence, Memory, and National Cosmology among Hutu Refugees in Tanzania* (University of Chicago Press, 1995); Philip Gourevitch, "The Poisoned Country," *New York Review of Books,* June 6, 1996, pp. 58–65.

15. Janie Leatherman, William DeMars, Patrick D. Gaffney, and Raimo Väyrynen, *Breaking Cycles of Violence: Conflict Prevention in Intrastate Crises* (West Hartford, Conn.: Kumarian, 1999), pp. 97–101.

16. Ahmed Rashid, "The Taliban: Exporting Extremism," *Foreign Affairs,* vol. 78, no. 6 (1999), pp. 22–35.

17. The UN recognized the regional dimension of prevention in its new approach to West Africa; see United Nations, *Report of Inter-Agency Mission to West Africa,* S/2001/434, May 2001.

18. For one example, see Barnett R. Rubin, "The Political Economy of War and Peace in Afghanistan," *World Development,* vol. 28, no. 10 (2000), pp. 1789–1803.

19. Barnett R. Rubin, with Susanna P. Campbell, "Introduction: Experience in Prevention," in Barnett R. Rubin, ed., *Cases and Strategies for Preventive Action,* vol. 2 of *Preventive Action Reports* (New York: The Century Foundation Press, 1998), pp. 1–21.

Chapter 8

1. The most notable effort was the so-called multidonor evaluation, which led to a six-volume report. The volume on early warning still remains probably the most profound treatment of this question. See, especially, Howard Adelman and Astri Suhrke, with Bruce Jones, *Early Warning and Conflict Management*, vol. 2 of *The International Response to Conflict and Genocide: Lessons from the Rwandan Experience* (Copenhagen: Joint Evaluation of Emergency Assistance to Rwanda, 1999).

2. Monique Mujawamariya, paper presented at conference on NGOs and early warning, Harvard University, John F. Kennedy School of Government, April 1995, partly summarized in Emily MacFarquhar, Robert I. Rotberg, and Martha A. Chen, introduction to Robert I. Rotberg, ed., *Vigilance and Vengeance: NGOs Preventing Ethnic Conflict in Divided Societies* (Brookings, 1996), pp. 9–10.

3. Steven L. Burg, "Failure of Early Warning in Kosovo," in Barnett R. Rubin, ed., *The Application of Prevention: Report of the Center for Preventive Action's Fifth Annual Conference, December 11, 1998* (New York: Council on Foreign Relations, 1999), pp. 5–11.

4. Carnegie Commission on Preventing Deadly Conflict, *Preventing Deadly Conflict: Final Report* (New York: Carnegie Corporation of New York, 1997); Alexander L. George and Jane E. Holl, "The Warning-Response Problem and Missed Opportunities in Preventive Diplomacy," in Bruce W. Jentleson, ed., *Opportunities Missed, Opportunities Seized: Preventive Diplomacy in the Post–Cold War World* (Lanham, Md.: Rowman and Littlefield, 2000), p. 29.

5. This debate is the source of the only known joke about preventive action: *Q:* Which is the biggest obstacle to preventive action, lack of early warning or failure of political will? *A:* I don't know, and I don't care. Of course, like much else in the field, this joke is derivative—in this case from an earlier joke about ignorance and apathy.

6. The OSCE did hold talks to defuse the tension between Crimea and Kiev. On the general problem of false negatives and false positives in preventive action, see Kalypso Nicolaïdis, "International Preventive Action: Developing a Strategic Framework," in Robert I. Rotberg, ed., *Vigilance and Vengeance: NGOs Preventing Conflict in Divided Societies* (Brookings, 1996), pp. 23–69. On the Ukrainian case, see David Callahan, *Unwinnable Wars: American Power and Ethnic Conflict* (Hill and Wang, 1997), p. 82–83.

7. Carnegie Commission on Preventing Deadly Conflict, *Preventing Deadly Conflict: Final Report*, p. 43.

8. Howard Adelman, "Difficulties in Early Warning: Networking and Conflict Management," in Klaas van Walraven, ed., *Early Warning and Conflict Prevention* (The Hague: Kluwer Law International, 1998), p. 52; Adelman and Suhrke, with Jones, *Early Warning and Conflict Management*. George and Holl, "The Warning-

Response Problem and Missed Opportunities," similarly argues for a unified system of warning and response, as has been developed in defense applications.

9. George and Holl, "The Warning-Response Problem and Missed Opportunities."

10. A framework for response also dictates investment of resources in warning. Warning, not just response, requires will and resources. In 1996-97, when the Rwandan government and Zairian rebels attacked Rwandan Hutu camps in eastern Zaire, organizations publicized vastly different figures of those missing and at risk of summary execution. Humanitarian organizations demanded that the U.S. government use its intelligence resources to find and count them. Because satellite imagery could not pierce the dense forest canopy, the United States sent out a low-altitude surveillance aircraft from Nairobi. The aircraft turned back, without collecting the information, after being fired upon. As one diplomat has pointed out, however, if the fugitives in the forest had been guerrillas massing for an attack on U.S. troops or any other action to which U.S. policy dictated a response, the aircraft—and others if necessary—would have braved enemy fire to track them down.

11. Jeffrey Cooper and Lewis Dunn, "Rethinking Warning in a Changing World," Science Application International Corporation, McLean, Va., December 1, 1999.

12. Commission to Assess the Ballistic Missile Threat to the United States, "Report of the Commission to Assess the Ballistic Missile Threat to the United States," Federation of American Scientists, 1998.

13. See various reports on the commission's website (www.nssg.gov).

14. For the most systematic attempt to link the two, see Barbara Harff and Ted Robert Gurr, "Systematic Early Warning of Humanitarian Emergencies," *Journal of Peace Research*, vol. 35, no. 5 (1998), pp. 551–79. Harff and Gurr argue that risk assessment in fact is not early warning, but I prefer to situate it as one of several categories of warning. Risk assessment studies using cross-national data may also use data from different time periods but, except for statistical procedures to handle the problem of autocorrelation, do not take sequencing or development over time into account.

15. Yahya Sadowski, *The Myth of Global Chaos* (Brookings, 1998).

16. Peter Wallensteen and Margareta Sollenberg, "Armed Conflict and Regional Conflict Complexes," *Journal of Peace Research*, vol. 36, no. 5 (1999), pp. 621–34. For a review of several such studies, see Anne-Marie Gardner, "Diagnosing Conflict: What Do We Know?" in Fen Osler Hampson and David M. Malone, eds., *From Reaction to Conflict Prevention: Opportunities for the UN System* (Boulder: Lynne Rienner, 2002), pp. 15–40. See also Monty G. Marshall, "Measuring the Societal Impact of War," in Hampson and Malone, *From Reaction to Conflict Prevention: Opportunities for the UN System*, pp. 63–104.

17. In statistical terms, large negative residuals (high predicted conflict, low actual conflict) are early warning indicators.

18. Harff and Gurr, "Systematic Early Warning of Humanitarian Emergencies," p. 556.

19. John L. Davies and Ted Robert Gurr, eds., *Preventive Measures: Building Risk Assessment and Crisis Early Warning Systems* (Lanham, Md.: Rowman and Littlefield, 1998), includes short descriptions of a broad selection of approaches. A good overview of more recent developments is Susanne Schmeidl and Doug Bond, "FAST Early Warning and Conflict Prevention: The Strengths and Limitations of (Automated) Event-Data Monitoring to Support Early Warning Analysis," paper presented at the meeting of the International Studies Association, Los Angeles, March 14‒18, 2000.

20. For details of these systems, see Schmeidl and Bond, "FAST Early Warning and Conflict Prevention."

21. Harff and Gurr, "Systematic Early Warning of Humanitarian Emergencies"; John L. Davies and Barbara Harff, with Anne L. Speca, "Dynamic Data for Conflict Early Warning," in John L. Davies and Ted Robert Gurr, eds., *Preventive Measures: Building Risk Assessment and Crisis Early Warning Systems* (Lanham, Md.: Rowman and Littlefield, 1998), pp. 79‒94.

22. Heinz Krummenacher and Susanne Schmeidl, "FAST: An Integrated and Interactive Early Warning System—The Example of Central Asia," *Soviet and Post-Soviet Review*, vol. 24, no. 3 (1999), pp. 147‒59.

23. Schmeidl and Bond, "FAST Early Warning and Conflict Prevention."

24. Ibid., p. 91.

25. Stephen John Stedman, "Conflict Prevention as Strategic Interaction: The Spoiler Problem and the Case of Rwanda," in Peter Wallensteen, ed., *Preventing Violent Conflicts: Past Record and Future Challenges* (Uppsala, Sweden: Uppsala University, Department of Peace and Conflict Research, 1998), p. 67.

26. Ibid., p. 69.

27. Robert Jervis, *System Effects: Complexity in Political and Social Life* (Princeton University Press, 1997).

28. The term was reintroduced to modern social science and policy discourse by James Scott in *Seeing Like a State: How Certain Schemes to Improve the Human Condition Have Failed* (Yale University Press, 1998). For a sample of its application in preventive action, see European Platform for Conflict Prevention and Transformation, *People Building Peace: Thirty-five Inspiring Stories from Around the World* (Utrecht, Netherlands, 1999).

29. Janie Leatherman, William DeMars, Patrick D. Gaffney, and Raimo Väyrynen, *Breaking Cycles of Violence: Conflict Prevention in Intrastate Crises* (West Hartford, Conn.: Kumarian, 1999), p. 10.

30. Ibid., p. 40.

31. Interviews (with confidential informants), Bujumbura, Burundi, October 1998.

32. I once observed a dejected commander from Wardak Province leave the Swedish Committee for Afghanistan offices after being told that he could not receive food aid until the mujahedin in his area stopped fighting with one another. Otherwise, he was told, the committee would be perceived as partisan rather than

humanitarian, and it would not be able to carry out its mission. These files are described in Barnett R. Rubin, *The Fragmentation of Afghanistan: State Formation and Collapse in the International System* (Yale University Press, 2002), appendix A.

33. Ahmedou Ould Abdallah, *Burundi on the Brink, 1993–1995: A UN Special Envoy Reflects on Preventive Diplomacy* (Washington: United States Institute of Peace, 2000). Of course, the success was only relative, as Ould Abdallah had no direct means to affect the security situation.

34. Margaret E. Keck and Kathryn Sikkink, *Activists beyond Borders: Advocacy Networks in International Politics* (Cornell University Press, 1998), p. 13.

35. Leatherman et al., *Breaking Cycles of Violence.*

36. Hassan Ba, "Six renseignements," Synergies Africa, Geneva, December 1997.

Chapter 9

1. This is suggested in quite different ways by Manuel Castells, especially in *End of Millennium,* vol. 3 of *The Information Age: Economy, Society, and Culture* (Oxford: Blackwell, 1998), and by George Soros in *The Crisis of Global Capitalism* (New York: PublicAffairs, 1998).

2. United Nations, *Report of the Panel of Experts on the Illegal Exploitation of Natural Resources and Other Forms of Wealth of the Democratic Republic of the Congo,* S/2001/357, April 12, 2001.

3. Adekeye Adebajo, "Economic Agendas in Civil Wars: A Conference Summary," International Peace Academy, New York, 1999; Jakkie Cilliers and Christian Dietrich, eds., *Angola's War Economy: The Role of Oil and Diamonds* (Pretoria, South Africa: Institute for Security Studies, 2000); and Global Witness, "Conflict Diamonds: Possibilities for the Identification, Certification, and Control of Diamonds," London, 2000.

4. National Public Radio and the National Geographic Society's *Radio Expeditions,* "Coltan and Eastern Congo's Guerrillas," May 2, 2001; United Nations, *Report of the Panel of Experts on the Illegal Exploitation of Natural Resources and Other Forms of Wealth of the Democratic Republic of the Congo.*

5. Mathea Falco, *Rethinking International Drug Control: New Directions for U.S. Policy,* research report prepared by the Independent Task Force on Rethinking International Drug Control: New Directions for U.S. Policy, Council on Foreign Relations, New York, 1997.

6. The definition of small arms and light weapons is somewhat complex: generally, they are weapons that can be carried or used by individuals. For attempts to define them more rigorously, see Edward L. Laurance, "Small Arms, Light Weapons, and Conflict Prevention: The New Post-Cold-War Logic of Disarmament," in Barnett R. Rubin, ed., *Cases and Strategies for Preventive Action,* vol. 2 of *Preventive Action Reports* (New York: The Century Foundation Press, 1998), pp. 135–68; and Swadesh Rana, *Small Arms and Intra-State Conflicts* (Geneva: United Nations Institute for Disarmament Research, 1995).

7. European Platform for Conflict Prevention and Transformation with the African Centre for the Constructive Resolution of Disputes, *Searching for Peace in Africa: An Overview of Conflict Prevention and Management Activities* (Utrecht, Netherlands, 1999), pp. 317–23.

8. Websites with extensive references and links include those of the Federation of American Scientists (www.fas.org), the British American Security Information Council (www.basicint.org), the Norwegian Initiative on Small Arms Transfers (www.nisat.org), and the International NGO Action Network on Small Arms (www.iansa.org). The latter is the main umbrella organization of the movement.

9. See the International NGO Action Network on Small Arms founding document at www.iansa.org/mission/m1.htm.

10. William D. Hartung and Bridget Moix, "Deadly Legacy: U.S. Arms to Africa and the Congo War," World Policy Institute, New School University, January 2000.

11. See, for instance, the OECD webpage on "Fighting Bribery and Corruption" (www.oecd.org/subject/bribery [May 7, 2002]); the home page of the Financial Action Task Force on Money Laundering (www.oecd.org/fatf [May 7, 2002]); and the home page of Transparency International (www.transparency.de [May 7, 2002]).

12. For information on a program on this subject that was launched partly at the suggestion of the CPA, see the website of the Watson Institute for International Studies at Brown University (www.brown.edu/Departments/Watson_Institute/programs/gs/targetedfinsan.html [May 7, 2002]). More general information on targeted financial sanctions is available from the "Smart Sanctions" home page of the Swiss government (www.smartsanctions.ch/start.html [May 7, 2002]).

13. Mark Duffield, "Globalization, Transborder Trade, and War Economies," in Mats Berdal and David M. Malone, eds., *Greed and Grievance: Economic Agendas in Civil Wars* (Boulder: Lynne Rienner, 2000), pp. 69–89.

14. Barnett R. Rubin, "The Political Economy of War and Peace in Afghanistan," *World Development,* vol. 28, no. 10 (2000), pp. 1789–1803.

15. For some ideas on modernizing border control in ways compatible with globalization, see Stephen E. Flynn, "Beyond Border Control," *Foreign Affairs,* vol. 79, no. 6 (2000), pp. 57–68.

16. Thanks to Cesare Romano and Thordis Ingadottir for helping me clarify my comments on the ICC. Although the court has jurisdiction over the crime of aggression, it cannot exercise that jurisdiction unless the statute is amended and a provision adopted defining the crime and setting out the conditions under which the court can exercise its jurisdiction with respect to this crime. According to the statute, amendments can be proposed within seven years from its entry into force.

17. Kalypso Nicolaïdis, "International Preventive Action: Developing a Strategic Framework," in Robert I. Rotberg, ed., *Vigilance and Vengeance: NGOs Preventing Ethnic Conflict in Divided Societies* (Brookings, 1996), pp. 23–69.

18. Center on International Cooperation and International Peace Academy, *Refashioning the Dialogue: Regional Perspectives on the Brahimi Report on UN Peace Operations* (New York, 2001).

19. "Stability Pact for South Eastern Europe, Cologne, 10 June 1999," in *Economic Reconstruction and Development in Southeastern Europe* (World Bank and European Commission, 1999) (www.seerecon.org/KeyDocuments/KD1999062401.htm [May 7, 2002]).

20. Barnett R. Rubin, "Prévention des conflits: L'Europe et les leçons de l'expéri-ence," in Robert de Bussière, ed., *L'Europe et la prévention des crises et des conflits: Le long chemin de la théorie à la pratique* (Paris: L'Harmattan, 2000), pp. 87–120. On the "pouvoir d'attraction" of the EU, see Sophie Clément, "La prévention des conflits dans les Balkans: Le Kosovo et l'Ancienne République Yougoslave de Macédoine," *Cahiers de Chaillot* (Paris), vol. 30 (December 1997).

Chapter 10

1. Michael S. Lund, *Preventing Violent Conflicts: A Strategy for Preventive Diplo-macy* (Washington: United States Institute of Peace, 1996), mainly links tools to stages of conflict, in accord with a life-cycle model. Janie Leatherman, William DeMars, Patrick D. Gaffney, and Raimo Väyrynen, *Breaking Cycles of Violence: Con-flict Prevention in Intrastate Crises* (West Hartford, Conn.: Kumarian, 1999), pp. 97–110, primarily links tools to sources of conflict. Michael S. Lund and John Pren-dergast, *Preventing and Mitigating Violent Conflict: A Practitioner's Handbook* (Washington: Creative Associates, 1997), attempts to integrate the two approaches and in so doing comes closer to a strategic approach.

2. Michael S. Lund, "Preventive Diplomacy for Macedonia, 1992–1999: From Containment to Nation Building," in Bruce Jentleson, ed., *Opportunities Missed, Opportunities Seized: Preventive Diplomacy in the Post–Cold War World* (Lanham, Md.: Rowman and Littlefield, 2000), pp. 173–208, makes a similar point.

3. Anthony Giddens, *The Constitution of Society: Outline of the Theory of Struc-turation* (University of California Press, 1984); Anthony Giddens, *The Nation-State and Violence,* vol. 2 of *A Contemporary Critique of Historical Materialism* (University of California Press, 1987); Alexander E. Wendt, "The Structure-Agent Problem in International Relations," *International Organization,* vol. 41 (Summer 1987), pp. 335–70.

4. Aryeh Neier, *War Crimes: Brutality, Genocide, Terror, and the Struggle for Jus-tice* (New York: Times Books, 1998); Human Rights Watch, *Playing the Communal Card: Communal Violence and Human Rights* (New York, 1995).

5. Richard K. Betts, "The Delusion of Partial Intervention, *Foreign Affairs,* vol. 73 (November–December 1994), pp. 20–33; John Mearsheimer, "The False Promise of International Institutions," *International Security,* vol. 19, no. 3 (1994–95), pp. 5–49; Steven Van Evera, "Hypotheses on Nationalism and War," *International Studies,* vol. 18, no. 4 (1994), pp. 5–39; Barry Posen, "The Security Dilemma and Ethnic Conflict," *Survival,* vol. 35, no. 1 (1993), pp. 27–47; Chaim Kaufman, "Possible and Impossi-ble Solutions to Ethnic Civil Wars," *International Security,* vol. 20, no. 4 (1996), pp. 136–75.

6. Organization for Economic Cooperation and Development, *Development Assistance Committee (DAC) Guidelines on Conflict, Peace, and Development Cooperation* (Paris, 1997); Jamal Benomar, "Governance and Conflict Prevention: Outline of a New UNDP Paradigm for Crisis Countries," United Nations Development Program, 2000; United Nations Development Program, *Governance and Conflict Prevention: Proceedings of Expert Group Meeting, 7–8 March 2000* (UNDP Emergency Response Division, 2000).

7. For a discussion of the relation among these values in the context of conflict resolution, see John Paul Lederach, *Building Peace: Sustainable Reconciliation in Divided Societies* (Washington: United States Institute of Peace, 1997). Lederach, one of the leading thinkers of the conflict resolution paradigm, insists on integrating justice with the other values.

8. Jeffrey Ira Herbst, *States and Power in Africa: Comparative Lessons in Authority and Control* (Princeton University Press, 2000).

9. United Nations, *Report of the Secretary-General on the Work of the Organization: Supplement to an Agenda for Peace: Position Paper of the Secretary-General on the Occasion of the Fiftieth Anniversary of the United Nations*, A/50/60, S/1995/1, January 3, 1995, paragraph 27; Kofi A. Annan, *Prevention of Armed Conflict: Report of the Secretary-General* (United Nations, 2001), p. 87.

10. Susan Woodward, *Balkan Tragedy: Chaos and Dissolution after the Cold War* (Brookings, 1995).

11. Anara Tabyshalieva, personal communication, Santo Domingo, January 2000.

12. See the website of the War-Torn Societies Project (www.unrisd.org/wsp).

13. Manuela Leonhardt, "Conflict Impact Assessment of EU Development Cooperation with ACP Countries: A Review of Literature and Practice," International Alert and Saferworld, London, 2000; Jonathan Goodhand, "Conflict Assessment: A Synthesis of Case Studies," paper sponsored by the United Kingdom Department for International Development, April 2001.

14. Organization for Economic Cooperation and Development, *Development Assistance Committee (DAC) Guidelines;* Benomar, "Governance and Conflict Prevention"; United Nations Development Program, *Governance and Conflict Prevention: Proceedings of Export Group Meeting;* Paul Collier and Anke Hoeffler, "Aid, Policy, and Peace," World Bank working paper, August 17, 2000 (www.worldbank.org/research/conflict/papers/aidpolicy.htm [May 4, 2002]).

15. Alvaro De Soto and Graciana Del Castillo, "Obstacles to Peacebuilding," *Foreign Policy*, no. 94, (Spring 1994), pp. 69–83; James K. Boyce, ed., *Economic Policy for Building Peace: The Lessons of El Salvador* (Boulder: Lynne Rienner, 1996).

16. James K. Boyce and Manuel Pastor Jr., "Aid for Peace: Can International Financial Institutions Help Prevent Conflict?" *World Policy Journal*, vol. 15 (Summer 1998), pp. 42–49.

17. Collier and Hoeffler, "Aid, Policy, and Peace," p. 14.

18. Development Assistance Committee and Organization for Economic Cooperation and Development, "Conflict, Peace, and Development Co-operation on the Threshold of the Twenty-first Century," Policy Statement, DAC/OECD, May 1997.

19. United Nations Development Program, *Governance and Conflict Prevention: Proceedings of Export Group Meeting.*

20. Jack Snyder, *From Voting to Violence: Democratization and Nationalist Conflict* (New York: W. W. Norton, 2000).

21. Fareed Zakaria, "The Rise of Illiberal Democracy," *Foreign Affairs,* vol. 76, no. 6 (1997), pp. 22–43.

22. Thomas Carothers, *Aiding Democracy Abroad: The Learning Curve* (Washington: Carnegie Endowment for International Peace, 1999).

23. See, for instance, the analysis of how institutional design could help prevent conflict in Macedonia in Steven L. Burg, "Nationalism and Civic Identity: Ethnic Models for Macedonia and Kosovo," in Barnett R. Rubin, ed., *Cases and Strategies for Preventive Action,* vol. 2 of *Preventive Action Reports* (New York: The Century Foundation Press, 1998), pp. 23–45.

24. Kaufman, in "Possible and Impossible Solutions to Ethnic Civil Wars," argues for partition; Radha Kumar, in "The Troubled History of Partition," *Foreign Affairs,* vol. 76, no. 1 (1997), pp. 22–34, argues against.

25. These terms come from Kalypso Nicolaïdis, "International Preventive Action: Developing a Strategic Framework," in Robert I. Rotberg, ed., *Vigilance and Vengeance: NGOs Preventing Ethnic Conflict in Divided Societies* (Brookings, 1996), pp. 23–69. Stephen John Stedman ("Implementing Peace Agreements in Civil Wars: Lessons and Recommendations for Policymakers," Policy Paper Series on Peace Implementation, CISAC-IPA Project on Peace Implementation, International Peace Academy, New York, June 2001) develops a similar typology for the implementation of peace agreements.

26. John G. Cockell, "Early Warning Analysis and Policy Planning in UN Preventive Action," in David Carment and Albrecht Schnabel, eds., *Conflict Prevention: Path to Peace or Grand Illusion?* (Tokyo: UN University Press, 2001); Sam G. Amoo, *The Challenge of Ethnicity and Conflicts in Africa* (UNDP Emergency Response Division, 1997), p. 32.

27. Boutros Boutros-Ghali, *An Agenda for Peace: Preventive Diplomacy, Peacemaking, and Peace-keeping,* A/47/277-S/24111, June 17, 1992 (United Nations, 1992), p. 20; United Nations, *Report of the Secretary-General Pursuant to the Statement Adopted by the Summit Meeting of the Security Council on January 31, 1992,* A/47/277-S/2411, June 17, 1992; United Nations, *Report of the Panel on United Nations Peace Operations,* A/55/305-S/2000/809, August 21, 2000 (Brahimi report); Annan, *Prevention of Armed Conflict: Report of the Secretary-General.*

28. Cyrus Vance and David Hamburg, *Pathfinders for Peace: A Report to the UN Secretary-General on the Role of Special Representatives and Personal Envoys* (Washington: Carnegie Commission on Preventing Deadly Conflict, 1996).

29. For a survey of these institutions, see Connie Peck, *Sustainable Peace: The Role of the UN and Regional Organizations in Preventing Conflict* (Lanham, Md.: Rowman and Littlefield, 1998).

30. Ahmedou Ould Abdallah, *Burundi on the Brink, 1993–1995: A UN Special Envoy Reflects on Preventive Diplomacy* (Washington: United States Institute of Peace, 2000).

31. See the website of Transcend: A Peace and Development Network (www.transcend.org [May 10, 2002]).

32. United Nations, *Report of the Panel on United Nations Peace Operations.*

33. Herbert C. Kelman, "Contributions of an Unofficial Conflict Resolution Effort to the Israeli-Palestinian Breakthrough," *Negotiation Journal,* vol. 11, no. 1 (1995), pp. 19–27; Harold H. Saunders, *A Public Peace Process: Sustained Dialogue to Transform Racial and Ethnic Conflicts* (St. Martin's, 1999); Shibley Telhami and Jack Snyder, eds., *The Role of Second Track Diplomacy in Ethnic and Nationalist Conflict* (Columbia University Press, forthcoming).

34. International Alert's Women Building Peace program (www.international-alert.org/women/default.html [May 10, 2002]); the NGO Women Waging Peace tries to link such efforts (womenwagingpeace.net [May 10, 2002]).

35. According to Human Rights Watch, "The [television] system was not . . . being used to incite violence (akin to Radio Mille Collines during the Rwandan genocide), which might have justified their destruction. At worst, as far as we know, the Yugoslav government was using them to issue propaganda supportive of its war effort" ("Civilian Deaths in the NATO Air Campaign," Human Rights Watch, February 2000).

36. Richard N. Haass, ed., *Economic Sanctions and American Diplomacy* (New York: Council on Foreign Relations, 1998); David Cortright and George A. Lopez, eds., *Economic Sanctions: Panacea or Peacebuilding in a Post–Cold War World?* (Boulder: Westview, 1995); Richard N. Haass and Meghan O'Sullivan, eds., *Honey and Vinegar: Incentives, Sanctions, and Foreign Policy* (Brookings, 2000); John Stremlau, "Sharpening International Sanctions: Toward a Stronger Role for the United Nations," report to the Carnegie Commission on Deadly Conflict, Carnegie Commission on Preventing Deadly Conflict, Washington, 1996; Thomas G. Weiss, David Cortwright, George A. Lopez, and Larry Minear, eds., *Political Gain and Civilian Pain: Humanitarian Impacts of Economic Sanctions* (Lanham, Md.: Rowman and Littlefield, 1997); Michael Mastanduno, "Extraterritorial Sanctions: Managing 'Hyper-unilateralism' in U.S. Foreign Policy," in Stewart Patrick and Shepard Forman, eds., *Multilateralism and U.S. Foreign Policy: Ambivalent Engagement* (Boulder: Lynne Rienner, 2002), pp. 295–322.

37. Haass and O'Sullivan, *Honey and Vinegar.*

38. Jane Holl, "Great Guns for Greater Goods: The United States and the Use of Force," in Ivo H. Daalder and Paul Stares, eds., *Force, Order, and Global Governance* (Brookings, 2000).

39. Ruth Wedgwood, "Unilateral Action in a Multilateral World," in Stewart Patrick and Shepard Forman, eds., *Multilateralism and U.S. Foreign Policy: Ambivalent Engagement* (Boulder: Lynne Rienner, 2002), pp. 167–89.

40. In 2000, the UN had thirty-two headquarters staff backing up twenty-seven thousand deployed peacekeepers (United Nations, *Report of the Panel on United Nations Peace Operations,* paragraph 181, table 4). For UN headquarters to back up troops in the field would require a hundredfold increase of headquarters capacity that member states would not permit and the UN does not want.

Chapter 11

1. Bruce W. Jentleson, "Coercive Prevention: Normative, Political, and Policy Dilemmas," *Peaceworks* (of the United States Institute of Peace), vol. 35 (October 2000); Francis M. Deng, Sadikiel Kimaro, Terrence Lyons, Donald Rothchild, and I. William Zartman, *Sovereignty as Responsibility: Conflict Management in Africa* (Brookings, 1996).

2. See, for instance, the *Millennium Report.* For an account of the secretary general's statement and subsequent debate in the Security Council, see United Nations, "Conflict Prevention Must Be 'Cornerstone of Collective Security in Twenty-first Century,' Secretary-General Tells Members, as Council Discusses Armed Conflict," Press Release SC/6892, July 20, 2000.

3. United Nations, *Report of the Independent Inquiry into the Actions of the United Nations during the 1994 Genocide in Rwanda,* S/1999/1257, December 16, 1999; United Nations, *Report of the Secretary-General Pursuant to General Assembly Resolution 53/35: The Fall of Srebrenica,* A/54/549, November 1999; United Nations, *Report of the Secretary-General on the Implementation of the Report of the Panel on United Nations Peace Operations,* A/55/02, October 20, 2000; United Nations, *Resource Requirements for Implementation of the Report of the Panel on United Nations Peace Operations,* A/55/507, October 27, 2000; United Nations, *Causes of Conflict and the Promotion of Durable Peace and Sustainable Development in Africa: Report of the Secretary-General,* A/S4/796, March 2000; and United Nations, *Minority Rights and the Prevention of Ethnic Conflicts,* E/CN.4/Sub.2/AC.5/2000/CRP.3, May 2000.

4. Group of Eight, "G8 Communiqué Okinawa 2000," July 23, 2000 (www.mofa.go.jp/policy/economy/summit/2000/documents/communique.html [May 10, 2002]); Group of Eight, "G8 Summit Cologne Communiqué 1999" (www.mofa.go.jp/policy/economy/summit/1999/documents/communique.html [May 10, 2002]).

5. Connie Peck, *Sustainable Peace: The Role of the UN and Regional Organizations in Preventing Conflict* (Lanham, Md.: Rowman and Littlefield, 1998); Center on International Cooperation and International Peace Academy, *Refashioning the Dialogue: Regional Perspectives on the Brahimi Report on UN Peace Operations* (New York, 2001).

6. See Oran R. Young, "Regime Dynamics: The Rise and Fall of International Regimes," *International Organization,* vol. 36, no. 2 (1982), pp. 277–97; Stephen D. Krasner, ed., *International Regimes* (Cornell University Press, 1983); Stephan Haggard and Beth A. Simmons, "Theories of International Regimes," *International*

Organization, vol. 41, no. 3 (1987), pp. 491–517. Michael S. Lund, *Preventing Violent Conflicts: A Strategy for Preventive Diplomacy* (Washington: United States Institute of Peace, 1996), pp. 180–94, argues for a "multilateral, multilayered, decentralized regime" of conflict prevention (p. 180).

7. Janie Leatherman, William DeMars, Patrick D. Gaffney, and Raimo Väyrynen, *Breaking Cycles of Violence: Conflict Prevention in Intrastate Crises* (West Hartford, Conn.: Kumarian, 1999).

8. Carnegie Commission on Preventing Deadly Conflict, *Preventing Deadly Conflict: Final Report* (New York: Carnegie Corporation of New York, 1997), p. 40.

9. On the organization of peace operations, see Antonia Handler Chayes and Abram Chayes, *Planning for Intervention: International Cooperation in Conflict Management* (The Hague: Kluwer Law International, 1999).

10. United Nations, *Report of the Panel on United Nations Peace Operations,* A/55/305-5/2000/809, August 21, 2000 (Brahimi report).

11. See Ernst B. Haas, *Beyond the Nation-State: Functionalism and International Organization* (Stanford University Press, 1964); John Gerard Ruggie, "International Responses to Technology," *International Organization,* vol. 29, no. 3 (1975), pp. 557–83; Peter M. Haas, "Do Regimes Matter? Epistemic Communities and Mediterranean Pollution Control," *International Organization,* vol. 43, no. 3 (1989), pp. 377–403; Peter M. Haas, "Introduction: Epistemic Communities and International Policy Coordination," *International Organization,* vol. 46, no. 1 (1992), pp. 1–35.

12. Leatherman et al., *Breaking Cycles of Violence,* argues for "cultivating networks" as a strategic goal in conflict prevention.

13. See these networks' websites at www.euconflict.org and www.fewer.org.

14. See the Global Compact website (www.unglobalcompact.org [May 10, 2002]); Jane Nelson, *The Business of Peace: The Private Sector as a Partner in Conflict Prevention and Resolution* (London: Prince of Wales Business Leaders Forum, International Alert, Council on Economic Priorities, 2000).

15. The OSCE website can be found at www.osce.org.

16. Margaret E. Keck and Kathryn Sikkink, *Activists beyond Borders: Advocacy Networks in International Politics* (Cornell University Press, 1998), pp. 12–13; see also Mary Kaldor, *New and Old Wars: Organized Violence in a Global Era* (Cambridge: Polity, 1999), especially pp. 112–52; Kumar Rupesinghe, with Sanam Naraghi Anderlini, *Civil Wars, Civil Peace: An Introduction to Conflict Resolution* (London: Pluto, 1998), pp. 128–34.

17. Hassan Ba, "Six renseignements," Synergies Africa, Geneva, December 1997.

18. See the reports listed at the FEWER website (www.fewer.org/pubs/main.htm#0 [May 10, 2002]).

19. The Harvard-UN website is at www.preventconflict.org.

20. See the report at www.preventconflict.org/portal/nepal/nepal_finalreport.pdf (May 10, 2002).

21. James D. Fearon, "Counterfactuals and Hypothesis Testing in Political Science," *World Politics,* vol. 43, no. 2 (1991), pp. 169–95.

22. See the unclassified version of the PDD (the only version I have seen) at www.fas.org/irp/offdocs/dpdd56.htm (May 10, 2002). Thanks to Eric Schwartz for drawing this to my attention and helping elucidate it further.

23. Thanks to Eric Schwartz for this information. He bears no responsibility for any errors of transmission on my part.

24. United Nations, "Note of Explanation on the Framework for Coordination Mechanism," undated. This four-page handout is the only document I have obtained on the FCM, though I have also spoken with participants. Whatever more elaborate documentation may exist for internal purposes (the "Note of Explanation" refers, for instance, to a letter from the UNDP administrator), it has been kept confidential to avoid arousing opposition from member states suspicious of prevention.

25. The eleven organizations are the UN Department of Political Affairs, the UN Office of the Coordinator of Humanitarian Affairs, the UN Department of Peacekeeping Operations, the UN Development Program, the Office of the High Commissioner for Human Rights, the UN International Children's Fund (UNICEF), the UN High Commissioner for Refugees, the World Food Program, the Food and Agriculture Organization, the World Health Organization, and the World Bank.

26. United Nations, "Note of Explanation on the Framework for Coordination Mechanism."

27. Ibid.

28. EISAS stands for ECPS (Executive Committee on Peace and Security) Integrated Strategic Analysis Service.

29. Michael Lund and Andreas Mehler, principal contributors, "Peace-Building and Conflict Prevention in Developing Countries: A Practical Guide," draft document, Stiftung Wissenschaft und Politik and Conflict Prevention Network, Ebenhausen, Germany, 1999.

30. Center on International Cooperation and International Peace Academy, *Refashioning the Dialogue.*

31. Leatherman et al., *Breaking Cycles of Violence,* p. 208.

32. Stewart Patrick and Shepard Forman, eds., *Multilateralism and U.S. Foreign Policy: Ambivalent Engagement* (Boulder: Lynne Rienner, 2002).

33. Steve Kull, "Public Attitudes toward Multilateralism," in Stewart Patrick and Shepard Forman, eds., *Multilateralism and U.S. Foreign Policy: The Cost of Acting Alone* (Boulder: Lynne Rienner, 2002), pp. 99–120.

34. See, for example, Condoleezza Rice, "Promoting the National Interest," *Foreign Affairs,* vol. 79, no. 1 (2000), pp. 45–62.

35. Thomas L. Friedman, *The Lexus and the Olive Tree: Understanding Globalization* (Farrar, Straus and Giroux, 1999); Manuel Castells, *The Rise of the Network Society* (Oxford: Blackwell, 2000).

36. From a rush transcript posted on the CNN Allpolitics website (www.cnn.com/allpolitics/stories/1999/10/28/gop.debate/transcript.html [May 10, 2002]).

Index

Abacha, Mohammad, 98
Abacha, Sani: death of, 83–84, 100; engagement with, 130; and international actors, 83–84, 94–95; looting by, 85, 98, 100, 155–56; military dissent, 88–89; and oil companies, 92; political manipulations of, 91, 135, 136; regime of, 83–84, 87, 89; repression of Muslims, 88. *See also* Nigeria
Abiola, Boshurun Moshood, 84, 86, 87, 93, 100–01, 130
Abiola, Kudirat, 93, 98
Abubakar, Abdulsalami, 100
Accelerators. *See* Escalation dynamics
ActionAid, 149
Adelman, Howard, 140
Adolat, 110, 118
AFDL (Alliance of Democratic Forces for the Liberation of Congo-Zaire), 49
Afghanistan: arms embargo on, 155; drug trafficking, 26, 135, 153; emeralds trade, 153; and end of cold war, 20; and engaged transnational monitoring, 149; exploitation of destruction of, 1–2; as failed state, 14; humanitarian crisis, 18; landmines, 55; linking with conflict in region, 14, 107, 121, 134, 135, 147; post-Soviet occupation, 200. *See also* al-Qaida; Ferghana Valley case study; Taliban
Africa Crisis Response Initiative, 50
Africa Fund, 91
Africa Growth and Opportunity Act, 50
Africa Rights, 127

African American Institute, 42
African National Congress, 97
An Agenda for Peace (Boutros-Ghali), 132, 176, 202; 1995 *Supplement to,* 167–68
Agip, 90
Aideed, Muhammad Farah, 126
AIDS, 6, 202–03
al-Qaida, 1–2, 6, 113, 117, 118, 120, 121, 147, 200
Albania: collapse of, 75–76, 135; as failed state, 14, 15. *See also* Albanians; South Balkans case study
Albanians, 57–81; conditions for discussions with Serbs, 128; CPA views of, 129; and international intervention on behalf of, 167; linking with conflict in region, 14, 134, 135; preventive efforts of CPA to deal with, 133. *See also* South Balkans case study
Albright, Madeleine, 6, 50, 80
Amnesty International, 90
Angola: diamond trade, 152; landmines, 55; linking with conflict in region, 14, 134; motives of leaders, 26; overthrow of Mobutu, role in, 50; revolt against Kabila, role in, 52
Annan, Kofi, 168, 186
Apostles of Peace (Les Apôtres de la Paix), 191
Armed conflict: among states, 5; domestic conflicts, 5; nonstate actors, 5; spillover of, 14. *See also* Conflicts; Military; Military force
Arms. *See* Small arms

Malloch-Brown, Mark, 115
Mamdani, Mahmood, 36
Man, the State, and War (Waltz), 19
Mandela, Nelson, 54, 133, 179
Maps: Burundi and Great Lakes Region of
    Central Africa, 34; Ferghana Valley in
    Central Asia, 104; Nigeria, 82; South
    Balkans, 56
Market-based model, adoption of, 21
Marks, John, 41
Marks, Susan Collin, 41
Mass media. *See* Media
Massoud, Ahmad Shah, 117, 118
McCain, John, 205
McHenry, Donald, 91
Media: and cooperative conflict manage-
    ment, 180; escalation of violence by,
    30; and foreign policy, 4; and growing
    disparities, 24; images of Rwandan
    genocide, 4; journalism projects, 64,
    180; and psychosocial dynamics, 31;
    role in conflict, 180
Metis, 148
Middle East. *See* Israeli-Palestinian con-
    flict
Military force: dissent in Nigeria, 88–89;
    "humanitarian" intervention, 52;
    limited-liability air offensive, 201;
    militias, contemporary, 13; new kinds
    of, 194; use of, 182–83. *See also* Armed
    conflict; Peacekeeping
Milosevic, Slobodan: agreement with
    Rugova, 72–73; arrest and overthrow
    of, 158, 159, 162; and CPA mission, 13,
    93; and Dayton talks, 68; internation-
    alization of Kosovo by, 64; and
    municipal elections, 75; opposition to,
    71; political manipulation by, 135,
    136; reaction to air strike threats, 57,
    77, 181; refusal of international inter-
    vention, 167, 181; relations with
    United States, 67, 73–74; repression by,
    61, 129. *See also* Kosovo; South
    Balkans case study
Mobil Oil, 90, 91–92
Mobutu Sese Seko, 42, 47–48, 50, 134,
    136, 155, 170. *See also* Zaire

Money laundering, 23, 98, 155–56; global
    early warning for systemic prevention,
    142–43; sanctions, 182; and systemic
    prevention, 203
Money Laundering Control Act, 98
Monitoring. *See* Conflict monitoring
Montenegro, 64, 65
Movement for the Survival of the Ogoni
    People (MOSOP), 88, 97
Mugabe, Robert, 52, 54
Muhammad, Murtala, 86
Mujawamariya, Monique, 139
Multinational corporations, 5
Museveni, Yoweri, 39, 50, 54

Namangani, Juma, 106
Namibia: linking with conflict in region,
    135; revolt against Kabila, role, 52
Nation-state, strengthening of, 126, 205.
    See also Stability
National Democratic Institute for Inter-
    national Affairs, 64, 101
NATO. *See* North Atlantic Treaty Organi-
    zation
Nazi genocide, 16
Ndadaye, Melchior, 39
Negotiations, 26, 176–81
Neier, Aryeh, 17
Nepal and Maoist insurgency, 193
Networks: accountability, 192, 194; advo-
    cacy role, 92, 188–94; economic and
    transborder alliances, 14; and ethnic
    diaspora, 13, 156; ExCom contact
    with, 197; in Ferghana Valley, 115–16;
    information technology, 193; Internet,
    189–90, 199; NGOs, 188–93; results of,
    202; transborder trade, 14, 156–57,
    174; transnational issues, 5, 149
NGOs. *See* Nongovernmental organiza-
    tions
Nigeria: as area of concern, 202; Christ-
    ian-Muslim cooperation and dialogue,
    180; civic groups, 134; civil society, 99;
    CPA involvement, 95, 100; elections,
    86, 94; financial sanctions against, 98;
    interethnic riots, 101–02; and NGOs,
    91–93, 100; Ogoni executions and

75; preventive efforts in, 64, 65; and three-plus-three group, 74; UN mission in, 65. *See also* Kosovo; South Balkans case study
Serbian Liberation Army, 57
Serbian Orthodox Church, 58, 71
Serbian Renewal Movement, 75
Settlements, negotiated, 26
SFRY. *See* Socialist Federal Republic of Yugoslavia
Shanghai Cooperation Group, 119–20
Sharia, 88, 102–03
Shell Oil, 88, 90, 91–92, 100
Sierra Leone, 134; amnesty in, 80; atrocities in, 152; conflict diamonds, 22–23, 26, 152–53; ECOWAS deployment on border with Guinea, 183; as failed state, 14; motives of leaders, 26; peacekeeping force in, 89. *See also* Nigeria case study
Sikkink, Kathryn, 92, 149, 190
Silk Route, 107
Skopje University, 64
Slovenia, 59
Small arms, 21–23; campaign against proliferation and misuse of, 157; embargoes, 155; global early warning for systemic prevention, 142–43; Islamic Movement of Uzbekistan, 132; limiting legal sales of, 154–55; marketing, 21–22, 107, 113; NGOs' campaign to limit, 153–55; sales after collapse of Albania, 76; and systemic prevention, 155, 203; transborder trade in, 156; UN programs, 153
Smuggling, 156–57, 174. *See also* Drug trafficking; Small arms
Social capital, 25–26
Social networks across borders, 136, 147
Socialist Federal Republic of Yugoslavia (SFRY), 59, 60
Socialist Party of Macedonia, 63
Sollenberg, Margareta, 14
Somalia: and al-Qaida, 2; effect of humanitarian organizations' actions, 126–27; and end of cold war, 20; as failed state, 14, 15; U.S. forces in, 4,

126, 179. *See also* Burundi and Great Lakes Region of Central Africa case study
Soros Foundation, 68, 92–93, 116
Soros, George, 64
South Africa, 11, 89, 97
South Balkans case study, 55–81; assassinations, 76; background, 57–63; bombing, 57, 66, 77, 78, 79, 81; civil society, 99; Contact Group, 74; cost of conflict vs. prevention, 81; CPA mission to, 66–69, 71, 132, 162; and early warning, 57; education, 62, 64, 69, 70; map of, 56; massacres, 57, 76–78; Muslims, 58, 59; and NGOs, 65, 67, 68; and post–cold war conflicts, 55–57; preventive efforts before CPA mission, 63–66; preventive efforts of CPA, 132–33; Rambouillet negotiations, 78–79; sanctions, 68, 72; three-plus-three group, 74–75; UN mission in, 63, 65, 74–75, 77–78; unemployment, 74; Yugoslav breakup and post–cold war conflicts, 55–57; Zajedno coalition, 75
Southeast Europe University, 62, 70
Soviet Union: Afghanistan occupation, 149, 156; collapse and post–cold war world, 19–21, 110; as ethnofederal state, 25; rule over Central Asia, 107–10. *See also* Russia
Soyinka, Wole, 87, 93
Spoilers, 146
Stability: benefits of, 163; economic development as key to, 114; and transnational relations, 5
"Stability pact" for Balkans, 159
State Department: Bureau of Intelligence and Research, 186; Secretary's Initiative on Preventive Diplomacy, 197
State-level conflict, 5, 24–29
Stedman, Stephen John, 146
Stiftung Wissenschaft und Politik, 74
Structural prevention, 168–70; and allocations decisions, 143–45; and Central Asia, 132; conflict-impact assessments, 169; defined, 131–32; and economic